J. Lawrence Rentoul

The Early Church and the Roman Claim

Third Edition

J. Lawrence Rentoul

The Early Church and the Roman Claim
Third Edition

ISBN/EAN: 9783337020576

Printed in Europe, USA, Canada, Australia, Japan

Cover: Foto ©ninafisch / pixelio.de

More available books at **www.hansebooks.com**

J. Lawrence Rentoul

The Early Church and the Roman Claim
Third Edition

ISBN/EAN: 9783337020576

Printed in Europe, USA, Canada, Australia, Japan

Cover: Foto ©ninafisch / pixelio.de

More available books at **www.hansebooks.com**

AND

THE ROMAN CLAIM

LECTURES BY

J. LAURENCE RENTOUL, M.A., D.D.,

Professor of N.T. Greek and Exegesis: and of Christian Philosophy.
(Formerly Professor of Hebrew and O.T. Exegesis)
Ormond College, Melbourne University.

IN REPLY TO ARCHBISHOP CARR

ON "THE PRIMACY OF THE ROMAN PONTIFF."

THIRD EDITION.

Melbourne:
MELVILLE, MULLEN AND SLADE,
1896.

MELBOURNE:
M'CARRON, BIRD AND CO., PRINTERS,
479 COLLINS STREET.

TO

The Rev. S. Robinson, D.D.

AND TO

THE ELDERS, MANAGERS, AND PEOPLE

OF

ST. KILDA PRESBYTERIAN CHURCH,

(IN WHICH THEY WERE FIRST SPOKEN),

THESE LECTURES ARE INSCRIBED

IN TOKEN OF

OLD FRIENDSHIP AND SINCERE REGARD.

J. L. R.

PREFACE.

In these Lectures our conflict is not with men, but with opinions. Frankness of speech in vindication of historic facts does not in any way alter the kindly personal feeling I entertain for those from whom I differ.

The Roman Claim would ban out of God's fold, and exclude from the brotherhood of the hope in Christ, myself, and half of Christendom. It becomes a Duty not to be shirked, in loyalty to Truth, and to the Common Faith, to test the basis on which such a claim affects to rest. This duty I trust I have performed with candour.

The following pages are intended at once for the ordinary reader, and also (by Notes and Appendix) to aid those who wish to make a further study of the subject.

J. LAURENCE RENTOUL.

ORMOND COLLEGE,
    THE UNIVERSITY, 1st *July*, 1896.

FORE-WORD.

FOUR LECTURES.

	PAGE
I.—THE ROMAN CLAIM, AND METHOD: PETER AND THE ROCK	16
II.—THE ROMAN LEGEND OF PETER—THE QUESTION AND MODERN SCHOLARSHIP.—WAS PETER "BISHOP OF ROME?"	72
III.—RISE OF A SACERDOTAL ORDER IN THE CHRISTIAN MINISTRY	103
IV.—EVOLUTION OF THE PAPACY: ITS EARLY STAGES	132
APPENDIX	183

Delivered on Sunday Evenings in the St. Kilda Church, and Redelivered in the Scots' Church, Melbourne.

FORE-WORD.

TO CHURCHMEN: ANGLICAN AND NON-ANGLICAN.

It was with much reluctance that I consented to prepare these lectures, and to enter, for the first time in my life, into controversy with Roman Catholic advocates.

The very large and representative audiences that followed the lectures, and the many kindly communications received by me from all parts of Victoria since their delivery, have touched and encouraged me. It seems evident that the public sense has been revolted by the sweeping claims and the assertions as to history made during the last few years by Roman Catholic ecclesiastics, and emphasised in Archbishop Carr's annual series of lectures, culminating in his attack, last year, upon the English Bible and the Reformers, and in his recent utterance on the *Primacy of the Roman Pontiff*. Not the least cordial and generous of the letters I have received have come from clergymen and laymen of other Churches than my own. The writers have been good enough to say that I have not spoken as an advocate for my own Church (however much I am personally loyal to her), but in vindication of the basis of Scriptural and historic truth on which the early Christian Church rested, and on which all the Churches of the Reformation rest still.

These lectures will, I hope, be found (especially from Part II. of Lecture I. onward) a treatment possessing interest quite apart from the temporary causes which called them forth. The questions raised have perennial claim upon all Christian men. Their immediate occasion, however, was the course of six lectures delivered by Archbishop Carr, of Melbourne, on *The Primacy of the Roman Pontiff*—oddly enough during the penitential season of Lent. An examination of the character of Archbishop Carr's dealing with "the Testimony of the Fathers," and with "Protestant testimony," and of his "quotations" and representation of historical facts generally, in the effort to present a plausible case for Papalism, will probably strike the intelligent reader with the impression that the six lectures might fitly have been followed by another and more adequate "penitential season."

The publication of large abstracts of my lectures in the *Argus* and the *Age* led to a correspondence between Archbishop Carr and myself. The one and only statement of mine which Archbishop Carr attempted to controvert was a mere side issue, viz., my criticism of one characteristic illustration of his "quotations," and what he termed "exclusively Protestant testimony." In my first lecture I protested both against his inclusion of Renan in that category, and (still more) against his drastic mutilations of the passage he quoted from Renan, so as to shape it into a testimony for "the Roman Primacy." That brief correspondence made, I have reason to know, a profound impression all over Victoria with regard to Romanist methods of controversy. (The full correspondence will be found in the Appendix.)

I refuse to be diverted from the central and all-important question by this side consideration. For,

I suppose, the public will agree with me that—even if all Archbishop Carr's "testimonies" had been solid, instead of mainly worthless or irrelevant or misleading, owing to the use of ambiguous terms like " Primacy," or thrown out of line with their original context—a mere array of *names* and *opinions* is a very secondary and unimportant element in an investigation like this. The facts of the New Testament, and of the Apostolic time, the facts of chronology, the real *facts of history—these* are the things which should be faced.

In the first letter of the above-mentioned correspondence, Archbishop Carr promised, however, that in " the book form " of his lectures he would " avail himself of the opportunity of developing (his) answers to meet the special phases of the difficulties which have been most recently presented." I replied :

"I shall be happy to examine the developed answers of the Archbishop. I venture to suppose that they will require development. For the difficulties which front the Archbishop and his Roman claim are solid and unanswerable historic facts." (*Argus* and *Age*, 20th May.)

In " the book form " of Dr. Carr's lectures nothing is more significant than the fact that the " developed " answers have not arrived. He does not in the least attempt to deal with the *chronological* facts I have adduced, proving the " Roman claim " to be an historic impossibility, and to rest on what is undeniably legend. *How Peter could be in two places at the same time* (which supposition is necessary to the "Roman bishopric of Peter"), Archbishop Carr has not attempted to show. How the Romanist advocate can harmonize the facts that Tertullian, in the close of the second century, declares that *Clement* was first bishop of Rome,[*] and that Irenaeus (Tertullian's contemporary) declares

---

[*] *Tert. De Præscr. Haer.* 32. "The context shows that he did not regard Peter as first bishop."—Prof. Bright, *Roman See* (1896), p. 11.

that *Linus* was first bishop of Rome; this, or any other of the many huge difficulties that beset even the first steps of the self-contradictory Roman tradition (necessary to Papalism), Dr. Carr does not venture to look in the face. His rôle is that of all Roman Catholic advocates—to shun actual facts of history, and to pile together (under the Romanist notion of the impressiveness of "*authority*" and *names*) a mass of odd "quotations" from "fathers," and from "Protestant" testimony. My readers will find this sort of thing analysed in the cognate parts of the following pages.

Archbishop Carr must have a limited belief in the intelligence of the public when he announces that the views of his "new adversary" differ radically from the views of "Anglicans" on "the primitive form of Church government and the necessity of Apostolical succession." This sentence resembles the rest of Dr. Carr's controversial utterances. It derives its only plausibility from the use of "*ambiguous* terms." When I turn to my dictionary, I find that the word "Anglican" means "English;" or, in a religious sense, "a member of the Church of England." But Archbishop Carr is always trying to use it, *when it suits him*, as if it meant what is known as "Anglo-Catholic." When it does *not* suit him in this sense then he uses it differently; and, like the other "ambiguous term," "*Primacy*," this word "Anglican" plays strange pranks in the Archbishop's rhetoric.

Thus, in his fifth lecture, Salmon (*i.e.* Professor Salmon of Dublin) is specially set amongst "Anglican controversialists," and is accused by Archbishop Carr of "downright dishonesty," and worse. Also, Bishop Lightfoot is grouped amongst "Anglican writers;" and Archbishop Carr knows very well that the views held by Lightfoot as to the primitive form of Church government are substantially identical with the views set forth in my lectures, instead of being, as he tries to hint, " radically different."

But *that* is not all. In his Lecture I., when it suits his purpose, Dr. Carr denounces "the utterly *un-Anglican and un-episcopalian theory* advocated by Lightfoot." Poor Bishop Lightfoot! Great scholar as he was, he was not acquainted with the methods of Archbishop Carr. Hence he supposed that the letter of Clement of Rome "does not proceed from the Bishop, but from the Church of Rome." That is how Archbishop Carr expresses the great un-Anglican sin committed by the late Bishop Lightfoot. And, unfortunately, any of us, reading Clement's letter from " *The Congregation of God sojourning in Rome*" would fall exactly into the same "sin" of interpretation into which poor Lightfoot fell.

But, as a simple matter of truth, to talk of an "Anglican view" and a "Presbyterian view" of the primitive form of Church government is to talk absurdly. There are two now dominant "views" amongst modern scholars as to "the primitive form of Church government." The one may be called the "Lightfoot view," held also substantially by such scholars as Sanday, Westcott, Alford, Perowne, Ewing, Reichel, Moorhouse, &c., by Stanley, Arnold of Rugby, Farrar, and a host of others. Are not these good "Anglicans"? The view (expressed briefly) is that, originally (as proven by the New Testament) "presbyters" and "bishops" were synonymous. They were the same in function, and their ordination the same. Then, gradually, one presbyter was elevated above the others, or, as Lightfoot puts it, "the episcopate was developed out of the presbyterate." All these Anglican scholars have rejected, just as utterly as I reject it, the figment of "the Apostolic Succession." A great and sensible bishop, like Lightfoot, knows too well within himself that, whatever else he is he is not an *Apostle*. But if we hold the Apostles' *faith*, it is well!

Professor Sanday, of Oxford ("the later Lightfoot," as he has been called) says distinctly that the early Church "passed through a Presbyterian stage," and the acknowledgment of that and cognate facts ought to be "the *eirenicon* between the churches." For himself he prefers Episcopacy, as in our days, he thinks, "the more excellent way." He is quite free to that opinion, and we to ours. But between him and myself there is no "radical difference" of any kind as to "the primitive method of Church government." Nay, Archbishop Carr knows this very well. He has, in past courses of lectures, declared that all the Reformers who shaped the Reformed Church of England held that view.

The other scholarly view is called the Hatch-Harnack view. It is still more destructive of the early-Episcopal notion, and of the "Apostolic Succession figment," than is the Lightfoot view. The early *episcopos* (bishop) according to Dr. Hatch's view, was the man who was *functioned* to the oversight, in *each congregation*, of the *alms* and charities and finance, in connection with the weekly Lord's supper and Agape (or love-feast). Hence he and the "deacons" were associated. Now observe that this theory also was set forth by an eminent "Anglican" (Dr. Hatch). It was adopted by the great Lutheran scholar, Harnack, and elaborated with his wonderful ability and research. The Presbyters were *over* the Episcopos; the Presbyters *ruled* the Christian community; "they were the persons of authority; they were honoured and obeyed." (*See* Clement of Rome.) Dr. Harnack admits, however, that practically and frequently "the functions of presbyters and bishops were not distinguished." And the "Lightfoot view" is certainly the dominant view at this moment amongst scholars.

Now look! Both Lightfoot and Hatch were "Anglicans." Nay more, *Jerome*, the authoritative Latin "father," on whose labours Rome's Latin Bible rests, says the same on this matter as Lightfoot does. He asserts, as Dr. Carr well knows, just what I have asserted, viz., that the early Church's government was in each place "by a common council of presbyters." Afterwards, in the epoch of the gnostic heresies, one presbyter was lifted into a single episcopos in each congregation or community. Then the thing soon spread till the bishop became a great fellow. Each bishop was called "papa" (Pope). Finally, one bishop in the biggest city became the most bumptious bishop, and then claimed to be the only "Papa" or Pope. Finally, he took the title of the extinct pagan Roman high-priest, and called himself *Pontifex Maximus*. This is the verdict of history.

I notice, and it shows the unworthiness of Archbishop Carr's attempt to confuse the public judgment on this matter, that one of the most scholarly Anglicans in Victoria, Canon Berry, the Bishop of Melbourne's Examining Chaplain, has written a frank and finely-toned letter to the *Argus* stating that he and all moderate Anglican Churchmen would accept the positions affirmed in my lectures; further, that the same position is substantially taken by Canon Spence in his work on the recently discovered early Christian writing, the *Didache (Teaching of the Twelve Apostles).*

One other thing I wish to say here. I call attention in my lectures to the attack made by Archbishop Carr on that noble scholar, Professor Salmon, whom he accuses of "downright dishonesty." Roman Catholic advocates are angry at what Dr. Salmon

---

* See Appendix.

has said about the early Roman "lists," and also about the "Clementine Romance," viz., that an early editor of it was the *inventor of the legend of Peter's Roman Episcopate*. Archbishop Carr's attempt to deal with this, and with Canon Potter's statements on the same subject, are in my judgment the most earnest attempt, to be met with in Archbishop Carr's lectures, to grapple with a great difficulty in a critical and historical spirit. It is quite evident that Dr. Carr *could* write with effect if he had facts to go upon. But here, again, as will be evident from my discussion of the Legend of Peter, the Archbishop has been misled by his very untrustworthy Achates, the Rev. Luke Rivington, and by the cross lights of an "ambiguous term," viz., "the Clementine Romance."

He quotes, and it is his one seemingly strong point, from Harnack's recent work. As I shall show, he quite misunderstands Harnack. The very words he quotes might have guided him better. Harnack is speaking of the Clementine writings "*in the form in which we have them*." But Harnack, like Lightfoot, Renan, and many another scholar, has shown that the Clementine writings, *as we have them*, rest upon *much older apocryphal writings* of the second century. And in those there lies at least one teeming source of the early legends about Peter. This will be seen in its own place. In this matter Archbishop Carr does not shake the substance of Canon Potter's argument: just as, on Irenaeus, his elaborate discussion and quotations do not impair the statement of Dr. Stacey Chapman.* To myself who used to sit in the class-room of a great German University listening to Harnack, with his union of rare knowledge and genius for teaching, Dr. Carr's use of him seems odd.

---

* *The Alleged Papal Supremacy*, 1895. This seems to have induced Archbishop Carr's course of lectures.

Just as I go to press my attention is called* to Professor Bright's latest book, *The Roman See in the Early Church*. It is startling to find that the conflict we are compelled to wage here is being waged just now in England, and over just the same field. Professor Bright is an outstanding man amongst the "Anglo-Catholics" at home. Archbishop Carr, in conflict with what he terms "Anglican controversialists," has frequently quoted him with great gusto—this "Oxford Regius Professor." Now this scholar, Canon Bright, has had to write his book mainly in criticism of *The Primitive Church and the See of St. Peter*, by the Rev. Luke Rivington, a convert from "Anglo-Catholicism" to Romanism. Mr. Rivington's arguments and "quotations," and "adventurous appeal," as Dr. Bright calls it, bear the same general family features as the modes and words of the various handbooks and pamphlets now being pushed out in advocacy of the *Cathedra Petri*. Prof. Bright points to the very grave issues "raised by a publication which is obviously part of a new Roman campaign against the English Church and the churches in communion with her."† Here is how Bright apostrophises "the Roman spirit, when it absorbs all other considerations into the supreme necessity of making out a case for Rome":—

"You will therefore *read that view into all your documents.* You will assume it as in possession of the ground, and throw on opponents the task of proving its absence. *Whatever seems to make for it, you will amplify; whatever seems to make against it, you will minimise, or explain away, or ignore.*"‡

On the next page he says:—

"*Loyalty to Rome will determine how much of a passage, or a sentence, should be quoted in the text;* or how far the reader is to be enabled by foot-notes *to refer to authorities and to judge of*

---

* By the Rev. Dr. Robinson.
† Bright, *Roman See*, p. 213.   ‡ P. 211.

their accuracy.* You will deal largely in assertion, and in repetition and reiteration of what has been asserted; you will not be afraid of paradox, *in maintaining the genuineness of what has usually been deemed spurious*, or the spuriousness of what has usually been deemed genuine. You will uphold the majesty of the Holy See with an air of superb confidence; you will apply to the defence of Papal authority the watchword of a great revolutionist—'*De l'audace, encore de l'audace, toujours de l'audace.*' Such boldness suits the Roman genius, and is traditional with those who have best understood Rome."†

Now, this is tolerably strong from a scholar whom Archbishop Carr has been fond hitherto of quoting. In my own gentler temperament I would not have ventured upon it, though it seems justified by the facts Canon Bright brings into evidence.

But what I quote it for is to emphasise the demand that is upon all of us to-day if we but understand our time, with the great world's need and sin-sickness weltering round us, while Christ's living Gospel and God's Scriptures are hid away from the eyes of men. Rome dreams of reconquering England—and mainly through a sacerdotal movement, gradually killing the Protestant tone and faith within the bosom of England's national Church. Every strong blow struck by Archbishop Carr in his writings against the Church of England and against Protestantism has come weighted by the quoted words of some Laudian, or non-juring, or "Anglo-Catholic" man within the Church of England herself. And, meanwhile, "Anglo-Catholics" are playing into the hands of Rome by a theory of mediating priesthood, and a kindred theory of the direct descent and inspiration of all bishops equally as "successors of the Apostles"—a theory of which the father was Cyprian of priestly North Africa

---

* I have had to spend days trying to put right the many utterly erroneous foot-references on Archbishop Carr's pages. Many of them are utterly wrong and unmeaning.

† Bright, *Roman See*, p. 212.

in the third century. And whether one hold that Cyprianite theory or hold the Papal theory, of which the father was Leo I. of Rome in the fifth century, it is essentially the same pagan theory—foreign to, and lacking faith in, the all-sufficient high-priesthood and accomplished sacrifice of Jesus Christ our Lord. It is disloyal to His perpetual spiritual presence in His congregation, in the hearts, wills, and lives of His believing people.

That theory of a priestly caste in Christ's ministry divides and distracts Christendom. I have spoken these lectures in the hope of emphasising, and drawing men's attention to, that which is the abiding centre of unity for all the Churches of God. The possession of *that* proves that there is far less *disunion* between the Protestant Churches than is seen in the Roman Catholic Church herself, with her iron-bound and authoritative external uniformity, and the ghastly internal self-contradictions and changes which have marked her tragic history.

Whatever may help to call us back direct to Christ and His Apostles—John, Paul, Peter, and all the men who bore His Evangel to the world—is said well—whatever causes us to build simply upon the one *Petra*, the one foundation set forth equally by St. Paul, St. Peter, St. Stephen, and the early "witnesses":—Christ, the Atoner, the life for men and *in* men. In this central substance of the living faith there is no distinction between Presbyterian Churchman, Anglican Churchman, Wesleyan Churchman, and the Churchmen of God's "independent" congregations.

(NOTE.—I have been unable to use Canon Bright, save for a few foot-notes, and one or two brief passages inserted in the final revision of my Lectures. These I have marked in square brackets. His Lecture on "The Reign of Elizabeth" is marked, unfortunately, by strong "Anglo-Catholic" bias, *e.g.*, his treatment of Grindal, &c.)

LECTURE FIRST.

THE ROMAN CLAIM AND METHOD: PETER AND THE ROCK.

"Paul, a servant of Jesus Christ, called to be an apostle, separated unto the Gospel of God, . . . to all that are in Rome beloved of God, called to be Saints: grace to you and peace from God our Father and the Lord Jesus Christ."—

St. Paul's Letter to the Christians in Rome. 58 A.D. (Rom. I., 1–7.)

"Peter, an apostle of Jesus Christ to the Elect who are Sojourners of the Dispersion in Pontus, Galatia, Cappadocia, Asia, and Bithynia."—

St. Peter's Letter to the Jewish-Christians scattered through various Provinces in Asia, where his ministry lay. (1 Peter I., 1.) [63-64 A.D., acc. to Lightfoot; 70-80 A.D., acc. to Prof. Ramsay; 45 A.D. (!!), acc. to the *Douay Version*.]

PART I.—INTRODUCTORY.—ROME.

THE city of Rome was not the cradle of civilisation or of Christianity. But, as the capital of the ancient "heathen" World-Empire, and long afterwards the central city of Western Christendom, Rome has left her impress, for good and for evil, upon both civil and Christian history. To all who have open heart and eye for the tragic story of the human race, and of the Christian Faith, that city of Italy by the yellow Tiber will always yield a vivid interest. Amongst the many features of that old-new city, fitted to arrest the gaze and to set the mind a-thinking, there are two which stand out now in startling contrast. They are symbols of two antagonistic forces, whose conflict has been from of old. They rise on opposite sides of the river; and the stream of Time, turbid with its movement, flows between. The one symbol is the palace of the King of a free people, with, not far away, the significant tokens of the Parliamentary Institutions and popular self-government that attend upon National order and liberties, and that brook dictation from neither priest nor Pope. Near to it on one hand lie, in the valleys and on the heights, the ruins of ancient "pagan" Rome, the once metropolis of the world, in their massive wonder of shattered and silent strength. On the other hand and in far circuit spread the streets and ways of the Modern City, like living arteries through which throb the movement and energies of a nation's life. The Christian King, Victor Emmanuel's son and Garibaldi's friend, walks in the garb of a simple gentleman along the Corso, or passes in his unpretentious carriage, with no pomp of attendant soldiery, a loyal King amid a loyal and enfranchised people. Then, away opposite, across the flow of the turbid Tiber, there rises on the view the other Symbol —the Symbol of the dead and dying Past. It is a huge dark palace, by a huge dark church, reached by the slope which (as a brilliant scholar of our time says) "the bad taste of the seventeenth century has occupied with a theatrical arcade," known as the Piazza of St. Peter. Within that palace, its approach guarded by rifle and bayonet, the aged Pope of Rome, calling himself the successor of Peter the fisherman of Galilee, and infallible Vicar of Christ, frowns from his sullen seclusion at the existence of the Christian King and the freedoms of the new Italy, and dreams of a restoration of the "temporal power of the Papacy" over Emperors and Peoples. A once predecessor of that Pope could march at the head of ruthless armies with sword and flame, and crush his adversaries, or could put a hostile King "under the ban," or could keep a Kaiser waiting barefoot and in sackcloth in the snow, and finally could plant his foot on that Kaiser's prostrate neck, pretending that the submission was "penitence." In a later century, an Emperor and a great German Diet would have to denounce "the power of the Pope as an Enemy of Peace, and his interference . . . as the act, not of a Vicar of Christ, but of a cruel and lawless tyrant."* But now, to-day, a Pope writes from that Vatican palace impotent encyclicals to a Protestant and amused England, consigning that sturdy Puritan realm as "the Dowry of Mary" to the mercies of St. Peter and of Mary "the Holy Mother of God." Nor can "Peter's Vicar," with all his ban and anathema, scare to-day even one wretched princelet of Bulgaria to keep himself and his child loyal to the Holy Roman Church, and to the "See of Peter;" not even though that princelet's heir be descended from the blood of "most Catholic Kings." The day for a Pope's banning of England's Magna Charta, the day for Canossa, or for the threatenings of a Council of Trent is past. To-day, the wholly different course needs to be taken—it is needful to manipulate dexterously the ambiguous term "primacy," and to strain out of their natural meaning "the early fathers," in order to get plausible apology for the beginnings, and rise, and development of a Papacy of any kind.

Nevertheless, to that city of Rome the perennial glamour clings. Not for its Pope and Papacy, but

---

* cf. Gibbon, Menzel, Milman *Lat.* Christ. Bk. xii., &c.

for what is older and more abiding than its Papacy, what was earlier than its Popes, does the interest of the student and of the man who has a human heart gather round Rome. The great Roman Republic— "*The parliament of Kings, the men of Rome*"—whose genius of practical state-craft and of conquering power culminated in the Empire of the Cæsars, worked out into actuality the splendid dream of one world-wide Realm. It made the Christian hope of a brotherhood of men possible. Though slavery weltered, as yet, at that great pagan Empire's heart, yet the justice and civil law of ancient Rome, abridged and arranged later on by a Christian Emperor, have left their impress upon the jurisprudence and life of all modern nations.*

But to the Christian thinker the city of Rome has a yet deeper interest. It was by Rome's Procurator, and by violation of Roman law, Christ was sent to the cross. Rome was at that time the centre and capital of the civilised world. All movements of men, good and bad, gravitated towards Rome. Early Christianity, which always sought the throng of men, soon reached to the Empire's heart. On the tide of traffic, which swept all things towards the great Central City of the West, the message of the Gospel in Christ was borne to Rome. Wandering Jews, like Aquila and Priscilla, passing from city to city bartering their wares, carried with them the new tidings which could give Life to the dying world.

PAUL IN ROME.

The new faith and brotherhood of Christianity, beginning at Jerusalem, soon broke beyond the barriers of Judæa and of Judaism. It made itself felt in all the great cities—in *Antioch* of Syria, in *Thessalonica* of Macedonia, in *Corinth* of Achaia, in *Ephesus* of Asia, in *Alexandria* of Egypt, in *Rome* of

---

* Prof. Bryce—Art. "Justinian," Encyc. Brit.

Western Europe. Soon the great Apostle of the Gentiles, Paul, set his thought on Rome as the world's centre of life and citizenship. He longed to come to it, to carry out from that metropolis the evangelisation of Western Europe. As early as the year 58 A.D. he wrote to the Christian congregation in Rome his greatest epistle. That Church was already in vigorous existence. No Apostle was at its founding. Three years later Paul himself reached Rome a prisoner, to be tried before Nero, the Emperor. Paul was the first Apostle who set foot in Rome. There was no Peter to welcome him when he came. Only three years later the first terrible persecution—the persecution of the year 64 A.D. under Nero—burst out against the Christians. It made Rome to be "filled with the blood of the Saints and of the martyrs of Jesus." To the early Christian imagination, Rome, next to Jerusalem, soon came to have most tragic interest. It was at once the forceful centre of the world's life, and glorified by the memories of faith's heroism and martyrdom. Paul himself, the great Apostle-prisoner—even if set free from his first imprisonment—certainly perished in Rome, under Nero's axe or sword. For the moment, the Christian "congregation" at Rome was swept away. When it again began to gather back into Rome, the memory of "the blood of the martyrs" was a quickening impulse to a swiftly-growing Christian community.

The Faith of the Early Church at Rome.

But *that* was not the Church of Popes, or of priests, or of prelates, or of altars, or of outer ceremonial. It was the congregation of Jesus, the gathering together of men and women in a living faith, which found the heart, and then from the changed heart, in its inner trust in Christ, changed the life—making its spirit and conduct Christ-like. The faith and practice of the Early Church of Rome in the Apostles' day we find quite clearly set out in St. Paul's Epistle to Rome, and in his Epistles written to other churches from Rome. Here is that faith :—

"We are justified freely by His (God's) Grace, through the redemption that is in Christ Jesus, whom God set forth to be a Mercy seat (or Propitiation), through faith by His blood to show His righteousness . . . that God might be Just and the Justifier of him that hath faith in Jesus." (Rom. iii. 24-26).

In that one sacrifice and righteousness of Christ for us, the Apostle says, all other priestly mediation is ended and done away. Here is the only priestly "service and practice" which still continues in the Church of God :—

"I beseech you, therefore, brethren, through the mercies of God that ye present *your bodies a living sacrifice*, holy, acceptable to God, which is your reasonable (rational or spiritual) service (*latreia*, ministration of worship)." (Rom. xii.*)

And here, according to St. Paul, is the *inner motive and state of heart* which constitutes men members of the Kingdom and Church of God, and renders their prayer and gratitude and purity of life *the* only true priestly " service" which God will accept:—

"As many as are *led by the Spirit of God*, these are Sons of God." (Rom. viii. 14-15.)

In all the writings of Paul, to Rome and from Rome, there is not a trace of what is now known to the world as "Roman Catholicism." The two are in direct antagonism—Paul and "Rome." There is nothing more tragic in history than this fact, which a study of the New Testament makes certain, that the thing Roman Catholic ecclesiastics hate with a fierce hatred, and which they condemn as "Protestantism,"

---

* A service to God such as befits the reason, as contrasted with dumb and dead Jewish or heathen sacrifices, or ritual ceremonial. —Prof. Sanday, Lightfoot, Meyer, Thayer's Grimm, &c.

is just the thing set forth in St. Paul's letter to the Romans as the Gospel that saves men. Very strikingly does even M. Renan, a brilliant modern scholar, educated for the Roman Catholic priesthood, but recoiling from it into scepticism, confess that the Roman Church afterwards "arrived at ideas which *would have revolted Paul.*" More strikingly still does he speak of that characteristic feature which has marked the history of the Roman Church, the "*ascetic and sacerdotal character opposed to the Protestant tendency of Paul.*" Penetrated with the "political and hierarchial spirit of old Rome," the old Rome of the Pagan Empire, "the city of the pontificate, of a hieratic and solemn religion, of *material sacraments alone sufficient for justification*"—in vain Paul speaks to her!

"In vain will Paul address to her his noble Epistle, expounding the mystery of the Cross of Christ, and Salvation by faith alone. She will hardly understand it. But Luther, fourteen centuries and a-half later, will understand it."*

I have quoted these words from Renan, whose faith in Christ Rome's training killed, because Archbishop Carr has, as we shall see, appealed in singular fashion to him as "testimony" for the ancientness and solidity of the Roman claim; and because, also, the words themselves, in their truth and exactitude have, as coming from a man like Renan who knew Roman Catholicism from the inside, a touching and tragic impressiveness.

In Rome, the material capital of the ancient world, the centre of forceful authority, the embodiment of the fusion of imperial and priestly rule, the city where the Pagan Emperor was also *Pontifex Maximus* (Chief Pontiff), the Christian faith and Church soon became a politico-religious force, all unlike in spirit and aims

---

* Renan's *Hibbert Lectures*, p. 60. Consult also pp. 59-172, *et passim*.

to what Christ had proclaimed as the spirit and method of His Kingdom. Not one of the martyrs, who died in the flames of Nero's gardens in Rome in the year 64 A.D. (could they revisit our earth to-day), would be able to recognise in the externalism of this Roman Catholic hierarchy, doctrine, and worship—in the "sacrifice of the Mass," the compulsory confessional, the images, the mariolatry, the indulgences, the purgatory, the claim made for a sinful man of infallibility as Christ's Vicar on earth—any resemblance to the faith for which those early martyrs died, or to the simple forms of worship in which that faith expressed its aspiration and its "service."

"Made Void by Tradition."

And yet here is a tragic thing! Away in, underneath all *that* external growth of priestly invention and of ecclesiastical state-craft, there lies, hidden out of view of the people, that truth of the Divine love and of a redeeming and living Christ, which *could* save and regenerate the nations, were it not "made void by traditions of men," and by unwholesome legends of "saints." The noblest hymns of both the Greek Catholic and the Roman Catholic Churches, those which express the Christian heart's devotion at its highest, are singularly free from any of those accretions either of doctrine or worship which form the characteristic substance of "Catholicism," whether Greek or Roman. Eminent men of our time have pointed out this great fact. What the Reformers brought to light again, and vindicated for God's modern Church, was what had lain at heart of the purest and greatest souls of the congregation of Christ in all the ages. This is the "unity and continuity of the Church"—the life of Christ in man. It is not the things for which Archbishop Carr contends, or for which Anglo-Catholics contend, that the great illumined souls of all the Christian ages and Churches have vibrated to, and have uttered into undying beauty of devotional song and gratitude. It is the Evangelic, the Protestant heart of the Faith, that speaks in the greatest hymns even of Roman Catholic singers. Not Peter's primacy, nor any priestly claim, nor any "sacrifice of the Mass," nor Mary's intercession, nor "saints' merits" voice themselves *there*, but the soul's direct living trust in God's fatherly mercy, and in Christ's redeeming love and High Priesthood, and in the indwelling of His Spirit within the hearts of believing men. The great Reformers re-discovered this central and life-giving truth of Christianity. They lifted it up again before men's gaze, bidding them come in their need and sin and penitence direct *to Christ himself*. And they made *thus* the modern world and the people's freedoms. They brought back into our life the faith and the Gospel which the Apostles preached, and for which the early martyrs in Rome died.

THE REASON FOR THESE LECTURES.

Religious controversy is personally distasteful to me. Unless absolutely necessary it should be avoided. It frets away time: and time with some of us is toilsome and precious. It is mere folly, however, to say that "controversy is always injurious." History gives that assertion splendid disproof. Controversy, when waged by true-hearted men, with rightful weapons of truth and argument, and for worthy causes, has been fruitful of great results. Every great epoch, religious, scientific, or political, has been an epoch of controversy. The Reformation day, the Puritan day, the day of Wesley's and Whitefield's rousing of England into new spiritual life, the day of modern missionary outburst and self-sacrifice—all these have been days in which men of strong intellect and spiritual elevation strove together for the faith of the Gospel, and for the good of the peoples. Let the heat of the conflict's temper be avoided; let the conflict itself be waged! For what is at stake is truth. The indifferent souls will grow eager and vehement at least when the question is a disputed "legacy" or "a boom in stocks!" They, too, will "contend" when the question is about the things of the pocket and the till, "the things of self." Christ's own ministry was often "a controversy," weary and hazardous—Paul's too, and even Peter's. *He* withstood the Judaeizers at Jerusalem. Paul withstood *him* at Antioch!

Yet I dislike controversy. It is, for the most part, the love and the life and the character of churches and of men that tell on the world, rather than argument. Also, there are good and there are bad in the best and in the worst churches. To myself, especially, argument with Roman Catholics is disagreeable, because of kindly memories which lie in the background of my life. Till now I have never publicly taken part, in pulpit or on platform, in such controversy.

The New Romanist Propaganda.

Of late, however, under the *régime* of Cardinal Moran in Sydney and of Archbishop Carr in Melbourne, the peaceful manner of the late Archbishop Goold seems to have been deliberately abandoned. There seems like a trumpet-blast along the whole Romanist line. Of late Archbishop Carr has persistently launched forth, not only against his "Anglican" antagonists, but against the positions common to all Protestant Churches, not excepting "the Protestant

Bible" from his attacks. He has also implicitly assailed myself, though I had, in word or act, given him no ground for reasonable annoyance. My sin apparently was that I attended a "British and Foreign Bible Society" meeting.* Archbishop Carr has further, in recent courses of lectures, made for his own Church (which is at best but a section of Christendom, and never was, even in its most potent days, aught but an organisation in Western Europe) such sweeping claims that all of us should be unchurched and un-Christed did we assent to those truculent demands. In presence of such claims, all who care for the spiritual heritage of Christendom find their judgment and common sense challenged. And all who prize the accuracy of historic facts must feel revolted by the strange assertions, and the equally strange "quotations," by which Archbishop Carr has sought to buttress his positions. When, therefore, I was urged from various quarters to speak on this subject, I could no longer refuse.

The Roman Claim.

Bellarmine, the authoritative Roman Catholic theologian, defines the true Catholic Church as consisting of all those, and of those only, who (1) profess the true faith, (2) partake of the true sacraments, and (3) subject themselves to the rule of the Pope of Rome as head of the Church "even though they may be false, wicked, and impious" (*etiamsi reprobi scelesti et impii sint*). This definition of the "Holy, Catholic, Apostolic, and Roman Church" obliterates the divine distinction between the Church visible and the Church invisible and spiritual, and makes the Church and Kingdom of Christ as external, "visible, and palpable" as is "the Kingdom of France or the Republic of the

---

* See his lectures on "The Church and the Bible."

Venetians."* It excludes out of God's Church, and out of the pale of salvation, not only all the Reformation Churches and all Protestant peoples, but also the whole Greek or Eastern Catholic Church. For the Eastern Catholic Church, though holding substantially the same faith as the Roman communion, and observing "the seven sacraments," rejects the supremacy and authority of the Pope, and denies him to be the successor of Peter, *declaring that " Peter's apostolic activity in Rome is unknown to history."*† The Romish definition of the Church thus seeks to exclude out of the pale of the Church of God, roughly speaking, the half of Christendom, with the majority of its most enlightened nations. We shall see, in our fourth lecture, that Leo I., "the father of the Papacy," took the same dreadful view in the fifth century, consigning to hell those who do not assent to the primacy of the Bishop of Rome.

Archbishop Carr, in his recent Lectures, takes the same ground. He says:—

"Catholics then maintain (1) that St. Peter was invested by Christ with supreme authority over His church; (2) that St. Peter finally fixed his see in Rome; (3) that the Roman Pontiffs are the successors of St. Peter in the see of Rome."

He boldly declares that this "primacy" does not mean any mere primacy of honour—"a first amongst his equals"—but an absolute "supremacy," a "supreme authority"—"authority to teach, to rule, and to correct." Further, "the limits of that authority are as wide as the Church of Christ upon earth." He further quotes and affirms the words of the Canon of the Vatican Council—words which, in common with the whole dogma of "infallibility," must, to the Pro-

---

* *De Conc. et Ecc.*, lib. iii., cap. 2.

† See Declaration of the Greek Catholic (or Orthodox) Bishops in Reply to the Pope's Encyclical (1895).

testant reason and conscience, in the light of the New Testament Gospel, sound as a foolish blasphemy:—

"If anyone say . . . that the Roman Pontiff is not the successor of Blessed Peter in the same primacy *let him be anathema.*"

This is a large claim! If it had power, it would be a ferocious claim. And, as I and all of us utterly reject it, we must run the gauntlet of that now futile "anathema." To all those three huge propositions of Archbishop Carr, and of his church, we answer that the facts of history and of Scripture compel us to reject them as without basis in truth, and as essentially foolish in substance. Christ did not invest St. Peter with any "supreme authority over His church." Both Peter himself and Paul declare just the opposite. St. Peter had never any "see" in Rome, probably never was in Rome, or in Europe anywhere. And the Roman Pontiffs are in no way "the successors of St. Peter in the see of Rome." They are, as a matter of historic fact, the successors of a long line of despotic priestly politicians, many of whom were amongst the worst figures in human history.*

ARCHBISHOP CARR'S "PROOFS" AND "TESTIMONY."

In support of his three propositions one naturally asks what *proof* does Archbishop Carr give? On examination of his Lectures, we find that the "quotations" he gives are many, but the proofs are sadly few. The attempts at "proof" are amusingly *irrelevant*. Archbishop Carr's method of argument must, to any one accustomed to the laws of evidence, seem extremely odd. But it is the method of "Roman Catholic controversy" to pile together a great number of names and of "quotations" from various "Protestant"

---

* cf. Gibbon, Milman, Menzel, Hallam, &c.; even frank Roman Catholic writers abundantly confess to this.

writers, and to read these out one after the other, torn from their context, and irrespective of age, or century, or value, as if this in some way strengthened the Archbishop's propositions. Archbishop Carr's first two lectures, for example (if we except their references to two "fathers," Clement and Irenaeus), are taken up almost wholly with the "padding" of fragmentary passages, forming what he is pleased to term "exclusively Protestant testimony." When one asks—"testimony" in favour of *what*? and when one begins to examine the so-called "testimony" itself, the result is like Rosalind's chin—"indifferently furnished." Most of the names quoted are either (1) so *antiquated* that they have no weight in our modern day of exact historic criticism; or (2) the "quotations" attached to the names have *no relevance* to the positions Archbishop Carr is trying to establish, but rather support the contrary; or (3) the professed "quotations" themselves are so completely *torn away from their original context*, or are so *mutilated* and altered in their inner substance that they convey to the general hearer or reader almost the opposite of the original meaning. Some of these instances are very venturesome and astonishing. [For Archbishop Carr's "quotations" and "Protestant testimony" see Appendix I.] If wit be "the juxta-position of the incongruous," then the topsy-turvy array of undated and obsolete names adduced by Dr. Carr's "testimony" is wit of a brilliant quality! When Archbishop Carr does condescend upon a few modern names, of commanding importance in the historic investigation of these subjects, such as Lightfoot, or Lipsius, or Harnack, or Renan, or when he appeals to an influential modern writer like Farrar, not one of those men can be got to say any of the three things—the three propositions—which Archbishop Carr's lectures took in hand to establish. Three of those scholars, viz., Lightfoot, Renan, and Farrar, express the opinion that Peter probably visited Rome for a few months at the time of Nero's persecution and died there. Lipsius, as we shall see, declares, on the strongest ground of historical fact, that Peter never was in Rome at all. Harnack, as we shall see, suspends his judgment. But all of them, with one voice, reject as impossible the entire chronological theory on which the "Roman claim" rests. They reject utterly what Archbishop Carr asserts, viz., that Peter "founded the Church in that City of Rome;" or that at any time " St. Peter was invested by Christ with supreme authority over his Church."

Mutilation and Misquotation.

During the perusal of Archbishop Carr's lectures I have been persistently forced to ask myself two questions—(1) Has he really read the books from which he professes to quote, so as to know the context of the passages "quoted?" Or (2) is not the kindlier explanation the true one, viz., that the Archbishop is culling from the various "Hand-books" of "Catholic Controversy" written in defence of the *Cathedra Petri*, the characteristic "quotations" which form the substance of all of them, without having the opportunity to compare them with the original? This latter explanation has seemed to *me* both the more gentle and the more feasible. [The methods of "quotation" adopted in Roman Catholic Controversy Canon Bright, of Oxford, has recently hit off by the striking phrase "to *Vaticanise*" history. "Loyalty to Rome," says he, "will determine how much of a passage or a sentence should be quoted in the text."*]

---

* *The Roman See*, p. 212. This has been read by me since the delivery of my lectures.

The Romanist Method of Advocacy.

I am exceedingly sorry to have to refer to this peculiarity of Roman Catholic Advocacy. I will take at present only a few of the startling instances in Archbishop Carr's Lectures. I feel the more free to speak of it because, in connection with one amazing "quotation" purporting to represent Bishop Lightfoot's statement regarding Irenaeus and the early "lists" of bishops of Rome, Archbishop Carr does much more than simply make Lightfoot appear as saying the opposite of what he *meant* to say. To render the thing more impressive he eulogises Lightfoot at the expense of Professor Salmon, of Dublin, and the Rev. F. Puller and other "Anglican controversialists," and actually accuses the latter of "downright dishonesty," both a "*suggestio falsi*" and a "*suppressio veri*," and of a *deliberate* ignoring of the facts! It is very bad, all this. And I can account for it only on the supposition that Archbishop Carr had not Lightfoot in his hands, but took the representation of his statement on the authority of others.

Professor Salmon's name, I need scarcely say, is (and will always be) a word of honour and renown to Dublin's great University, and to its Schools of Classical, of Mathematical, and of New Testament learning, with which its fame is inseparably associated, and in all of which his singular ability has been proven. He is not only of world-wide reputation as an expert in these questions which lie close to his special chair of New Testament teaching, but he is trusted for his unswervingly fair, and judicial temper. In many matters I do not agree with Professor Salmon. But all of us, in all Churches, who are special students of Biblical and Early Christian learning, owe to him a debt of reverence. That Archbishop Carr could permit himself to apply such epithets to such a man, and at a time when he himself is just about to misquote and misrepresent another pre-eminent scholar, viz. Bishop Lightfoot, only shows that the Roman Catholic Claim, at these crucial points of Early Christian hisory, is anything but strong.*

Dr. Carr on Lightfoot and Irenaeus.

[I will put in parallel columns what Archbishop Carr asserts Lightfoot says about Irenaeus' "list" of the early Roman "bishops," and what Lightfoot says himself.

A.	B.
Carr on Lightfoot.	Lightfoot Himself.
"I cannot pass from these lists of the first Popes without protesting against the downright dishonesty of Anglican controversialists, such as Salmon and Puller, who deliberately ignore the character of the list of St. Hegesippus and the twofold enumeration of St. Irenaeus. Such a *suppressio veri* is more than a *suggestio falsi*. Amongst Anglican writers, however, Bishop Lightfoot is a remarkable exception, and	"It will thus be seen that Irenaeus, in the passage quoted, *separates the Apostolic founders of the Roman Church from the bishops, and begins the numbering of the latter with Linus.* Accordingly, elsewhere (iii. 4-3), he describes Anicetus as the *tenth* bishop; but in two other places (*Hær.* i. 27 I, iii. 4-3), speaking of Cerdon, he says that this heretic appeared in Rome in the time of Hyginus, whom he describes as the

---

* The passages which follow, down to the words "The above instances," on page 39, and included in square brackets, were not spoken in full when this lecture was delivered. The matters dealt with need the *eye* to discern clearly the details of the misquotations here censured. The general facts of the misrepresentation regarding Lightfoot, Irenaeus, Ignatius, and Cyprian, were simply stated rapidly. Then I passed on to take in detail one only of Dr. Carr's "quotations," viz., that from Renan, "as a *sample of all*." In view of the additional matter introduced into the Archbishop's published *Lectures*, with the additional amazing "quotations" there, I deem it better to set these passages in their proper place in the text of my lecture. The "quotations" have been compared in each case with the published form in Dr. Carr's lectures.

I gladly acknowledge the fact. Though his conclusions are sometimes in strange conflict with his premises, still he never suppresses any important fact connected with his subject. For instance, *he admits that all authorities "are agreed as to the authenticity of St. Irenaeus' enumeration of the Bishops of Rome, which includes St. Peter; and he admits, also, that there could be no accidental tripping,"* because St. Irenaeus gives the enumeration in the very next chapter to that in which he had given the list of the *successors* of the Apostles in the see of Rome. But *for no other reason, apparently, than that such an enumeration does not harmonise with his own theory, he* (Lightfoot) *coolly says that he believes St. Irenaeus was mistaken."*— (Lect. V., p. 169-170).

'ninth' in the episcopal succession from the Apostles, 'the ninth bishop.' Here, therefore, *if the readings be correct*, either the Apostolic founder or founders must have been included in the enumeration, so that Linus would be the second bishop, *or there must be some accidental tripping in the number."* — Lightfoot, *Clement of Rome*, vol. i., p. 204.

In a footnote Lightfoot points out that, as to "the two places" in which Irenaeus seems to contradict his own list, beginning as it does with Linus, and excluding Peter and Paul, there is a confusion of the text—

"In the first passage (i., 27, I.) the text of the old Latin translation has *nonum* (ninth), and this reading is confirmed by Cyprian and Eusebius, as well as by Epiphanius. Here, then, all the authorities are agreed. In the second passage (iii., 4, 3) the Greek is preserved only in Eusebius, who has *enatos* (ninth) but the *Latin translation of Irenaeus has octavus* (eighth). *I am disposed to think that in both passages—in the latter certainly—the 'ninth' was a later emendation, so as to include the Episcopate of Peter.*"*

At the risk of weariness, I have been at pains to set out this matter in full. It illustrates the value of

---

* In the above passages I have put the emphatic sentences in *italics*.

Archbishop Carr's charges against Salmon and other Protestant scholars, and the worth to be attached to his "quotations" throughout. Just let us look at this one instance for a moment. He asserts that, according to Lightfoot, "all authorities are agreed as to the authenticity of St. Irenaeus' enumeration of the Bishops of Rome, which *includes St. Peter*." But what Lightfoot says is that Irenaeus' list *excludes* "*the Apostolic founders*," that is, both Peter and Paul, and "*begins with Linus*;" and that in another passage of Irenaeus (*Haer*., i, 27, I) there is a reading describing Hyginus as *ninth* bishop, and this word *ninth* is confirmed by the later "fathers," Cyprian, Eusebius, and Epiphanius ("all' the authorities" as to these singular Irenaean "lists" of early Roman bishops). I will here turn to Irenaeus, and quote the passage:—

"Cerdon was one who took his system from the followers of Simon (Magus), and came to live at Rome in the time of Hyginus, who held the ninth place in the Episcopal succession from the Apostles down."—(Iren. *Haer*. I., 27, i.)

It does not say a word about Peter, or his inclusion in the list of bishops. And Lightfoot, further, points out that the word "*ninth*" must be a mistake, because in the other passage the Latin text of Irenaeus calls Hyginus the *eighth*, thus showing that Peter was not counted "bishop" of Rome.

Then, further, Archbishop Carr actually asserts that Lightfoot "admits there could be no accidental tripping." But what Lightfoot says is—"*or there must be some accidental tripping*." Again, Archbishop Carr asserts—"Lightfoot coolly says that he believes St. Irenaeus was mistaken," and "for no other reason than that such an enumeration does not harmonise with his own theory." But, as an actual fact, Lightfoot says—and his reason is *solid grounds of textual criticism*—that the text of Irenaeus has been tampered with or emended "so as to include the episcopate of Peter."

[NOTE.—In *The Roman See and The Papacy*, by Prof. Bright, of Oxford, received since the above was written, it is funny to find that in his conflict with the Rev. Luke Rivington, that Anglo-Catholic convert to Romanism, and author of *The Primitive Church and the See of St. Peter*, he has had to deal with this same sort of "representation" regarding the "list" of Irenaeus. He says that the language of Irenaeus, who calls both Paul and Peter "founders," shows that neither was ever counted *Bishop* of Rome. "The phrase 'from the Apostles' excludes either Apostle from the Episcopal list. . . . The Latin version of Irenaeus reads 'eighth' in the second passage; and *Stieren considers that it originally read 'eighth' in the first passage also.*" (Bright, pp. 10, 11.) The *manes* of Prof. Salmon ought to feel avenged. It is interesting also to learn from Bright that not only, as we already knew, does Salmon think that "Peter's Roman Episcopate" was first invented by "an editor of the Clementine Romance," but our own Bishop Moorhouse, now of Manchester, has been in the fray too, and thinks "the Clementine fiction" has played odd tricks with the original history of the Roman Church. Of that fiction I have spoken lower down.]

DR. CARR ON LIGHTFOOT AND HARNACK AS TO IGNATIUS.

Another illustration of the daring method pursued by Roman Catholic advocates, in dealing with historic facts and Protestant scholars in relation to those facts, is seen in Archbishop Carr's description of *Ignatius'* letter to Rome in the second century, and Bishop Lightfoot's statement regarding it. As all candid and competent scholars now agree, the remarkable thing in connection with the letter of Ignatius to the Roman "Church," or congregation, in the second century, is that he makes *no reference to its having any bishop*. He writes to the Church or congregation itself:—

"The Church which has obtained mercy . . . which also presides in the place of the region of the Romans."

The eminent scholar Harnack holds that at this time (130-140) "the Episcopate" had not yet begun in the Roman Church. But the Church itself, in its vigorous life and influence as the Church of the Metropolis, had a *pre-eminence* or "presidency" "amongst the sister communities," and an energetic activity in "supporting and instructing the other communities." You might say as much of the Wesleyan Methodist Centre in Melbourne in relation to the outlying Methodist congregations. But Archbishop Carr actually twists this and Lightfoot's similar words about it into a testimony to the Roman Papacy and its Universal Supremacy! "This singular appellation of the Roman Church," Archbishop Carr tells the public, is a proof of the Papal Supremacy! In fact, the ambiguous term "Primacy" is made to play fantastic tricks of varied meaning in Dr. Carr's lectures. This is how he does it:—

CARR (p. 141).	LIGHTFOOT.
"Protestant writers feel the importance of this inscription to the 'Church of the Romans,' and make every effort to explain it away. Still, however, there are non-Catholic authorities of the very highest eminence who *agree with the Catholic interpretation*. Bishop Lightfoot admits that it testifies to a pre-eminence of rank, 'a Primacy,' in fact, in the Roman Church. . . . "Harnack is still stronger."	"We might read the Epistle from beginning to end without a suspicion that the Episcopal office existed in Rome at this time, if we had no other grounds for the belief."—(*Ignat.*, vol. ii., 186). "In the letter (of Ignatius) to the Church of Rome there is not the faintest allusion to the Episcopal office from first to last."—Lightfoot's *Clement*, vol. i., p. 71. "Yet at the same time he assigns a primacy to Rome. The church is addressed in the opening salutation, as she who hath the presidency (prokathetai) in the place of the region of the Romans.' *But immediately afterwards the nature of this supremacy is defined. The presidency of this Church is declared to be a presidency of love (prokathemene tes agapes).*

> *This then was the original primacy of Rome, a primacy not of the bishop, but of the whole church, not of official authority, but of practical goodness,* backed, however, by the *prestige* and the advantages which were necessarily enjoyed by the *church of the metropolis.*"—Lightfoot's *St. Clement of Rome,* vol. i., p. 71.
>
> "The idea of the Cathedra Petri (chair of Peter), therefore, has no place here."—Lightfoot's *Ignat. ad Rom.,* vol. ii., p. 191.

Harnack truly is "still stronger!" But it is in antagonism to all the propositions and misrepresentations of Archbishop Carr. Harnack shows that not only does Ignatius, in the letter to Rome, not allude to any bishop of Rome, but, further, that *there was no such bishop as yet!* Nay, still later than Ignatius, Hermas (142 or 145 A.D.) is, says Harnack, a distinct witness *against* the existence at that time of any bishop of Rome. That Irenæus' "list of bishops of Rome" is legendary and "is false *can be proved,*" says Harnack. And when Harnack says so, he has the proof in his hands.*

Interpolations of Cyprian.

Still more glaring, if possible, is the fact that Archbishop Carr, in "quoting" from Cyprian, the North African father of the third century, publishes to the unwary crowd sentences ascribed to Cyprian, but which critical editors have long ago condemned as manifest interpolations. Thus:—

---

* Harnack, *Ignatian Epis. Exp.,* Ser. iii., No. xiii.

CARR.	CRITICAL EDITORS.
"But St. Cyprian is not content with pointing out the unity of the Church; he is very precise in insisting on the source of this unity:— The Lord saith unto Peter: 'Thou art Peter, &c. *Upon him, being one, He builds His Church.*'" (Lect. iv., p. 104.)	"This passage ('Upon him being one He builds His Church') is beyond all question spurious." Prof. Roberts; Dr. Donaldson; Dr. R. Ernest Wallis; Ante-Nicene Lib. *Cyp.*, vol. i., p. 381. "Falsifying of the text by Romish editors." "Here is interpolated 'Upon him being one He builds His Church,' &c." Dr. Cleveland Coxe; *Ante-Nicene Fathers*, vol. v., p. 422, notes.
St. Cyprian:—"He who opposes and resists the Church, *and who deserts the Chair of Peter, upon whom the Church was founded, does he trust that he is in the Church?*" (Lect. vi., p. 180.)	"Beyond all question *spurious.*" Roberts, Donaldson, and Wallis; "*Writings of Cyprian,*" Ante-Nicene Chris. Lib. *De Unit. Ecc.*, vol. i., p. 381. "Here is interpolated:— '*Who deserts the Chair of Peter upon whom the Church is founded.*' This passage also is undoubtedly spurious." Bishop Coxe; (*Ante-Nicene Fathers*, vol. v., p. 422, n.) See also Lightfoot—*St. Clem.*, vol. ii., pp. 484, 485; [also Bright—*Roman See*, pp. 42, 43]; Burgon — *Letters from Rome*, p. 417; Coxe—*Elucidations* ii.

It is to me sad and irksome beyond all words to have to follow and refute thus Archbishop Carr through all the pitiful *minutiæ* of his "quotations" and purported evidence. Part of the unwelcome fate allotted to me in life, as a teacher of New Testament and Early Christian learning, has been the necessity of acquiring a knowledge of the "patristic" writings of the first three or four centuries. It is a tragic study and story. None but those who have had to familiarise themselves every day with this study can understand the drastic distortion of facts to which Roman Catholic advocates have recourse. Surely, at least, Archbishop Carr ought to have felt himself bound in honour to indicate that those passages he quotes as authoritative and distorts out of relation to their context, are deemed spurious by eminent critical Editors of the "Early Fathers." He dogmatically quotes those passages as if no doubt had ever existed regarding them.]

The above instances, alas! are not at all isolated. They are simply specimens of the method of Roman Catholic "quotation" and argument. But there is worse than that. What impresses me most, on examining the "quotations" and references in these Lectures of Archbishop Carr, and of other recent "Catholic Controversy," is that a forced meaning, a quite unnatural interpretation, is stamped frequently upon the fragmentary passages quoted, an interpretation which those passages were originally never intended to bear. Cyprian of Carthage, as we shall see later, was the earliest great spokesman and inventor of "the episcopate;" "the one undivided episcopate" resting equally upon all the Apostles. This original Unity of the Church is according to him "the root and matrix" of the Church.* Cyprian is the father of what is called "Old Catholicism," the grandfather of what is called "Anglo-Catholicism." North Africa fashioned its cradle. Yet Archbishop Carr represents him as a champion of the Roman Papacy and of the Roman Pope!

---

* cf. Coxe, *Cyp. Ep.* xliv. [Bright p. 46]; Lightfoot, *Phil.*

Archbishop Carr and Renan.

I am surprised at the Archbishop's boldness in quoting from the brilliant critic, Renan, in support of the Roman claim for the Papacy.* I am still more surprised that the quotation is so maimed and mutilated that it gives a sense almost the opposite of what Renan intended to say.

I protest against the implication in Archbishop Carr's lectures that Renan was a Protestant. He

---

* The controversy in the *Argus* and in the *Age*, to which this gave rise between Archbishop Carr and myself, I have gone to the trouble and expense of publishing in the Appendix. In this way the facts will stand before the public impartially and without possibility of change. It is noticeable that, in his published lectures, Archbishop Carr has added much new matter to his first lecture as it appeared in *The Advocate*, and which lecture he had, in his letter of 21st May, declared was "published *in extenso* in the *Advocate* of the 14th and 21st March." More noticeable still, the new matter breaks the original connection just at that crucial stage (forming the context of the matter of our correspondence) where Dr. Carr had worked up along his chain of "Protestant testimony" towards Renan. The connective links were *Nevin—Neander—Renan*. Now, between Nevin and Neander, is inserted a page (pp. 21-22), beginning "A Catholic could hardly," &c., thus throwing the connection out of gear. The further new passage now concluding Lecture I. extends from the words "Church's Existence" to the end of the lecture (pp. 41, 42). This new passage begins:—"It will seem to many that I have deliberately *put myself at a disadvantage in quoting so exclusively from Protestant authorities regarding St. Peter's relations with Rome.*" In the next sentence he attempts a subtle distinction between this and "the Roman Primacy of the Prince of the Apostles," about which "there is no controversy amongst Catholic writers." (The *italics* are mine.) But the correspondence and the beginning of his second lecture and the whole make-up of his first lecture prove that this will not do. (1) "That St. Peter was in Rome;" (2) That he "fixed his See in Rome;" (3) That his Primacy "was transmitted to his successors in the Roman See;" all these were what he declared he had "quoted exclusively Protestant testimony to prove." Thus after Nevin, *Neander* was "quoted" as testifying "to the antiquity of the Papal claims to a Primacy of jurisdiction," and then came *Renan's* admissions "*in favour of the Roman Primacy as the irresistible outcome of the facts of history.*"

never was. He was educated for the Romish priesthood. Recoiling from it, and from the incredible demand which its absolute authority, and its ecclesiastical miracles and legends make upon the human reason, he abandoned belief in the supra-natural of Christianity altogether. Renan gravitated towards a kind of Agnostic Pantheism. Probably he had not soul or earnestness enough for more. Nothing more sad, with a mixture of brilliant flippancy, can be found in literature than Renan's description of his own revolt from the teaching of the priests, prepared as he was for such disbelief by his mother's witty rehearsal of "the grotesque legends of the Breton saints." The very diverse kinds of teachings his priestly instructors gave him accelerated the process. One of his clerical teachers—M. Gosselin, polite, slim, fastidiously neat, and hating all enthusiasm—possessed, as almost his only ardour, an exceeding dislike of all the relics and all the ancient ecclesiastical saints. His reason was—

"Their disregard of personal cleanliness, their deficient education, and their striking lack of common sense."*

Renan says:—

"I imagined that in being polite like M. Gosselin, and moderate like M. Manier, I was a Christian."

I am no admirer of Renan, save for his literary brilliance. I must again say, also, he was not a Protestant, although he confessed that Protestantism was, "in a sense, a returning to the religion of Jesus."

Now, if Archbishop Carr had told from what work of Renan he professed to quote, and had given its full title, the public would have got some glimpse of its meaning. I will tell you what it is. It is the *Hib-*

---

* *Souvenirs*, p. 230. Cf. Professor Elmslie.

bert Lectures for 1880, on the Influence of the Institutions, Thought, and Culture of Rome on Christianity, and the Development of the Catholic Church. The main thought of that book is that the Papacy has been a Roman development mainly due to the peculiar condition of the City and Empire of Pagan and Imperial Rome. The Second Lecture in that book is entitled "*The Legend of the Roman Church: Peter and Paul.*" In that lecture Renan declares:—

"If there is anything in the world which Jesus did not institute, it is the Papacy; that is the idea that the Church is a monarchy."

In a later lecture in that book Renan declares that what "set order above liberty" was the "Episcopate." Moreover, the chapter just preceding that from which the Archbishop takes his "quotation" is entitled: "*Rome, the Centre of Growing Ecclesiastical Authority.*" In it, Renan says he agrees with *Lightfoot* as to the letter of Clement of Rome. In Clement's letter, Renan declares: "*We find no trace as yet of a presbyterus superior to and about to dethrone the rest.*" At the end of the First Century the highest rulers of the Christian Church, he says, were "the presbyteri" (elders), (p. 130). He then shows, as Lipsius does, how the legend of Peter's "bishopric in Rome" arose. It sprang, he explains, in large measure from the strange mingling together of "Ebionite," or Jewish gnostic, and other heresies, whose *apocryphal writings* form so curious a feature of the second century. These "heretic" factions took for their "shibboleth" the most eminent Apostles' names, especially Peter's and Paul's. The "Ebionite" gnostics opposed the name Paul by the name Peter.

"*A vast Ebionite legend arose in Rome,*" continues Renan, "*and under the name of 'the Preaching,' or 'The Journeys of Peter,' took a fixed shape about the year* 130 A.D." (P. 134.)

Then he shows how this legend, glorifying Peter, "was insulting, it is true, to St. Paul" (p. 136). But Piety took hold of it; the spirit of growing ecclesiasticism blended it with the facts of Paul's labours in Rome, and his martyrdom.

"In all that concerns Peter and Paul the work of legend was rich and rapid." (P. 142.)

Then, in the opening of the very chapter from which Archbishop Carr "quotes," Renan points out the shrewd advantage which this legend of "a Church founded both by Peter and by Paul" gave to Rome, in the growingly despotic atmosphere of the Second Century.

"To have succeeded in establishing this belief was the masterpiece of that cleverness which characterized the Church of Rome." (P. 107.)

But even in Rome, Renan points out, the introduction of one presbyter or bishop as superior to the others was strenuously opposed even as late as 145 A.D.

"This revolution, however, was effected not without protest; the author of 'The Shepherd' (Hermas), for instance, still attempts to maintain the primitive equality of the presbyteri against the growing authority of the bishops." (P. 155.)

Then, to illustrate the new autocratic spirit which was invading the Church everywhere, Renan quotes from an Asian writing, which (in common with many great scholars) he deems "apocryphal."* The age or time he is picturing is the *latter part of the Second Century*, some 140 years after the death of Jesus. It is the time, according to Archbishop Carr, the facts regarding which make such impress upon Rationalistic writers that we must "regard their admissions in favour of the Roman Primacy as the *irresistible*

---

* *Ign. ad Eph.*

outcome of the facts of history." It is, as he also declares, the time when, according to Protestant teaching, "*the faith of the Church was pure, and the sanctity of the Roman Pontiffs conspicuous.*"* That sounds well! But, as we know, Lightfoot and others have pictured the state of things just then in Rome as sadly different.† And to speak of "Roman Pontiffs" *then* is to speak "at large." Here, now, is the picture of what Renan means by the "Catholicity" which grew up at Rome. It is strangely different from the impression Archbishop Carr's hearers would draw from this use of the word "Catholicity."

Here is the context in Renan (pp. 171-172)—

"This was written about the year 160 or 170. A purely ecclesiastical piety took the place of the ancient ardour which, for more than a hundred years, had been kindled by the recollection of Jesus. Orthodoxy is now the chief good; docility is salvation; the old man must bend before the bishop even if he be young. It was thus that, by pushing to an extreme the principles of Paul, men arrived at ideas which would have revolted Paul. Would he, who was unwilling to listen for a moment to salvation by works, ever have admitted that a man could be saved by simple submission to his superiors?" (Renan, *Hibb. Lect.*, pp. 171-172.

Now, here is the passage as Archbishop Carr quotes it, without any hint of its contextual or central meaning, and with its damaging sentences dropped out, and he prefaces it with the declaration: "there is no room for mistake in his (Renan's) words":—

Archbishop Carr's Quotation from Renan.	Renan Himself.
"Rome," says M. Ernest Renan, "was the place in which the great idea of Catholicity was worked out. More and	"Rome was the place in which this great idea of Catholicity was worked out. More and more every day it became the capital of Christianity, and

---

* The *italics* are mine.   † Cf. Lect. iv.

more every day it became the capital of Christianity, and took the place of Jerusalem as the religious centre of humanity. Its Church claimed a precedence over all others which was generally recognised. [All the doubtful questions which agitated the Christian conscience came to Rome to ask for arbitration, if not decision. Men argued—certainly not in a very logical way—that, as Christ had made Cephas the corner-stone of His Church, the privilege ought to be inherited by his successors.]. . . The Bishop of Rome became the Bishop of Bishops, he who admonished all others. Rome proclaims her right—a dangerous right—of excommunicating those who do not walk step by step with her. . . . At the end of the second century we can also recognise, by signs which it is impossible to mistake, the spirit which, in 1870, will proclaim the infallibility of the Pope!"

took the place of Jerusalem as the religious centre of humanity. Its Church claimed a precedence over others, which was generally recognised. All the doubtful questions which agitated the Christian conscience came to Rome, to ask for arbitration if not decision. Men argued—certainly not in a very logical way—that as Christ had made Cephas the corner-stone of His Church, the privilege ought to be inherited by his successors. *By an unequalled tour de force, the Church of Rome had succeeded in giving itself the name of the Church of Paul also. A new and equally mythical duality replaced that of Romulus and Remus.* The Bishop of Rome became the Bishop of Bishops, he who admonished all others. Rome proclaims her right—a dangerous right — of excommunicating those who do not walk step by step with her. *The poor Artemonites — a kind of Arians before Arius, have great reason to complain of the injustice of fate which has branded them as heretics, although up to the time of Victor the whole Church of Rome was of one mind with them. From that time forth the Church of Rome put herself above history.* At the end of the second century we can already recognise by signs which it is impossible to mistake the spirit which, in 1870, will proclaim the infallibility of the Pope."

Notice Dr. Carr's use of the word "*the*," and the quite different suggestion it conveys—"*the* great idea of Catholicity." Renan says "*this* great idea of Catholicity." And he had defined it just above as the notion that "*docility is salvation*," that "a man can be saved by simple submission to his superiors" —ideas which "would have revolted Paul." Notice, again, how Dr. Carr says "precedence over *all* others," while Renan says the largely different thing —"precedence *over others*."

(I have *italicised* the sentences the Archbishop omitted.) Now I suppose very few in Melbourne could have dreamt there had been dropped out of that "quotation," at the little blanks where the Archbishop has made a few dots, two passages of tremendous force,* which destroy the very basis on which the Archbishop seeks to stand. In the one passage Renan declares that the Church of Rome gradually invented the Apostolic succession, and the dual foundation by the two Apostles, Cephas and Paul. This duality Renan declares to be as "mythical" as the pagan-Roman legend of "Romulus and Remus." In the other passage, omitted by the Archbishop, Renan declares that the Church of Rome was at that very time *Arian* in doctrine, the very time when the Archbishop is representing it as supreme over Christendom and singularly pure in faith, and as the guardian of the truth of Peter and of Christ.

---

* In the above column, which reproduces Archbishop Carr's "quotation," I have marked in square brackets *two* sentences— "All the doubtful, &c."—which did not appear in the *Argus* abstract of his Lecture (an abstract report which was carefully made from his MS.), but which appeared afterwards in the *Advocate in extenso* report (see his letters). I quoted from the *Argus*. It will be evident that the two sentences referred to do not affect in the slightest my charge. The passage, as the Archbishop quoted it, was drained of its whole meaning by the excision of the sentences to which I refer. cf. *Append.*

Here is the first passage Archbishop Carr drops from out that plausible-looking "quotation":—

"By an unequalled *tour de force* the Church of Rome had succeeded in giving itself the name of the Church of Paul also. A new and equally mythical duality replaced that of Romulus and Remus."

Here is the second passage the Archbishop drops out:—

"The poor Artemonites—a kind of Arians before Arius—have great reason to complain of the injustice of fate, which has branded them as heretics, although up to the time of Victor the whole Church of Rome was of one mind with them. From that time forth the Church of Rome put herself above history."

I will make no comment on these startling facts. I simply ask two questions:—(1) Why did Archbishop Carr drop those damaging sentences out of Renan's statement, if he chose to quote from him? (2) What is the value of Archbishop Carr's "quotations" in reference to the matter in hand?

Part II.

SIMON PETER AND THE ROCK.—PETER'S "SEE" AT ROME.

"Other Foundation can no man lay than that which is laid, which is Jesus Christ."—St. Paul, 1 Cor. iii., 11.

"Behold I lay in Zion a Chief Corner-stone. . . . a Stone of stumbling and a Rock (PETRA) of offence."—St. Peter, 1 Pet. ii., 6—8; St. Paul, Rom. ix., 33.

"For I (Paul) reckon that I am not a whit behind the very chiefest Apostles."—2 Cor. xi., 5.

"James, and Cephas, and John, who are reputed to be pillars, &c."—Gal. ii., 9.

"If there was any primacy at this time it was the primacy not of Peter but of Paul."—Lightfoot, *S. Clement of Rome*, vol. ii., p. 490.

OF Archbishop Carr's three propositions, essential to the Papal claim, the *first* is—

"That St. Peter was invested by Christ with supreme authority over His Church."

This huge assertion the advocates of Papalism seek to base upon one solitary passage of one Gospel, viz., the highly figurative words of our Lord to Simon when Simon confessed Him as Messiah: "Thou art *Petros*, and on this PETRA I will build my congregation" (Matt. xvi., 18).* Now let me say, plainly, I do not myself feel in the least concerned as to the question whether the word PETRA (rock) in this figurative passage is to be interpreted as having special reference to Simon Peter and as a play upon his name, or as meaning only *Our Lord Himself* in His Messiahhood, to which Simon, had just then so strikingly confessed. It does not in the least affect the truth of the Protestant faith, nor does it alter the falsity of the Roman claim *which* view we take. We Protestants (to use a colloquialism) "have no axe to grind" as regards the interpretation of this passage. A large number of eminent Protestant scholars in our modern day have held the opinion that our Lord, when speaking of the rock, made special reference to Peter "in virtue of his steadfast faith,"† or in virtue of his confession, faith, and courage.‡ That the interpretation which affirms a *personal allusion* to Simon Peter does not in the least make for the Roman claim is sufficiently evident from the fact that such stalwart Protestants in our day as Alford and Lightfoot in England, Fritsche, Meyer,

---

* Compare the accounts in the three Synoptic Gospels, Mark viii., 27—33, Matt. xvi., 13—25, Luke ix., 18—24. If the Romish notion that Peter is the Rock-foundation of the Church had any truth in it, it would be unaccountable that Mark and Luke have no reference even to the metaphor.

† Meyer, in *loco*. ‡ Lightfoot, *S. Clem.*, vol. ii., 483—487.

and Weiss in Germany, Briggs and Schaff in America, and Dr. David Brown in Scotland have affirmed that view. And, on the other hand, scholars just as free from bias and as large in vision have taken the contrary view. They have felt bound, by the whole force of the passage and the true meaning of terms, to conclude that the word "rock," with its Old Testament prophetic associations, refers to *Christ himself*, just then so strikingly confessed by Simon, as the Messiah.

It is part of the unvarying tactics of Roman Catholic apologists to ascribe any view save their own to "*bias*," or the "exigencies of controversy." These allegations provoke a smile. I will not now spend time upon them. It is sufficient to point out here that the huge difficulty of the modern Romanist interpretation is that it has against it not only Protestant scholarship, but the whole weight of the opinion of the earliest and greatest "fathers." Whether the word "rock" refers to Peter personally or not is surely little to the point, as regards the marvellous Roman claim, viz., that the bishops in Rome are Peter's only successors, and that Peter was made Supreme Prince of all the Apostles and head of God's Universal Church, and that the bishops of a city in Italy, and they only, speak with Peter's infallible voice and authority. These statements are so incongruous the one with the other that the whole thing, calmly looked at, seems grotesque.

DIFFICULTIES OF ROMAN VIEW.

To begin with, the Roman interpretation has in its path four insuperable difficulties:—(1) Peter himself was quite ignorant of it; so was Paul; so was John; so were all the New Testament writers; it is contrary to the whole spirit of the Gospel of Christ. In the very chapter (Luke ix., 20, compare 46·47) in which the Evangelist tells of Peter's confession of Christ, it is also told:—

"*And there arose a reasoning among them which of them should be greatest (greater).*"

"And Jesus took a *little child,* and set him by His side," as a symbol of *greatness* in His Kingdom. (2) The Roman interpretation did not come into existence *till the fifth century.* We shall show this in a later lecture. The early Fathers knew nothing of this "succession of Peter" existing only in the Church of Rome. (3) If there could be any such thing as an "Episcopal Apostolic succession" depending on a "chair of Peter," or "throne of Peter," or "seat of Peter," that chair would belong to *Antioch* and other cities of the East rather than to Rome. The same legends, exactly, on which Rome depends for her marvellous "Petrine bishopric" and Petrine infallibility assign that "Petrine bishopric" *to Antioch earlier and more certainly than* to Rome. So the great "Greek Fathers" of the fourth and fifth centuries call the Bishop of Antioch, the "successor of Peter," and affirm of "the great City of Antioch" that it possesses "the throne of Peter." Owing to the wealth and political power and situation of the City of Rome in the West, owing to the legends it industriously intertwined with its political and priestly arrogant claim, it came to assume the title to "Peter's Chair" and "Peter's Succession." But the facts of history prove that its claim to these is later, weaker, and even more legendary than that of Antioch and other Eastern cities. And (4) that Peter ever was Bishop of Rome, or ever founded the Church of Rome, is opposed, at once, to historical truth, and to all that is even probable. It violates every canon of the credible.

The treatment of this latter question will come in its own place. Let me at present look at the true and simple interpretation of

Christ's Saying to Simon Peter.

The language, as recorded in St. Matthew's Gospel,* with its figurative terms—" Petros," " Petra," " Congregation," "Keys of the Kingdom," " Gates of Hades —can be understood only by comparing it with kindred language in the Old Testament. It is especially the impassioned and figurative language of the Prophet Isaiah, in describing the kingdom of the Messiah (language which was often on Our Lord's lips, as also on the lips of his forerunner, John Baptist) that unlocks for us here the simple yet grand meaning. All of us will agree, I suppose, with the judgment of Harnack that, whatever be the precise signification of that passage, it indicates that, amongst the twelve earliest Apostles, Simon Peter was the most efficient and influential by force of will and character :—

"It seems to be in harmony with other passages of the synoptic gospels which indicate not only that Peter was foremost among the Apostles by virtue of natural force of character, but that he was also their ordinary leader and representative."†

Until Paul arose, Peter was foremost in action. He is mentioned first in the early Apostolic list, though always on an equality with the other eleven:—"Have not I chosen you, the *twelve*, and one of you is a devil?" Simon also was always associated with the two or three who were the Lord's most intimate friends, the two brothers, James and John (sons of Zebedee), and his own brother Andrew. In the garden, he and the sons of Zebedee were asked to watch with Christ

---

* *Cap.* xvi. 13-20.   † Harnack, *Pet.* cf. also Texten u. Untersuch.

one hour, and failed. In every society of men some one or two stand out prominent, by influence of character. But of any supremacy of one Apostle over the other, there is never a hint. On the contrary, Christ firmly represses any such question, on their part, as "*Which of us is the greater?*" It is significant that the Apostles ask that question *after** those words about the "rock" and "keys" were spoken to Peter, proving that they did not in the least understand the words as giving any supremacy to *him*. If the misused and ambiguous word "primacy" may be at all applied to Peter, it was, as Lightfoot says, only a "primacy *of historical inauguration.*"

Peter's True Claim.

He was *earliest* in reaching clear-sighted faith; he had force of *initiating* energy. He *first*, in a moment when the great multitudes seemed forsaking Jesus, and men were doubting *who He was*, asserted boldly He was God's Messiah. He *first* at Pentecost opened, as with a key, the gate of the New Testament Church, the Kingdom of Christ, to the multitude of Jewish believers.† He first opened it also—reluctantly, but none the less surely—to Cornelius the Latin centurion, and to the Gentiles in Cæsarea. In fact this seems his true and only connection with Latins or with Rome.‡ A little later he defended, at Jerusalem, the reception of the Gentiles into Christ's Kingdom, apart from all Jewish ritual-restrictions, in presence of those who would keep the gate still closed. Peter firmly used the metaphoric "key," and threw that gate of entrance open. Then his initiative was done. The forward movement of the Church's spiritual progress depended on another; the larger "key" of

---

* cf. Matt. xviii., 1.   † Acts ii., 41, 42.   ‡ Acts x.

its wider door passed into the hands of a greater than Peter—namely, Paul. "I laboured more abundantly than they all," says that great pioneer and "founder," who founded—as did all of them—well, because he founded on Christ. Paul was greatest, not by "sovereignty" or lordship, which was a thing unknown and forbidden in Christ's society or kingdom, but "greatest" because the greatest is "he that doth serve."

PETER'S CONFESSON.

Now, in the light of these facts, let us look at the occasion when our Lord spoke his striking words to Simon Peter. The crowd had deserted. Christ was not the King they had expected. He was no Messiah with David's sword and power, conqueror of the Gentiles, bringer of material good, "restorer of the Kingdom to Israel." As Harnack puts it—"His miracles of healing and feeding had not been followed by the assumption of the *national leadership*. Many of the disciples had begun to drift away. Those who were looking for the (national) Messiah saw in *Him* only one of the prophets. Those who remained were tested by a direct question—'Who say ye that I am?' or (as St. John gives it) 'Will ye also go away?' Then it was Peter who answered, and at once: '*Thou art the Christ.*' "

I will not stop to discuss whether Dr. Harnack does Peter less than justice in saying:—

"Although Peter was foremost in expressing the confident belief of the disciples that Jesus *was the Messiah*, it seems clear that, *in his conception of the Messiah, he did not rise above the current ideas of his countrymen.*"

The "national Leader," the Restorer of the World-Kingdom to Israel—this notion was certainly in Peter's mind, as in the minds of all, materialising their vision. Harnack points, as all of us have pointed, to the startling facts that for this quite material view Christ had immediately afterwards to rebuke Simon as very "Satan" and adversary; and, later, when all hope of the national Kingdom was shattered by Christ's capture, "Peter gave way to utter despondency, and denied that he knew Him!"

Yes; but, along with that material aim, there was, we think, in Peter's soul, and in the others, something of a spiritual vision, a faith (which Peter voiced, and which God reveals within) setting Christ high, as Lord of a new undying Age and Realm, Maker of a deathless Kingdom.

Christ's Reply.

This, anyhow, is what is expressed in our Lord's reply to Peter's prompt answer.

As over against the "Gates of Hades"* (viz., all that makes for destruction, and for the darkness and doom awaiting the falsity of Power and the glory of World-Kingdoms) Christ lifts up the vision of His Spiritual Kingdom, like a new kingly spiritual *house*, founded on the Spiritual Rock, in Zion. This "Rock," and on it founded a house of enduring Messiah-Kingship over the World, had been the dream and word of hope spoken by the greatest prophets. The day for its manifestation had come *now*. Simon Peter, voicing the faith of others round him, saw this with spiritual insight, and strongly said it:—" Here is the King-

---

* "Gates of Hades—by a well-known oriental form of speech—the *power of the Kingdom of Death.*"—Alford, in *loco*.

Hades—Sheol—"primarily—the inexorable doom which *demands and swallows* up everything upon the earth."—Delitzsch.

"The realm of the dead, or the region of death and destruction, is represented as an edifice with gates . . . rearing itself aloft as if in *antagonism to life*."—Dr. James Morison, in *loco*.

dom: Thou art its King! Thou art the Messiah of God." In that hour of seeming desertion it was a great confession. Swift came the answer of Christ back:— "*Thou art Petros (Rock-man or Stone) and on this Rock* (Petra) *I will build my Church*"—the community of those that believe in the Messiah, and form the Messiah-Kingdom; "and the Gates of Hades shall not prevail against it."

Now *that*, with these two distinct emphatic words *petros* and *petra*, is the exact form of the sentence in the *Greek* of it. And *that* is the only first-century form of it we have in the Gospels. Let us take all theologic "goggles," whether Protestant or Romanist, from off our eyes, and look simply and frankly at it, in the light of the Old Testament Scriptures, and especially in the light of the figurative language of Isaiah, in which Christ's mode of speech was undeniably steeped.

Manifestly the metaphors in Christ's saying to Peter are a fusion of three striking passages in Isaiah —two of which, viz., those about the *Rock*, are emphasised afterwards by both St. Peter* and St. Paul.† *Both* Apostles (a fact very significant) apply the word *Petra*, and the *Stone laid in Zion* (called also by Peter "*Chief Corner Stone*"), to *Christ only*, as the foundation of the Messiah-Kingdom of God.

The Kingly House on Its Rock.

The three striking passages of Isaiah whose figurative language blends in Our Lord's saying to Peter are—Isa. xxviii. 16-22, and Isa. viii. 14, and Isa. xxii. 22. The first two of these three passages give us the picture of the *Rock* on which the abiding Kingdom of God was to be builded, like a kingly

---

* I. Pet. ii., 6-8.   † Rom. ix., 32, 33.

house.* Over against that Rock-founded Kingdom is pictured the league of "Great Ones" trusting in the world-forces—a Confederacy of Hades, "a Covenant with Death, and with Hades an Agreement." But it is all in vain! Calmly there rises, over against it, what Jehovah "lays in Zion, the precious Corner Stone—*whosoever believes on it shall never be shaken*."† Yet, though it *is* a strong Centre of Refuge—so that "whatsoever escaped from doom, in the Old Testament, stood upon THIS STONE"‡—it will be also a "Rock of offence,"§ on which "the proud shall be broken to pieces."—Mat. xxi. 42-44.‖ It was Jehovah himself in the Old Testament that was called the Rock. But the prophetic eye, and the later consciousness of the Jews, applied all these thoughts to the expected Messiah. *The word "Rock" was "a name for the Messiah amongst the Jews.*'

The other passage from Isaiah gives us the simple meaning of the word "*Keys*," in connection with this Messiah-Kingdom, pictured thus by the Old Testament figure of a Royal House upon the Rock. In Isa. xxii. 15-25, the proud "House-Steward" of the House of David, who lifted himself up in arrogant trust upon the World-Kingdoms and their alliances, is "*pulled down from his standing place.*" Another and worthier Steward of the house is appointed in his stead. "And the Key of the House of David" is hung upon his shoulder "to open and to shut" the King's house to the approach of those outside.

---

* Delitzsch's memorable treatment of Isa. xxviii., and Cheyne's lucid exposition of the same chapter should be read.

† Isa. xxviii. 16.   ‡ Delitzsch.   Isa. viii. 14-15.   ‖ Delitzsch.

¶ Sanday.—See the very striking group of quotations from Jewish writers and Justin given by Sanday and Headlam.—*Romans* (1895), pp. 280, 281.

"THE KEYS."

"A key" is just *what opens a door*; any good and believing and winsome man who loves Christ can surely open the door of the New Testament Church (*that is* the Kingdom of Heaven), and can win those who are outside into it. And Peter, as we all gladly affirm, was the first man who, in an hour of defection, proclaimed Christ as Messiah, the foundation on which the Church rests. He was also the first man who opened wide the door of the New Testament Church to the approach of the multitudes outside.* Delitzsch shows that the phrase "*binding and loosing*" is another figure just "similar in sense."†

When one sees thus the simple meaning of these Jewish Old Testament metaphors, which were familiar to Christ's hearers, the "fitness" and force of his words to Peter are evident. Simon Peter had just boldly announced his belief in Christ as the King of the Messiah-Kingdom, its establisher—the Messiah answering to the people's hopes of "the Rock," on which the Kingdom should be made perpetual. Christ answered—"Thou art true to thy name: kin to the Rock, and on this Rock I will build my Church, the gathering of my faithful ones."

For many years, I myself believed that Our Lord referred to Peter, personally, in the words "*this Rock,*" thinking of him as the *earliest* "living stone" in the building of His spiritual house. I have no bias, as a Protestant, not to believe that still, for it in no way strengthens the Roman claim. But, the more fully one studies into Old Testament language, and into Christ's habitual modes of speech, the more does one feel driven to the conclusion that

---

* Meyer, Lightfoot, Alford, Mansel, Morison, &c
† Del. *Isa.* in *loco* ; cf. Meyer, &c.

Augustine, in abandoning his earlier opinion (viz., that "the Rock" was Peter), and in finally deciding that "the Rock" meant *Christ Himself* (on whom, as Messiah, God's congregation is built), was deciding according to *criteria* of true interpretation.

Both Peter and Paul Make Christ the Rock.

It is to me an arresting fact *that both St. Peter and St. Paul* apply the word *Petra* to Christ only; they represent believing men as but "living stones," built upon that one foundation-stone. I am arrested, too, by the fact of St. Paul so boldly declaring, "Other foundation can no man lay than that is laid, which is Christ Jesus." The whole New Testament chimes with *that*. [When, in Eph. ii. 20, believers, as the "household of God," are said to be built on the foundation of Apostles, &c., of course the genit. is *subjective*, viz., the *foundation laid by Apostles* (Mey., Stier, Ellic.), or possessed and held firm by Apostles, Alford, &c.]. I am impressed, further, with the fact that nowhere, in all the New Testament, or in the "Apostolic fathers," is there any hint of Peter being the "rock," or foundation of the Church. Paul and the others regard Peter as being a *pillar* (στῦλος) resting on the Rock, and strengthening and helping to support the fabric of the Church's stability. But James and John are equally "reputed" as "pillars." This interpretation also preserves us from the startling mixed metaphor which would make Peter both *rock* on which the House is built, and also *steward* having "the key" of that House.

In any case, whatever interpretation we take of the passage, three facts (as Lightfoot urges) must be kept in mind—(1) "In the Old Testament *Jehovah* is 'the Rock;'" (2) "In the New Testament, in like manner, Christ is the *solid basis* on which the Christian Church rests;" (3) "Obviously, Peter cannot be the rock in any sense which trenches upon the prerogative of Christ." Whatever "primacy" be claimed for Peter, it must be only "the primacy of historical inauguration."* Then, "his primacy was completed."

PETROS AND PETRA.

But, it is said by Romanists, and by some Protestant scholars, that *Petros*—the name assigned to Simon ("Peter")—is just the *masculine* and personified form of *Petra* (rock). I answer it is nothing of the kind. A scholar of both Greek and Hebrew will, at least, be slow to accept that. As a matter of fact, the words *Petra* = rock, or cliff (fit to be the basis of a fortress, or house)†, and *Petros* = a piece of rock,‡ a stone § (fit to be flung or to be builded upon the *petra*,|| are very old Greek words and always quite distinct. The distinction between them is as old as Homer and older. The distinction is as clear in "Hellenistic," or Biblical Greek, as in Classical Greek.¶ The attempt to make *petros* equivalent at times to *petra* is treated with scant courtesy by Liddell and Scott (large edition—"*there is no evidence*," &c.)

But we are told by Dr. Carr that "the demonstrative pronoun *this* identifies the petra or rock with Peter." I answer that one should be careful in making such assertions, in view of the New Testament and of Hebrew modes of language and gesture. It would seem to me that the "demonstrative" reference of the word "this" to Christ, the speaker himself, is characteristic of His method throughout. In fact this argument about the "demonstrative" force cuts

---

* *Clem. of Rome*, vol. ii., pp. 486-7. † Matt. vii. 25. ‡ Morison.
§ Lidd. and Scott, &c.; Thayer on Grimm.
|| Schmidt *Syn*. 51, 4-6. ¶ 2 Macc. i. 16; iv. 41.

the other way. For there has never been any adequate answer to the statement of the elder Lightfoot :—

"If he (Christ) had intended that the Church should be built on Peter, it had been plainer and more agreeable to the vulgar idiom to have said—"*Thou art Peter, and upon thee I will build my Church.*"*

Accordingly, one finds that some of the most liberal and broad-minded of modern British New Testament scholars, such as Plumptre and Morison, affirm that by "this Rock" is meant Christ himself, and others, like Professor A. B. Bruce, that "not Peter's person but Peter's faith (resting on the Rock† of the Eternal Truth) is the fundamental matter in Christ's mind."‡

PREDICAMENT OF THE ROMISH INTERPRETATION.

We shall see that modern Roman Catholic advocates are, on this question, at hopeless variance with the early Fathers. And Rome stands in this most awkward predicament that she is now, in this matter, propounding as doctrine, not only what has not "the unanimous consent of the Fathers," but what is directly opposed to that "unanimous consent."

ROMAN VIEW LATE.

The Romanist interpretation was an afterthought, so as to make Scripture square with the notion that Rome was the seat of empire and authority, and that Peter, as Bishop of Rome, was, in his so-called "successors" (the Roman prelates), the centre of unity and the source of jurisdiction. It was a hard task to find

---

* Light. *Works*, Ed. Pitman, vol. xi., p. 225.
† On the argument that Christ "spoke in Syro-Chaldaic," see Appendix.
‡ *Training of the Twelve*, cap. xi., pp. 163-5.

any Scripture which could be bent to *that* shape. But Rome, which had done many astute things, managed this also. In the fifth century, Celestine,* Bishop of Rome, and his strong-willed genius of an Archdeacon, Leo, afterwards Pope Leo the Great, for the first time mooted the theory which Leo, afterwards, so daringly elaborated. For the first time there was invented that anti-scriptural theory of Matthew xvi. 18, which is now in the mouth of every combative Romanist, viz., that Peter, as Prince of the Apostles, was the one "Rock" on which Christ's Church is built, and that he was supreme over the other Apostles, and that the Bishops of Rome represent him, and speak with his voice of authoritativeness, and from his chair.† "St. Peter," says Archbishop Carr, "was invested by Christ with supreme authority over His Church." In my fourth lecture we shall find this theory, championed by Leo, trying to fight its way to acceptance. But we shall see that, from the first, it was determinedly resisted by Christendom. Now, and here, I shall show that the very basis of Scripture interpretation on which it attempted to structure itself

---

* "Even the Western Fathers of the fourth and fifth centuries, such as Hilary, Ambrose, Jerome, and Augustine, as also Innocent I., had still interpreted the πέτρα (*Petra*) of Matthew xvi. 18, partly of the confession of Peter, partly of the Person of Christ."—Macpherson's Kurtz, vol. i., p. 269.

† If any "Father" earlier than Celestine and Leo seems to approach their notion, it is the obscure Optatus of Milevi, in North Africa, in the close of the fourth century (A.D. 384). His writings are much interpolated. "In their present shape we may call Optatus," says *Harnack*, "the father of that *objective* theory of the *Sacrament* which has played so vast a part in Western dogmatics." In fact, we owe to the peculiar mood of North Africa much, both of the *despotic* and of the superstitious and *sacerdotal* spirit, which has stamped the Western or Roman Church."

See also, as to the views of the "Fathers," Schaff—*Nicene and Post-Nic. Chris.*, vol. i., p. 303. Lightfoot—*St. Clem.*, vol. ii., pp. 482-485.

was a thing unknown to "the Fathers," for at least three and a-half centuries after our Lord's ascension.

Archbishop Carr ventures to say:—

"Indeed, St. Augustine is perhaps the only one amongst the Fathers who appears in two passages to interpret in a literal sense the *petra* or rock of *Christ*."

This is, to say the least of it, daring. For, a little above, the Archbishop had to confess that there are:—

"passages from St. Cyril, St. Augustine, St. Jerome, St. Ambrose, and Origen which are usually relied on by our adversaries to minimise the force of the text of St. Matthew.*

Archbishop Carr, true to the Roman method, is "equal to the occasion." He makes a fine-spun distinction between "a primary" and an "accommodated" or "secondary sense of the same text or texts." After this preliminary, we are not astonished to find the Archbishop continuing:—" In this way we can easily reconcile the passages from St. Cyril, St. Augustine, St. Jerome," &c. Oh, certainly! I do not doubt that, "*in this way,*" you can reconcile the most glaring contradictions in any "passages." By this Roman method of "reconciling passages," by putting a "primary sense" upon one, and a "secondary sense" or "accommodated sense" upon another, you can, in the region of interpretation, (just as, by the Roman doctrine of "intention," you can, in the region of Ethic) get astonishing results. Hence, Archbishop Carr can, apparently, satisfy himself by having to confess:—

"These Fathers in particular passages interpret the rock of Christ, as well they might, for Christ is, as St. Leo says, the fundamental and independent rock, while Peter is the secondary and dependent rock."

Now I never went to school in this kind, either of architecture, or of exegesis. These hair-splitting dis-

---

* Carr. *Six Lectures*, pp. 84, 85.

tinctions between "primary sense" and "secondary sense," between "fundamental rock" and "secondary rock," do not appeal to me. The Archbishop's words seem to yield, sorely against his will, the very thing Protestants say, and against which he seeks to contend.

Rome's View not known to Early Fathers.

What I want to get at is, not the ingenious "reconciling of passages," but actual facts. Now the actual facts are that the "*Early Catholic Fathers*," east and west, are as widely at variance with one another regarding the interpretation of Our Lord's words to Peter, (in Matt. xvi. 18) with respect to the *Rock*, as Protestant scholars are to-day. "Uniform" or "infallible" basis for an infallible Church, in the interpretation of this passage by "the Fathers," we can find nowhere! "Unanimous consent of the Fathers" we can find nowhere! Nay more, Archbishop Carr's assertion—"Indeed St. Augustine is perhaps the only one amongst the Fathers" to "interpret in a literal sense the petra or rock of Christ"—is quite contrary to fact.

As a matter of simple historic truth, the interpretation which makes the Petra (Rock) mean Christ, and the other non-Romish interpretations, meet us in the earliest Fathers who allude to the passage. And they recur and reappear through all the early centuries. *The only interpretation which does not meet us in the early Fathers is the Romanist interpretation.*

Four Views in Fathers.

We find in the "Early Fathers" *four*[*] distinct interpretations given to Christ's words—"*Upon this*

---

[*] This analysis will, I venture to think, be found, by scholarly readers, more adequate and exact than the *two* categories into which Lightfoot groups the views.

Rock I will build my congregation." (1) "The Rock" is *Christ Himself.* This meaning is expressed as early as Tertullian.* It recurs afterwards, again and again. It is affirmed by the great Latin Father, Augustine, and even by Cyril.

(2) The Rock has reference to the faith of Peter, as spiritually illumined to confess Christ "the spiritual Rock," and as representative of *every believing man.* This is the view of Origen, the great Alexandrian exegete in the third century, and he expressed it beautifully :—

> "If we also, like Peter, say *Thou art the Christ, the Son of the living God* . . . the Spirit from heaven having illumined our heart, *we become a Peter,* and it would be said to us through the Word 'Thou art Peter,' and the rest. For *every disciple of Christ is a rock.*"

So, further, declares Origen—*every Apostle* is as much a *foundation* for the Church as Peter, and has the keys of the Kingdom's door as much as he :—

> "But, if thou supposest that the whole Church is built by God on that one Peter alone, what would'st thou say concerning John the Son of Thunder, or any one of the Apostles? Otherwise, shall we dare to say that against Peter the gates of Hades shall not prevail, but that they shall prevail against the rest of the Apostles?"†

He goes on to say that the same "promises" spoken to Peter are given "to every one" who has *faith* like Peter. "For all become namesakes of the rock who are imitators of Christ the Spiritual Rock."‡

---

* Tert. *Adv. Marc.* iv. 13. "Again He changes the name of Simon to Peter. . . . But why Peter? . . . Was it *because Christ was both a Rock and a Stone?* For we read of his being placed for a Stone of Stumbling and for a Rock of Offence." It is odd that writers on the subject seem not to have noted this striking passage, for its distinct echo is in Augustine's famous treatment.

† Orig. *Comm. on Matt.* xvi. 13-20; c.f. also Lightfoot, *Clem.,* vol. ii., 483.

‡ *Ibid.*

(3) The "Rock," according to other "Fathers," has reference to Simon Peter in his *personal position as earliest* to confess Christ's Messiahhood, and earliest in throwing open, at Pentecost and at Cæsarea, the door of Christ's New Testament Kingdom to believing men. In that sense, Peter was the *first stone* in the building of Christ's historic Spiritual House, as no one else can be. This is the interpretation given by Tertullian in two different works* of his, one of them written while he was still a foremost spokesman of "the Orthodox Church," and before, as Jerome ruefully declares, the jealousy and tyrannical treatment of the Roman clergy drove him into Montanist revolt. Peter, says Tertullian, is called rock. But in the next sentence John is put on perfect equality with him as "the Lord's most beloved disciple," and "whom He commended to Mary as a Son in His own stead."

Tertullian on Paul's Rebuke of Peter, &c.

In the next chapter (23) Tertullian finds it necessary to defend Peter's apostleship, and equality, in view of Paul's rebuke of Peter. In the next chapter (24) he finds Peter's thus damaged claim, to equality and apostleship, vindicated again by the fact that he too as well as Paul, had died a martyr's death.

"It is a happy fact that Peter is on the same level with Paul in the very glory of martyrdom."—(*De Praescr. Haer.* 24.)

In his other writing, where he makes the word "rock" refer specially to Peter, Tertullian shows that, by this was meant only that the Church at Pentecost *began* with Peter, and with his throwing open its

---

* *De Praescr. Haer.* 22 ; *De Pudic.* 21. It is substantially the view of Alford and Lightfoot. It is finely put by Briggs—*Messiah of the Apostles*, p. 28, blending with it the Origen view.

message of repentance and remission of sins to believing men.

"[Peter] himself, therefore," says Tertullian, "was *the first to unbar*, in Christ's baptism, the *entrance to the Heavenly Kingdom*."

"This is," says Tertullian, "the Key." And the "loosing," he declares, meant the taking away and lifting off the *restrictions* which, like a yoke, had been imposed by the legalism of the Past.

"*The power of loosing and binding*, committed to Peter, had nothing to do with the capital sins of believers,"* cries Tertullian.

That is a noble protest from this Latin Father in the opening of the third century, to which, had the Church of Rome in later centuries listened, there would have been no need of a reformation. For there would have been no Popery.

(4) A fourth interpretation of the early Fathers was that Peter, in his confession, is spoken of as "rock," as spokesman and representative of *all the Apostles, in their common faith and equal authority,* "*with a like partnership both of honour and power.*" This is the view advocated, in the middle of the third century, by Cyprian,† the influential North African bishop. By this theory of the equality and unity of the Episcopate, Cyprian is the true father of, what we may call, an incipient "Old Catholicism;" all bishops, as representing the Apostles, *equal*, and the unity of the faith voiced through them, just as all the Apostles were equal. Their equality and unity is affirmed in what Christ said to Peter as spokesman for them all. This is the passage of Cyprian which Rome so strikingly interpolated;‡ but its meaning stands out clear through all.

---

* *De Pudic.* 21.   † *Cyp. de Unit. Eccl.*, 4.   Also *Epist.* lxxv.
‡ See Part I.   Also Lightfoot, *Clement*, vol. ii., 484-485 [and Bright's *Roman See*, 42. 43].

"*And although He gives equal authority to all the Apostles after His resurrection.*"

And again—

"The rest of the Apostles verily were, what Peter was, endowed with an equal partnership of honour and power, but the beginning proceeds from unity," &c.

RESULT—ROMAN VIEW UNKNOWN.

Now, I have been at pains to set out all these actual facts. Look straight at them. The interpretations of that passage in Matthew's Gospel differed as widely in the close of the second, and in the third centuries, as now. But, differ as they might, there is not a trace, east or west, of the Romish notion of Peter's supremacy, or of a Roman bishop's supremacy as successor of Peter. This very Cyprian, who for the first time spoke this theory of an absolute unity of the Church as standing in the "inspired Episcopate," spoke in terms of absolute equality to the Bishops of Rome, for no one bishop was higher or lower than another. As we shall see in a later lecture, Cyprian was consulted as to whether Cornelius, Bishop of Rome, was a proper bishop. And he resisted Stephen, a forceful and later Bishop of Rome, on a question of Church administration and discipline, and carried the day against him. The Roman clergy, writing to this Cyprian, Bishop of Carthage, call him "Papa" (Pope),* *Ep.* xxx.

Everywhere, in those early centuries, we search in vain for the Romish interpretation. As late as the fourth century, even the Latin Fathers nearest Rome, such as Ambrose of Milan, and even Jerome himself

---

* In their letters they (Cyprian and the Bishops of Rome) wrote in terms of perfect equality. "*Cyprian to Cornelius, his brother*, greeting," "*Cornelius to Cyprian, his brother*, greeting, "Cyprian to Stephen, *his brother*, greeting," &c. *Ep.* xl.—lxvi.

knew nothing of *Peter's supremacy.* Jerome says:—

"The Rock is Christ, who bestowed upon His Apostles that they also should be called 'rocks.'"—Amos vi. 12.

Ambrose calls the "primacy" of Peter only a "*primacy of confession, not of honour; a primacy of faith, not of rank.*"*

In fact, with Ambrose it is still, what Lightfoot happily terms, "a primacy of historical inauguration." Even Jerome, as Schaff and others have shown, "vacillates in his explanation of the *petra,* now, like Augustine, referring *it to Christ, now to Peter and his confession.*"

AUGUSTINE.

Then we are met by Augustine's judgment in his matured years.

"For the reason why the Lord says 'On this rock I will build my church' is that Peter had said: 'Thou art the Christ, the Son of the living God.' 'On this rock which thou hast confessed,' says he, 'I will build My church." *Petra enim erat Christus* (for Christ was the rock) upon which also Peter himself was built; "for other foundation can no man lay than that is laid which is Jesus Christ."†

That is said by the greatest Father of the Western Church.

Elsewhere Augustine says:—

"For it was not said to him :—'Thou art a rock (*petra*), but thou art Petrus (Peter) and the 'Rock' was Christ, through confession of whom Simon received the name of Peter.'"‡

Even Cyril of Alexandria, in the fifth century, flatterer of Rome for his own purposes though he was, yet says in his *Expos. on Isai.*, that the words "On this rock" mean "Our Lord Jesus Christ."§

---

* *De Incar. Dom.*, cap. iv.   † *Tract. in Evang. Joannis,* 124.
‡ *Retract.* I., i.21.
§ Schaff points out that even Gregory VII. (Hildebrand), "the greatest Pope of the Middle Ages," endorsed Augustine's interpretation.

Here then is a strange spectacle. I do not care to follow Archbishop Carr into his laboured casuistry in answer to the charge that the modern Romanist interpretation violates the principle of the Tridentine Confession of Faith, viz.:—

"Neither will I ever take and interpret them (the Scriptures) otherwise than *according to the unanimous consent of the Fathers.*"

I will leave Dr. Carr to his ingenious apologetic against his "Anglican antagonists," Dr. Littledale, and the rest, on this matter.

Rome Against Rome.

What I want to emphasise is that Rome's boast of uniformity of doctrine and of interpretation is a pompous phrase, having no reality of fact to correspond with it. And the phrase about "unanimous consent of the Fathers" is equally unmeaning and convenient. Rome, when it suits her purposes, as a great German scholar puts it, simply sets aside Scripture under the plea of "tradition;" and *who* is to interpret tradition? —*The Pope!* So "the Fathers," whose interpretation is awkward for Rome's purposes, are set aside; and even the solemn decisions of earlier Popes are set aside when inconvenient. One Pope denounced the withholding of the cup from the laity as sacrilege. A later Pope and Council decreed that "sacrilege." Similarly if there is one interpretation of Scripture more than another which is *contrary to "the unanimous consent of the Fathers," it is the modern Romanist interpretation of Peter's sole supremacy and Rome's supremacy based on Christ's saying about the rock.*

No Father and no Bishop of Rome knew anything of it till the close of the fourth century. The Bishop of Antioch was then, amusing to relate, called

"Successor of Peter," and Antioch had "the throne of Peter"—that is "his faith." If by "the Fathers" be meant the faith of Christendom in the first four centuries, then certainly the modern Romanist doctrine of Papalism and of the supremacy of the Bishop of Rome is contrary to the unanimous consent of the greatest Fathers east and west. It is a small thing to Rome to say that it is against *Scripture*. For the priestly arrogance which has not hesitated to force the Apocrypha into the canon of inspired Scripture, though Jerome excluded it, and to strike the second commandment out of the Decalogue, splitting the tenth into two commandments, is easily equal to the task of resting the huge fabric of the modern Papacy on a wild theory of Peter's sovereignty over all other Apostles, founded on a forced interpretation of "key," and "Gates of Hades," and "rock," and "binding and loosing," which (were it true) would condemn the greatest of the Fathers as arch-heretics.

"What a gigantic system of spiritual despotism," says Professor A. B. Bruce, "and . . assumption has been built on these two sentences concerning the rock and the keys! How nearly by their aid has the Kingdom of God been turned into a Kingdom of Satan."* Yes, that name—"Satan"—remember, Simon bore too. The Romanist interpretation is additionally hampered by this startling fact that in the same hour when our Lord called Simon "Petros" for confessing His Messiahhood he also called him "Satan," and bade him get behind Him, for being blind to the fact that His Kingdom was not one of worldly force and temporal power, but was to be won through redeeming love and sacrifice. "Get thee behind me, Satan," just as He did to the Tempter, in the wilderness, who offered Him "the

---

* *Training of the Twelve*, cap. xi., p. 165.

kingdoms of the world" and their glory. The attempt of the Douay version to explain those words away, and to get rid of the fact that if the Roman Church is built on Petros it is also built on Satanas, is of the sorriest description and can satisfy no candid mind.

"The Holy Fathers expound them otherwise; that is, *Come after Me*, or *follow Me*; and" . . &c.

Peace to the "Holy Fathers!" We have seen how *they* and Rome square. But the worst of all the evil is that, by building thus an external hierarchy on this external "rock" at Rome, there has been hidden from the view of the peoples that living Christ who, in His Spiritual Messiahhood, without any external power of world-kingdom, was once so nobly confessed by the Rockman, Simon Peter. Once, in the spiritual sway of His gospel over the souls of men, He could come into the world's cities—when His Church had no altar or High-Priest except Himself—and could say, "Come unto Me." And all who did come repentant, taking of His Spirit into will and heart, He made "kings and priests unto God." All His ministers He made (as St. Peter himself declares) not "lords over God's heritage," but simply teachers and ensamples to His flock."

LECTURE SECOND.

THE ROMAN LEGEND OF PETER.—THE QUESTION AND MODERN SCHOLARSHIP.—WAS PETER "BISHOP OF ROME?"

"Behold how much wood is kindled by how small a fire."—St. James iii., 5 (Rev. Vers.)

THE first proposition of the Roman claim was, as we saw in last lecture—

"That St. Peter was invested by Christ with Supreme authority over His Church."

The second proposition is, and it is *this* we are now to examine—

"That St. Peter finally fixed his See in Rome."*

So the "rock" has got transferred, by some strange geographical shift, from the east to the west, from the great limestone plateau of Zion to the slope near Janiculum by the yellow Tiber at Rome. The married fisherman of Galilee, Simon Peter, was destined to a strange fate, topographical, sacerdotal, political. He was to become the legendary head of a vast system of celibate monks and priests, bishops, archbishops, and prince-cardinals, and of a line of papal monarchs reigning in a great palace at Rome and at Avignon, and carrying both "the keys" that admit into the heavenly gates, and also the sceptre-staff under which

---

* Carr. *Primacy*, p. 8.

peoples, parliaments, kings, and emperors should be commanded to bow. Poor Peter, had he but known it! From the substance of his teaching and his epistle I judge he would not have been gratified. To Cornelius, the Latin centurion, who bowed down at his feet, he said:—" Stand up, I myself also am a man!"* The Elders away in his wide field of missionary work in Asia and " by the shores of the Black Sea"† he, as their fellow-elder, counselled not to " lord it over their charge" but to " make themselves ensamples to the flock." And he told them there is only one " Chief Shepherd," therefore they should be lowly, and " serve." For, adds he, "God resisteth the proud, but giveth grace to the humble."‡

Now, I need not stop to show the huge anachronism involved in the Romanist assertion that "St. Peter fixed his See in Rome." Here, again, there is that fatal "ambiguity of terms." The word " see" meant, originally, simply " seat," the *sedes*, or seat, of a teacher. How words alter their meaning; the simple gets ghostly; the noble, through Time's wear, gets vulgar! The word " silly" once meant "*blessed.*" On the other hand, one awesome priestly garment, much in vogue at present, meant originally, as Max Müller and Dean Stanley have shown, a *kerchief* for the nose. Another, the " dalmatic," was a common piece of raiment of a Dalmatian peasant. So the simple word "see,"§ at first innocent of any priestly meaning, now suggests awesome and lordly things of Diocesan crozier, mitre, and despotic authority. As Professor

---

* Acts x., 26.   † " Harnack" on 1 Pet. i.   ‡ 1 Pet. v., 1—5.

§ Thus Our Lord, in denunciation, says :—" The Scribes and the Pharisees sit in Moses' *seat*." (Douay—Rheims version—following Wycliffe, translates it "*chair.*") The French word for pulpit is *chaire*, which is shortened for *Cadera*, Greek *Kathedra*, as above. The history of this word, till at last it became the pompous *Cathedra Petri*, is significant. So "a Professor's chair."—Cf. Morison on Matt.

Sanday, treating of the once simple word "bishop," says:—"*We are slaves of words.*"

But apart from this, in Archbishop Carr's lectures, two quite different things are shrewdly mixed together—the question, viz.: Did Peter ever visit Rome? and the quite different question, which involves a glaring anachronism: Was Peter bishop of Rome, as the Roman legend affirms, for twenty-five years?—Did he, as the Roman claim affirms, found the Roman Church, and institute a line of Popes who have descended in unbroken succession from him?

Now, those two questions we must keep distinct. They have really little to do the one with the other. Even if you could prove that Peter ever was at Rome, (and I wish you could prove it), this would not in the least prove that Peter founded the Church of Rome, or ever was a "bishop" there. There was no such thing in those days as a single bishop ruling a church anywhere. And a wandering Missionary Apostle was just as unlike as could be to your modern hierarchical notion of "a bishop."

Did Peter Visit Rome?

Now, the Archbishop, like Roman advocates generally, says it is "for controversial purposes many Protestant scholars find difficulty in assenting to the affirmation that Peter visited Rome." I answer that it is certainly for nothing of the kind. A supposed visit by Peter to Rome would not in the least give any basis for the Roman claim, or imply *a bishopric* of Peter at Rome, any more than a visit of Paul or of Timothy or of John to Rome would imply, that *they* were "bishops of Rome." As Bishop Lightfoot, an eminent Anglican scholar (who thought that, for a few months, Peter probably did visit Rome) says, the question is to be pursued simply "as a historical study." And, from the facts of history, he not only rejects as an anachronism the notion that Peter could be " bishop of Rome," but further declares—

"Now I cannot find that any writers for the first two centuries and more speak of St. Peter as bishop of Rome."*

Sieffert and Schaff, eminent Presbyterian scholars, who also thought it probable " that Peter died in Rome as a martyr under Nero," say further—

"For the Roman Catholic fiction of a twenty-five years' Roman bishopric of Peter there is no foundation. The New Testament is surely against it."†

So that, evidently, Protestant scholars, have no controversial prejudice in dealing with this question— "Did Peter visit Rome?"

Carr on Calvin.

Even the Archbishop of an infallible Church may err. Even Popes, as we shall see, have badly erred. Here is what Archbishop Carr said in 1893 :—

"That St. Peter resided in Rome, and died there, and that he was Bishop of Rome, are historic facts, which were never disputed before Calvin's time."‡

That is an amazing sentence! Someone, in the meantime, has been priming the Archbishop. Now, in his *Primacy* lectures of 1896, he says—

" Before the fourteenth§ century no one, however hostile to the Holy See, had ever ventured to deny the fact of St. Peter's sojourn in the imperial city. It was reserved for Marsilius, of Padua, in furtherance of political purposes, to assert that St. Peter had never been at Rome, &c."‖

---

* *S. Clem.*, vol. ii., p. 501.
† Professor Sieffert in Schaff's *Herzog*.
‡ Carr, *Origin of the Church of England* (1893). Append. p. 83.
§ In a footnote Dr. Carr confesses that the Waldenses in the thirteenth century denied it. ‖ *Primacy*, p. 9.

And Dr. Carr goes on to say:—

"Their cry was taken up by Wycliffe and by Luther. Calvin evidently did not care to risk his reputation for learning by running counter to the universal testimony of fourteen centuries. 'There is nothing repugnant in the statement that Peter died at Rome" is, however, the extent of his (Calvin's) admission.'"*

Here, again, Archbishop Carr leaves quite an incorrect impression. But he is making progress. He has now learnt that on this matter (as on all matters of historic investigation and of exegesis) that great Augustinian thinker and scholar, Calvin, whom even flippant Renan called the greatest and "most Christian man of his century," was careful always not to "risk his reputation for learning." He had certainly a great reputation for that; and kept true to truth. He always looked facts straight in the face, and never shirked them even when it made against his own theology. And nowhere in literature will you find, for calm and fair historic analysis, and for quiet yet brilliant humour, anything finer than Calvin's criticism of Peter's so-called Roman Episcopate. After showing the strange contradictions of early writers as to Peter and Rome, Calvin says:—

I do not dispute that he died there (non pugnot quin illic mortuus fuerit), but that he was bishop, particularly for a long period, I do not believe. I do not, however, attach much importance to the point, since Paul testifies that the Apostleship of Peter pertained specially to the Jews, but his own (Paul's) specially to us. . . . We ought to pay more regard to the Apostleship of Paul than to that of Peter, since the Holy Spirit destined Peter for the Jews, and Paul for us. Let the Romanists, therefore, seek their primacy somewhere else than in the Word of God, which gives not the least foundation for it.

[NOTE.—Dr. Carr's foot-reference is here—as often —unmeaning. The following are some of Calvin's sentences:—"By what

---

* *Id.*, p. 9-10.
† I suppose this is what Dr. Carr funnily translates by "there is nothing repugnant." ‡ Instit. Bk. iv., cap. vi., 15.

authority do they annex this dignity to a particular place, when it was given without any mention of place?" "Let us see how admirably they reason. Peter, they say, had the first place among the Apostles. . . . But where did he first *sit?* At Antioch, they say. Therefore, the Church of Antioch justly claims the Primacy." "Nay, in the Epistle to the Philippians (written from Rome) . . . he (Paul) complains that *all seek their own.* And to Timothy he makes more grievous complaint that no man was present at his first defence—that '*all men forsook*' him (2 Tim. iv., 16). *Where, then, was Peter ?* If they say that he was at Rome, how disgraceful the charge which Paul brings against him of being a deserter of the Gospel." "But these authors are not agreed as to who was his (Peter's) successor. Some say *Linus* ; others, *Clement.* And they relate many absurd fables concerning a discussion between him and Simon Magus." (Bk. iv., cap. vi., 11-12-15.) Oh, rare John Calvin!

In fact, a course of Augustinian John Calvin and of that daring Marsilius of Padua, Rector of the University of Paris, who, as early as A.D. 1323 in Rome's days of greatest splendour, dared to tell the Pope that "the Priest should have no secular power ;" that "the New Testament knows no difference between a presbyter and a bishop, and no difference between Peter and the other Apostles ;" and that "the sole head of the Church is Christ," would be good for Archbishop Carr. And then, if he comes to be Pope, as I hope he will (for most ungratefully they have never yet elected an Irishman as Peter's successor) there will be some chance of the reunion of Christendom.]

I need not make comments on these wonderful self-contradictory readings of history spoken by Archbishop Carr on Calvin and others, nor on the spirit of them. Calvin, just like Harnack and other scholars of our later day, saw no reliable proof that Peter ever visited Rome. He saw the huge legends that surround the Roman assertion regarding it. But he personally had no objection to the theory ; and he seems to have been inclined to accept the statement made by certain "Fathers" that Peter died at Rome.

I myself would like to believe that if I could ; and I have tried hard to find some evidence. I would gladly prove, if it were possible, that Peter came to Rome. Unfortunately I am not able to do it. My reasons for wishing it are two ; (1) There are some interesting questions about the New Testament gospels on which the decision of this question, one way or the other, might cast some light; (2) secondly, I should at once become famous. And this, for a hard-worked Australian parson or professor, would be a pleasant thing. Any man who can prove that the Apostle Peter actually visited Rome will awake next morning and find himself famous, in the world of scholars, writers, and publishers. The publishers and magazine editors will be running after *him* then, as they now run after some latest discovery of a "novelist," who will describe in artistic fashion a hypnotised washerwoman's unclad foot, or make "idylls" in which rural persons sob and sin in a little less natural way than ourselves, and in a largely unintelligible dialect.

Modern Scholarship and Peter in Rome.

The study of the whole question has been revolutionised, in our day, by the profound investigations into the subject made by Professor Lipsius,* of Germany. He holds the very highest place of fame as a historian and archæologist. As the result of his investigations, he declares that the Romish tradition of the twenty-five years' bishopric of Peter at Rome is a fable, the result of the growth of legend. He also shows how that legend arose. We shall, later on, trace that legend. Then, as to the other and different question—"Did Peter ever come to Rome?"—Lipsius decides against it. The historic facts and probabilities, he holds, are all opposed to such a belief. This view other modern scholars of the foremost rank have taken—such as De Wette, Winer, Baur, Mayerhof, Holtzmann, Hausrath, Zeller, and Schwegler. The

---

* *Lipsius, Chronologie der römischen Bischöfe*, and various other works. Hort, Harnack, Duchesne, and others engaged in the discussion. See the literature given in Lightfoot, *S. Clem.*, vol. I., 201-2. Lightfoot sets the very highest value on Lipsius and Harnack.

force of the facts adduced by these scholars shook even Neander, formerly an eminent champion of the other view.

On the other hand, a number of eminent modern scholars, such as Wieseler, Ewald, Bleek, Hilgenfeld, Sieffert, Lightfoot, Renan and Sanday have inclined to the opinion that Peter did probably come to Rome for a brief time to encourage the Jewish Christians there, in the epoch of the Neronian persecution. But they admit that for this there is no clear and distinct contemporary proof. And his stay in Rome could have been at most only for a few months. Harnack, probably the greatest living scholar on the religious history of the early centuries, suspends his judgment. He declares that "the probabilities of the case are evenly balanced." But the notion of Peter as having founded the Church of Rome, or as having been bishop of Rome, is impossible. These scholars unanimously declare the Romanist tradition of Peter as founder of the Roman Christian Church, or as claiming "primacy," or as having established in Rome an "apostolic succession," or as having been bishop of Rome for twenty-five years, or "bishop of Rome" at all, to be beyond belief.* The more learned and candid of even Roman Catholic theologians have now yielded so far, to the force of facts, as to admit that Peter's visit to Rome, to use Farrar's words, "could only have been very briefly before his martyrdom."† Here arises a huge difficulty for the Roman Catholic

---

* Lightfoot holds that if Peter came to Rome at all it could only have been after Paul was set free from his "first imprisonment." "S. Peter would then arrive in Rome in the latter part of 63 or the beginning of 64. The Neronian persecution broke out soon afterwards (summer of 64), and he (Peter) would be one of the most prominent victims." *S. Clem.*, vol. ii., p. 497.

† Farrar gives a list of R. C. writers to the same effect. Döllinger, one of that list, abandoned Rome when the dogma of infallibility was carried. Other Roman Catholic theologians, *e.g.* Ellendorf, have cast doubt on the whole scheme of Peter's "bishopric" at Rome. Cf. Bleek and Weiss.

position. The twenty-five years' episcopate of Peter at Rome is inwoven with Roman tradition since Jerome's day, and with the "Pontifical list," and is part of the warp and woof of the authoritative Rheims-Douay Romanist Bible. Papalism depends upon it, yet it is an absolute impossibility. And any visit at all to Rome by Peter is a matter of the greatest uncertainty. It is awkward for an "infallible" Church and Pope to be built on what, at best, is an utter UNCERTAINTY. *For "more than a hundred years" after the death of Paul,* and of what must have been in the ordinary course of nature the approximate date of Peter's own death, as Harnack points out, not a single item of *clear contemporary proof can be found in favour of the notion that Peter ever was in Rome.* The earliest writing in which it is stated is the letter of Dionysius of Corinth * (cir. 170) in the latter part of the second century. Apparently the sacerdotal mind has no notion of what the lapse of a century means in the growth of legend and of wild imaginings of all kinds.

THE "FATHERS" AND LEGEND.

As we shall see later, the "testimony" of "Fathers" like Dionysius, Irenæus, and Tertullian in the close of the second century, regarding matters such as this, more than a hundred years before their time, is worse than worthless. For they "testify" too much. They testify what is self-evidently ridiculous. Meanwhile, during that second century, both from within and from without the Christian community at Rome, there had taken place the swift growth of what all scholars admit to be a fantastic legend, combining and interlacing together the two Apostles, the Apostle of the Jewish Christians, Peter, and

---

‡ Euseb. H.E., ii., 25.

the Apostle of the Gentile Christians, Paul. When Clement of Rome, probably in the last decade of the first century,* writes his letter to Corinth, he knows nothing of the Paul-Peter legend. At least he says nothing. Paul is, with him, the important fact. Eighty to a hundred years later, when Dionysius, Irenæus, and Tertullian wrote, with no contemporary facts to check them, the Peter-Paul legend fills the whole air at Rome. In their Apologetic of the Christian faith against hostile and clever Jew and Pagan attacks,—and especially against a swarm of heresiarchs, each one using some one Apostle's name for *shibboleth*,—these Fathers are busy *vindicating* the *unity* of the Apostles; busy *proving* that Paul did not *very strongly* conflict with Peter at Antioch. St. Paul himself, writing to his factious Corinthians, had shown his real unity with Cephas and Apollos;† but that had nothing to do with Rome. The second century "Fathers" had to justify that unity to the *outside world*, and to the heresiarchs in the distant west. And they did it strongly. *They did it too strongly.* That is their weakness. They made use of a fantastic legend about Peter's journeyings, which had caught hold of the pious imagination, to strengthen their argument for the faith's unity. When a modern historical critic, like Lipsius or Harnack, tests their statements by facts (as Calvin tried to do long ago) then the *second* century legend can be easily peeled off, and split away from the *first* century kernel of Apostolic truth.

Hast thou not read the French version of Waterloo, or the French story of their warship *Vengeur*, destroyed by the villainous British? The gallant *Vengeur* will not strike her flag! . . . . "Ocean

---

* Lightfoot says 95 or 96 A.D., Harnack 96.
† This is really *one root* of the later imagination that Peter and Paul together founded the Church both in Corinth and in Italy.

yawns abysmal: down rushes the *Vengeur*, carrying *Vive la Republique* unconquerable, into eternity," with all her officers and men refusing to yield. How beautiful the story! All France believed it soon, and would have continued to believe it, had not contemporary facts existed to refute it. But Carlyle turns the page—applies the historic lancet.

"Alas, alas! the *Vengeur*, after fighting bravely, did sink altogether as other ships do, her captain and above two hundred of her crew escaping gladly in British boats."*

That is a small matter compared with the second century Apocryphal writings regarding Paul and Peter, which had birth and growth between the time of Clement of Rome (95 A.D.) and the time of Irenæus (cir. 190).† I shall look at those legends immediately. Just now let me put the result as to the "Roman Visit of Peter *thus*:—To all candid students of history the Peter-Paul founding of the Church of Rome is palpably and provably a legend. The contemporary facts of Paul's, and Peter's, and Luke's, and the other New Testament writings are all against it. And Peter's visit to Rome, I very much fear is a legend‡ also. *There*

---

* *French Revol.*, vol. iii., bk. v., cap. vi.
† Lightfoot date for *Adv. Haer.*
‡ Prof. Ramsay's new theory is the only one which would make it feasible. He thinks that Peter's "First Epistle" was not written till "about A.D. 80," § instead of in (63 or) 64 to which Lightfoot, Harnack, Westcott, Farrar, &c., assigned it. Else he thinks it would be spurious. So Peter might live in Rome *after Paul's* death, and till 80. Some north-east Scotchmen live, and deserve to live, a very long time, and have great faith in the vitality and toughness of the Apostles, mentally and physically. Prof. Ramsay's book was received with special honour at the Vatican. It gives a chance to Peter in Rome! But the Vatican has made many blunders. This is surely one. For this new theory would obliterate the whole Roman chronology, Jerome, the "papal lists," and the Douay Bible. It would make an end of Linus and the main part of Cletus—the two first so-called Roman "bishops"; would vindicate the historic worth of Clement's letter to James, and drive us back on the queer theory of Rufinus as to Linus and Cletus. I am greatly indebted to Prof. Ramsay for much; but the only reason for his new theory is to preserve Peter's authorship of an epistle.
§ *Church in the Rom. Emp.*, p. 282.

is for it no contemporary proof. There is a good *deal* of contemporary disproof."

The Roman Tradition : Early " Papal Lists."

A "chain" of "infallible" inspired successors of the Apostle Peter, Vicar of Christ, ought to have no uncertainty about its links. *Especially its first links!* If the Romanist theory had any truth, the Church of Rome would, from the beginning, have made sure that no mistake, contradiction, or gap would cause utter uncertainty and confusion about *the earliest so-called links,*—the "bishopric" of the blessed Peter, and then of the so-called "bishops," who (on that theory) were to "succeed" Peter. But, alas, for the whole theory, we find the Roman Church herself, and the weightiest early Fathers, and the early "lists" in hopeless contradiction on this subject.

There are various "Fathers" who speak about the early Roman "presbyters" and "bishops." And there are various "Catholic *lists*," or catalogues, of the early "bishops" of the Christian Church in Rome. These Fathers and these lists vary badly. *They contradict each other.* And, do what you will to "straighten them out," they contradict each other still. It is dreary work. Lightfoot himself made a most kindly, most heroic effort to straighten out these contradictory statements of "Fathers," like Tertullian, and Irenæus, and Hippolytus, and "lists" like the "Irenæan," the "Eusebian," the "Jeromean," and the "Liberian;" and he, too, has failed.* In the first place, the

---

* I heartily agree with Professor Ramsay's criticism, *Church in Roman Emp.*, p. 284 n., on Lightfoot's dealing with Tertullian's statement regarding Clement's "Ordination." Tertullian knew Rome far better than Irenæus did, and his statement is a flat contradiction to the "list" of presbyter-bishops in Irenæus. I am greatly struck also with Professor Bright's conclusion to the same effect: *Roman See* (just received), pp. 11-12. He shows the two striking differences between Tertullian and Irenæus.

Succession itself you cannot straighten. The very first names are, as Professor Sanday calls them, "shadowy figures." We cannot, as Lightfoot confesses, confidently call them "bishops" at all. Harnack speaks more strongly still. Then, secondly, the *Chronology*, or dates for these so-called early "bishops" of Rome, with the legend of Peter at the top, presents a tangle more self-contradictory. A politician (in England), I am aware, made out for himself a genealogical succession from Alfred the Great, and also from two famous, female Scottish martyrs who had no descendants. But that is as nothing to the difficulties presented by the effort to get Peter into Rome, as its first founder and "bishop," and then to fix dates and names for the successive infallible Peters who followed him in the "Popedom." Now, I cannot, in a popular lecture, go into this thing in detail. I will sketch the exact facts in their general lines.

The Early Bishops of Rome.

1. As to the so-called early "bishops" themselves, Tertullian of Rome and Carthage, in the close of the second century, presents *Clement* as first bishop of Rome, declaring that he was ordained by Peter.* But Irenæus of Gaul, near to the same date, says that "Peter and Paul preached and founded the Church at Rome," and then those "blessed Apostles entrusted the ministration of the Church to *Linus* (*Haer*. iii., 3, 2, 3, and Lightfoot, *Clem*. vol. ii., 495; vol. i., pp. 63, 64). Now, what do you think of that stark Roman contradiction in those two blessed "Fathers?" But that is only to begin with. In all these earlier

---

* Tert., *De Praescr.* 32 [see Bright, p. 11]. In the later shape of "the Clementine fiction" Peter says, "I lay hands upon this Clement, as your bishop, and to him I entrust my *chair* of discourse." Epis. of Clement to James.

"Fathers" neither Peter nor Paul is ever spoken of as "bishop." They are "Apostles" and "founders." Then further Irenæus says, both Peter and Paul entrusted the episcopate to *Linus*. Tertullian says, Peter ordained *Clement*, and further that this was the view of "the Church of the Romans" itself, and he makes no reference to Paul ordaining anyone.* That only commences the trouble.—We have, I said, several early "lists" or "catalogues" of the so-called Roman bishops. We have one called the *Liberian* catalogue greatly honoured at Rome. It may be called the truly "papal catalogue." It was made out under Pope Liberius in the fourth century, and came into authoritative painting in the later Catacombs through his successor Damasus. It seems to rest on Hippolytus in the beginning of the third century. Of him we shall hear again. Its order of so-called Early Popes is followed in "the famous series of mosaics in the basilica of St. Paul at Rome." It gives the order, Linus, Clement, Cletus, Anacletus, &c., putting Clement second. Then there is the catalogue given in the tradition of Irenæus and which Eusebius in his history in the fourth century follows.

The succession in Eusebius is Linus, Anencletus, Clement, &c., thus putting Clement as *third* Bishop of Rome, and extirpating poor Cletus altogether. This is supposed by Lightfoot to be the "traditional" order. In the numbering of the bishops, Eusebius (as Lightfoot and others point out) always omits the names of the Apostolic "founders," and begins with Linus; and

---

* Lightfoot, though it makes for Dr. Salmon's view, confesses "Even Tertullian speaks of Clement as the *immediate* successor" of Peter the Apostle. If Ramsay's view ever gets accepted as to the late date of Peter's death, it will strangely fit into this, and make Clement first presbyter bishop at Rome. But then, as Sanday shows, till Hermas (145) the *presbyterial* government continued in Rome.

he always gives the precedence to *Paul* before Peter in speaking of the founders.*

Then we have Jerome presenting a shape of this list, with Peter alone set at the top of it. But Jerome has not forgotten that Tertullian spoke of Clement as immediate successor of Peter.† And although Jerome gives the list in the "Irenæan" way, yet he says the other, viz., with Clement topmost, was believed by "most of the Latins."

Now what do you think of *that* contorted and disputed, and (all of it) hugely questionable succession for your Rock of an infallible Church, and yet each of those lists has been endorsed by infallible Popes‡ or eminent saints. Great scholars—Lipsius, Mommsen, Harnack, and Lightfoot, have been investigating, trying to explain these catalogues. Lightfoot, the most favourable, says we have to choose between "a tradition (the Irenæan), a fiction (the Clementine), and a blunder (the Liberian)." He thinks we should choose the *tradition*. But, oh! remember the Liberian was fondly endorsed by infallible Popes and "most of the Latins." And then underneath them all is that huge legend, unknown to the first Fathers—Peter's bishopric at Rome. So I think we had better not choose any of them, but say with Professor Sanday, of Oxford, that Hermas in the second century (cir. 145 A.D.) "marks the point at which the Presbyterial form of government is passing into the Episcopal." Here let me set a synopsis of the "lists" in simplest condensed form :—

---

* Lightfoot, *Clem.*, vol. i., p. 206.

† *De Vir. Illust.*, i., 15 (c.f. Bright, p. 15.)

‡ Lightfoot says of the papal Liberian list—"Its details are confused." Its notices of time irreconcilable. Vol. i., pp. 65-6.

EARLY LISTS OF "BISHOPS" OF ROME.

TERTULLIAN. cir. 190–198.	IRENÆUS. 190.	"LIBERIAN." (Based on Hippolytus?) cir. 354.	EUSEBIUS. (Based on Irenæus.) cir. 330–335.	JEROME. cir. 392.	OPTATUS. 370. followed by AUGUSTINE.
1. Clement. Ordained by Peter the Apostle (So also "most of the Latins"—Jerome.	1. Linus.	1. Linus.	1. Linus.	1. Peter. (Bishop 25 years, A.D. 42–67 ?)	1. Peter.
	2. Anacletus.	2. Clement.	2. Anencletus.	2. Linus.	2. Linus.
	3. Clement.	3. Cletus.	3. Clement. Places Clement as *third* bishop. Does not count the Apostolic founders. Gives precedence to *Paul* as *founder*.	3. Anacletus.	3. Clement.
	4. Euarestes. (Linus appointed by the Apostles Peter and Paul. Supposed to rest on a lost writing of Hegesippus?	4. Anacletus.	This appears in two forms: in the Hist. and the Chronicle. The latter appears in three variant shapes: (1) Armenian; (2) Syriac; (3) Jerome.	4. Clement. &c. Confesses "most of the Latins" held differently.	4. Anencletus, &c.
		5. Aristus. This is at base of the whole *Liber Pontificalis*.*			

* In the form of it, as arranged by "the Liberian editor" (Lightfoot), Peter stands at the head, with a career at Rome from A.D. 30 to A.D. 55 ! ! ! (See Mommsen and Lightfoot).

[NOTE.—Archbishop Carr (p. 163), under the guidance again of the Rev. Luke Rivington, seeks aid out of Eusebius' *Chronicle* in its Armenian Version (5th cent.), where Peter is called in the Latin translation *Antistes Ecclesiae* (president of the Church). This had been answered by anticipation in Lightfoot (pp. 207, 215), and others [also Bright]. But the amusing thing is Dr. Carr's courage in venturing on this. The *Armenian Chronicle* not only presents what Lightfoot calls "very patent errors," but it makes Peter *Bishop of Antioch* before he "proceeds to the city of the Romans" (or as Jerome has it, " is *sent* to Rome"). Also his stay in Rome it makes twenty years, beginning in the year 39 ! Also there are two Bishops of Rome called " Linus," one beginning in the twelfth year of Nero and one in the second of Titus. Also Bishop Aggripinus (who according to other lists was a Bishop of Alexandria) here holds office after Soter as " Bishop of Rome." No wonder that Archbishop Carr says below this (p. 163) :—" The value of these versions of the Chronicle of Eusebius is independent of their chronology, so far as the Roman Episcopate of St. Peter is concerned," &c. Certainly ! *that* is quite manifest. The value of the whole Roman scheme is independent of chronology, and of Scripture too. And that is what Harnack—that adept in chronology as to these things—in his dealing with the dressed-up lists of the " Bishops" of Antioch and of Rome, says :—" A cautious critic will be just as slow to accept the chronology of a list of Antiochian Bishops first appearing in the third century as to admit that Linus was first Bishop of Rome." (*Ignat. Epp. Exp.*, 1886.)]

The above contradictions are small, however, compared with what meets you when you come to the *dates* connected with the Romanist " bishopric " of Peter. Here the utter defiance of historic reality, the superb contempt for Time's flight and years, is of the most marvellous description. In order to leave any room for Peter as Bishop of Rome, and for the other successive "shadowy figures," whom Catholic tradition has produced as " Bishops" of Rome in the first century, and in order to get Peter martyred at Rome, the catalogues have to bring Peter into Rome at an impossibly early period. Thus the Liberian papal list brings Peter to Rome A.D. 30, and places his death in A.D. 55. Linus succeeds him, A.D. 56. Another list gives him a twenty years' bishopric at Rome, beginning in the year 39 A.D., during the reign of the third Emperor, Caligula. The earlier lists left his bishopric out altogether. Another set of lists gives him a bishopric of twenty-five years, beginning in the year 42 A.D., in the second year of the fourth Emperor Claudius. This is the tradition followed by Jerome—the authoritative Latin Father—on whose vulgate translation of the Bible the Catholic version of the Scriptures, including the Rheims-Douay version, is founded. That Douay version, with its marvellous notes, affirms that Peter wrote his first epistle

"at Rome, which, figuratively, he calls Babylon, about fifteen years after our Lord's ascension."

The Douay version affirms also that the second Epistle of Peter

"was written a very short time before his martyrdom, which was about thirty-five years after our Lord's ascension."

Now, the date of our Lord's crucifixion is fixed by the best of modern chronologists as the year 30 A.D.* Thus the Douay version, in a heroic attempt to square with Jerome, makes Peter to have written his first Epistle in Rome about the year 44 or 45 A.D.† Yet we had supposed that 44 A.D. was the year of his imprisonment *in Jerusalem* by King Herod Agrippa. Peter's martyrdom the Douay version makes to have been at Rome about the year 65 A.D., during the Neronian tyranny, two years before the date named for it by Jerome.†

The Liberian papal catalogue had given this badly mishandled Peter the *quietus* of his bishopric ten years before, viz., in 55 A.D. (Light., *Clem.*, i., p. 253).

---

* Cf. Wieseler, Lightfoot, &c.

† The Douay note-writers probably meant to follow *Eusebius*, who placed Our Lord's ascension in 33 A.D., and Jerome, who gave it as 32 A.D. See Douay Chronology in Appendix.

Paul and Peter.

But that is only to begin with. The Roman tradition, in its early shape, joined Paul and Peter together in the founding of the Roman Church. THEY BOTH together—those two "blessed Apostles"—says, *e.g.*, that Irenæus over whom Archbishop Carr has spent so many words—"having founded and built up the Church" "entrusted the ministration of the bishopric to Linus."* But this is not all—the great snowball of legend gathers as it goes. One shape of it made Paul and Peter suffer martyrdom at the same time. One form of the legend represents them together; another form apart. One shape of it pictures Peter as fleeing from the Gate of Rome along the Appian way and meeting Christ, who, in answer to Peter's startled question, "*Domine quo radis?*" ("Lord, whither goest thou?") made answer, "I go to be again crucified." In the little church of *Domine Quo Vadis*, on the Appian-road, built to keep this legend in remembrance, I have sat and pondered. Along another Roman road, outside the Latin gate, and nigh to the Ostian way, there are the *Tre Fontane*—three fountains which sprang up where St. Paul's head, the legend saith, fell and rolled in martyrdom. Also, and in the earlier shape of the legend, we meet with Peter's wife as having part in the suffering and honour. Peter is seen encouraging his wife as she goes to martyrdom. A little later the legend represents the Apostle Peter as crucified with his head downward. It only wanted, as Renan characteristically says, some narrator to work all these touching items into some beautiful narrative—"a man at once of genius and a simple mind." But he was not forthcoming. Instead of a beautiful narrative, the legend was made the

---

* *Haer.* iii., 3, 3, 3.

basis in Rome for a gigantic system of priesthood, dominating with this once simple name, "Peter," the reason and the faith of Christendom.

II.—PROOF FOR PETER'S ROMAN BISHOPRIC.

When we ask what proof is given by Roman advocates that Peter founded the Church at Rome, or that he was ever Bishop of Rome, or, again, any proof even for the quite different assertion that Peter, perhaps, visited Rome for a brief time, the answer is amusing by its meagreness. The proof consists of these three elements :—

1. In the close of John's Gospel it is indicated that Simon, who had betrayed Christ, should suffer imprisonment and death for His sake.* Even in the drinking of that "cup" of suffering Peter had no "supremacy." James, the brave "Son of Thunder," drank it before him.† Stephen, a greater than either—though no Apostle—drank it first.‡ "But of the time and place of that death" of Peter (as Harnack says) "we know nothing with even approximate probability."

2. In Peter's Epistle, written to (probably *Jewish*) Christians, "sojourners of the Dispersion in Pontus, Galatia, Cappadocia, Asia, and Bithynia,§ he says :— "The co-elect that is at Babylon saluteth you, and (so doth) Marcus, my son."‖ Romanists, in common with some Protestant scholars, take this word "Babylon"¶ to be a hidden name for Rome. This

---

* John xxi., 18,19.   † Acts xii., 2.   ‡ Acts vii., 60.
§ 1 Pet. i., 1.   ‖ *Id.* v., 13.

¶ Sanday says this would be the "most decisive" proof "if it had good." Yes, it would be the *only* proof, as Harnack shows. Sanday confesses—"There is a natural reluctance in the lay mind to take Babylon in any other sense than literally."

would, of course, be likely enough had Peter been writing a symbolic Apocalypse, but unlikely in a simple, practical prose letter. Besides, were "Babylon" a symbolic word, it might just as readily mean *Jerusalem*, from which Christ had warned His disciples to come out and "flee" (as from Babylon long before) when the conquering armies drew near, or it might mean "Antioch," the Roman headquarters in the East.* In the Apocalypse, Jerusalem is called both "*Sodom* and *Egypt*."† But, in sooth, there is in Peter's beautifully direct "immediate" manner nothing of the Apocalyptic method or spirit.‡

CLEMENT OF ROME.

3. The third§ element of "proof" is that in the Epistle of *Clement*, the Presbyter of Rome, sent to the Corinthians in the close of the First Century (this, about 95 or 96 A.D., is the earliest known Christian writing after the New Testament) reference is made to Peter:—

"Who, by reason of unrighteous jealousy, endured, not one nor two, but many labours; and thus, having borne his testimony, went to his appointed place of glory." ‖

That is all. It does not say a word about the place, or the date, or the circumstances of Peter's death. It never hints, in any way, that he was ever in Rome, or ever suffered there. Nay, the *context shows that*

---

* Lightfoot, *Clem.* i., 355. † Apoc. xi., 8.
‡ See Harnack on this below.

§ I will not spend time on "the hint" some think they see in what Papias quotes from "The Presbyter" about Peter's connection with Mark. Harnack says:—"He says nothing of the *place* at which they were together." Nor need we pause regarding *Ignatius*, who gives not the slightest hint of Peter's connection with Rome. Harnack and Sanday pass both by.

‖ Clem., c. 5.

such a thought is quite foreign to the mind of the writer. He is writing, in the name of the Christian congregation at Rome, to the Christian congregation at Corinth deprecating the jealousy, and division, and "making of parties" which characterized the Corinthian congregation, and which had led them to oppose some of their faithful presbyters (or "bishops"), and even to remove them from office. Clement points out that God's best servants in all ages have been opposed through jealousy "through which also *death entered into the world.*"* *Abel* was opposed through jealousy; so was *Jacob*, so was *Joseph*, so was *Moses*, so was *David*.†

"But to pass from the examples of ancient days, let us come to those champions who lived very near to our time. Let us set before us the noble examples which belong to our generation. By reason of jealousy and envy the greatest and most righteous *pillars*‡ of the church (congregation) were persecuted, and contended even unto death. Let us set before our eyes the good Apostles—Peter, who by reason of unrighteous jealousy endured, &c."

Such is the connection ; and Clement then goes on to speak of Paul :—

"By reason of jealousy and strife, Paul, by his example, pointed out the prize of patient endurance."

I have been at pains to set out the exact words and meaning of this letter of the Christians at Rome to the Christians at Corinth (written by Clement's hand) for two reasons :—1. Archbishop Carr funnily calls it the "authoritative" letter of "Pope St. Clement" of Rome, who, Dr. Carr is good enough to state, "was

---
* C. 3.   C. 4.
‡ Observe that word "*pillars*" used equally of Peter and Paul, just as Paul used it of "James, Cephas, and John." Clement has no knowledge of Peter's "primacy."

third Pope in succession from St. Peter." He also is good enough to inform us that, in this letter, we really had no right to expect—

"Such clear-cut evidence as it affords of the exercise of supreme jurisdiction on the part of the reigning Roman Pontiff in the affairs of a distant and Apostolic Church."

Dr. Carr on Lightfoot's "Discreditable" Evasion.

Also, Archbishop Carr launches out fiercely at Lightfoot for telling the truth about the contents of this epistle of Clement, and for his (Lightfoot's) demonstration that the letter "does not proceed from the bishop, but *from the Church*" in Rome. As coming from—

"the representative of a Church which is constantly flaunting its claims to an Apostolic descent, the contention [of Lightfoot] is," says the Archbishop, "at once destructive and discreditable."

Also, Dr. Carr declares that Lightfoot's

"transparent object is to evade the strong proof of the Primacy contained in the whole Epistle of St. Clement"! (p. 29).

But Archbishop Carr surely did not suppose any educated people were present at his lectures when he ventured on the following :—

"It would seem that a few unruly members [of the Church in Corinth] had driven out probably *their bishop and some of his priests* or presbyters, and *the Church of Rome came to the rescue*" (p. 25).

That is good ! If *that* should ever happen to get to the eye of Professor Sanday, or Professor Bright, of Oxford, I can imagine the Oxonian smile.

Archbishop Carr further informs his auditory that, in this epistle, " Pope St. Clement" lays—

"claim to submission and obedience on the ground that his words were the words of God, and were dictated by the Holy Ghost."

Also, he affirms that in this letter the Pontiff " St. Clement" teaches—

"the absolute necessity of *Apostolical succession* for a legitimate ministry, mentioning explicitly the *threefold order of bishops, priests, and deacons.*"

Finally, Dr. Carr surpasses himself by informing his audience that the " Sovereign Pontiff, Pope St. Clement," sent—

"his own legates in order to secure the acquiescence of the Church of Corinth *to his will* !"

After all this, it is rather disappointing to find that he feels it necessary to explain to his hearers the singular fact that Clement *omits all reference to himself, and never even mentions his own name!* So wholly unlike a modern Pope. He suggests *two* explanations :—1. "*It may have been his humility.*" This, which would be quite a rare quality in a " Sovereign Pontiff's" encyclical, sounds an odd explanation, seeing that "Pope St. Clement," according to the Archbishop, had just been declaring that " his words were the words of God, and were dictated by the Holy Ghost!" So Archbishop Carr tries another explanation :—

"It would be very *unsafe* to give the name of the head of an organised Christian community in Rome!"*

It is very astonishing this. Here is "the opening paragraph" of Clement's letter, and there is not a hint of any reminder about " unsafeness" or the withholding of any name:—

---

* Carr, p. 38.

"The church (ecclesia = congregation) of God which sojourneth in Rome to the church (ecclesia) of God which sojourneth in Corinth, to them who are called and sanctified by the will of God through our Lord Jesus Christ. Grace to you and peace from Almighty God, through Jesus Christ be multiplied. By reason of the sudden and repeated calamities and reverses which are befalling us, brethren, we consider that we have been somewhat tardy in giving heed to the matters of dispute that have arisen among you, dearly beloved," &c.*

There is here simply a salutation from one sister Church to another, with an apology for not having written sooner. Clement never mentions his own name, or speaks with any authority of his own, or claims any jurisdiction whatever. "The very existence of a bishop of Rome itself could nowhere be gathered from the letter," says Lightfoot.† It is a letter from the congregation at Rome to that at Corinth, with counsel and advice, and with no appeal to any constraint but that of the common love and faith of Christ. Just so, a congregation in Edinburgh might write to one in Glasgow; or, so a convention, or presbytery, or gathering of churchmen in Melbourne might write to one in Sydney. Twice during recent months I myself have written to distant churches two letters more authoritative, and more decisive of the case, than this letter of Clement. One letter was to a church in another colony; one was to the Christian people of a group of South Sea Islands. They even asked me to nominate their sole minister— a far more "popely" act than was ever done by Clement or by Clement's Epistle. And yet Archbishop Carr has never thought of calling me "His Holiness the Pope." The *second* reason for my emphasis of this passage of Clement is that, as Professor Harnack, of Berlin, says—This passage of

---

* Clem. 1. Lightfoot's Trans.
† Lightfoot, *Clem.*, vol. i., p. 352, &c.

Clement is "the only historical mention we have of Peter for more than a hundred years" after the date of the death of Nero and of Paul.

Now, I ask sane men, looking at that passage quoted by me from Clement, what has it to do with Peter's presence in Rome? Was "Abel" in Rome? Was "Jacob" in Rome? Was "Moses" in Rome? Was "David" in Rome? Was "Peter" in Rome? All that Clement says is that all these were *opposed* " *through jealousy*;" but he does not connect any of them in any way with Rome. He does not connect Peter with Rome.*

Later on in that chapter Clement speaks of the Apostle Paul, but in what different terms! Paul, also, he says, had to face jealousy and strife; and after he

"had been driven into exile, had been stoned, had preached in the East and in the West, he won the noble renown which was the reward of his faith, having taught righteousness unto the whole world, and when he had come to the boundary of the West (τὸ τέρμα τῆς δύσεως), and when he had borne his testimony (suffered martyrdom) before the prefects (rulers), so he departed from the world."†

If that language indicates that Paul suffered at Rome, certainly it gives no hint that Peter did, or that he was ever in Rome, or in the West at all.

Origin of the Peter Legend.

But the fact of the two names, Peter and Paul, having been mentioned together in the same chapter of this epistle, written by Clement, from the Christians, *at Rome*, to the Christians in Corinth (just as St. Paul himself had mentioned them together in *his* Epistle to

---

* Clem. 4, 5. † Clem. 5. ‡ Compare Lightfoot's & Donaldson's translations.

the Corinthians, less than forty years earlier, as an evidence of the unity of the Church of Christ) was quite enough to set the ball of patristic imagination and legend rolling. This was one direct source of the Peter-Paul legend. But other legendary elements of fantastic kind, and drawn from Judaeo-gnostic sources, soon mingled with those impressive Apostolic names, and during the second century swiftly developed. In various apocryphal writings, Peter's journeys were dressed up into a romance to rival Paul's, then to blend with Paul's. By the close of the second century, the story has grown and consolidated into a huge legend.* Dionysius, of Corinth,† in the close of the second century, is the first Father to say that Peter visited Rome. But his words carry their own disproof. In large imaginative language he talks o the unity of—

the trees of the Romans and Corinthians planted by Peter and Paul. For they both alike came also to our Corinth, and taught us; and both alike came together to Italy; and, having taught there, suffered martyrdom at the same time.‡

Every one can see that this "planting of trees" is just a legendary echo of Paul's words to the Corinthians, "I planted." Somewhat later, Irenæus§ of Gaul surpasses this. He describes Peter and Paul as "preaching and founding the Church in Rome."‖ Tertullian of Carthage makes the ball larger still. He describes Peter as baptising in the Tiber; and, not content with this, he adds the Apostle John also. Peter and Paul, he says, suffered martyrdom at Rome, and the Apostle John, "after being plunged in boiling oil without suffering any harm, is banished to an

---

* See Appendix for special note.
† 170 A.D., Lightfoot. Harnack places it later.
‡ Euseb. *H.E.* iii., 25, as in Lightfoot.
§ 190 A.D., Lightfoot.
‖ *Haer.* iii., 1, 1, and 3, 2, 3. Irenæus will meet us later on.

island."* Oh, these Fathers! What an infallible voice of authority to trust to—"the consent of the Fathers." How could they tell the facts as to what happened 100 or 130 years before?† Think of even Clement and "the Phœnix!" Stick to your New Testaments, you laymen; there, at least, you will be sure you are not being befooled by some gnostic legend that got accepted by "the Fathers." There you will not build on a foundation of sand. There is not an item in all this traditional stuff written by Dionysius, Irenæus, and Tertullian, that is not provably erroneous. This same Irenæus tells that Christ lived to be an *old man*, and that his public ministry lasted nearly twenty years. (*Hæer.* Bk. ii., xxii., 5, 6). And the Romans, Tertullian says, could not *boil* John. All the value that can be set on these statements of Fathers on the verge of the second and third centuries is just this:—They show that, at the end of the second century, there was a prevalent tradition that Peter, as well as Paul, had been at Rome in the first century, and had died there in martyrdom.

Four Recent Scholars.

Now, take the opinions of perhaps the four most eminent of our recent scholars, who have specially studied this question—*Was Peter ever in Rome?* Lipsius says "No." Lightfoot and Sanday think he probably did come for a brief visit, to encourage the Jewish Christians in Rome at the time of the Nero persecution.‡ Harnack regards the balance of probabilities on both sides as equal. But three things he says are weighty against the opinion

---

* *De Bap.* 4. *Scorp.* 15. *De Praescr.* 36.
† Between the years 58 or 61-63 and 170 there is quite time for legend to grow up —Sanday.
‡ In 64, Lightfoot *S. Clement*, vol. ii., p. 490 sq. So also Sanday.

that Peter ever was in Rome—1. There is for it *no contemporary evidence*, no testimony "for more than a hundred years." The interpretation of "Babylon" as meaning Rome, in a matter-of-fact epistle, he characterises as unlikely; beyond that there is no *proof* of any kind. 2. The tradition of Peter's presence in Rome was *not uniform* in the Early Church. It is in direct conflict with the other stream of tradition—

"which represents 'Peter as having worked in Antioch, in Asia Minor, in Babylonia, and in the country of the barbarians, on the northern shores of the Black Sea.'"

Peter was the "Apostle of the Circumcision," to the Jews of the "Dispersion." His own epistle is in keeping with this, and so is the statement that his letter was written from Babylon, which

"is best understood, not as a crytographic expression for Rome, but, like the geographical names of the epistles of the New Testament, in *a literal sense*."

So says this great scholar.*

Then, further, the tradition of Peter in Rome is discredited because it is—

"Almost inextricably bound up with a story of whose legendary character there can be little doubt—that of the Simon Magus of the Clementines."

So Harnack, while on the one hand he recognises that "it is difficult to suppose that so large a body of tradition (speaking of Peter and Rome) has no foundation in fact;" on the other hand sums a weighty array of facts "which render the ordinary patristic statements doubtful"—the want of all contemporary proof, "the complete silence as to Peter (and Rome) in the Pauline Epistles," the legendary character of the "patristic" statements, and the fact that the Roman legend is directly contradicted by

---

* Dr. Marcus Dods says so also.

strong tradition, which places Peter's ministry wholly in the East.

In short, the whole thing is so legendary, I would not stake on that notion of Peter's having visited Rome the value of a sparrow's life, never to speak of the value of men's everlasting souls, and the undying destinies of Christendom. But, in any case, all these scholars agree that Peter's "bishopric" in Rome is fabulous.

IV.—THE NEW TESTAMENT DISPROOF.

Was Peter for twenty-five years Bishop of Rome, as Jerome conjectured and Romanists allege, viz,, from 42 A.D. until 67 A.D.?

Here the evidence is no longer negative, but of the most positive and undeniable kind. It is history *versus* fable. In the year 42 Peter had not left Palestine. In the year 44 he was imprisoned by Herod Agrippa in Jerusalem. About the year 51, at the Council in Jerusalem, Paul and Barnabas met James, Cephas, and John, who were "reputed to be pillars" of the Churches in Judea. They agreed that Paul should go as Apostle to the Gentiles, and the others to the Jews. A short time later Paul conflicted with Peter in *Antioch*. Then followed Paul's second and third great missionary journeys. Then, in the spring of the year 58 A.D., from Corinth Paul wrote his great Epistle to Rome. That epistle makes no reference whatever to Peter having ever been in Rome, or having founded the Church there. That fact of itself, as Harnack, Lightfoot, and Sanday all say, proves the Roman tradition to be impossible. Later still, in 61 A.D., Paul himself arrives in Rome. In his Philippian and other letters, and in Acts, we know the history of that Roman Church down to the year 63, on the eve of Paul's trial and the outbreak of Nero's persecution. But Peter is never mentioned. Up to this point all modern scholars of any standing are in unanimous agreement. Lipsius, Harnack, Lightfoot, Renan, all of all shades of opinion, declare that the tradition of Peter's having founded the Church of Rome, and having been bishop of it, is simply incredible.

If Peter was in Rome at all, says Lightfoot, it could only have been for a few months, " in the latter part of 63 or the beginning of 64. The Neronian persecution broke out soon afterwards." In that persecution, Peter, if there at all, must have fallen. If Paul then escaped and wrote his three Pastorals—1 Timothy, Titus, and 2 Timothy—these bring us down to 67 A.D. And still there is no word of Peter having ever come to Rome.

We have thus seen this huge legend, on which the Titanic structure of the Roman papacy has been gradually built up, crumble piece by piece, under the test of actual historic facts. The result can be expressed in three propositions :—1. The assertion that Peter was, at any time, in Rome can find for itself not a shred of actual proof. He may have been, or he may not have been. But it is at best unlikely; and it cannot at all be proved. 2. The assertion that Peter founded the Church of Rome, and was for twenty-five years Bishop of Rome, is absolutely impossible. 3. Of any " primacy," of rule or authority of Peter over the rest of the Apostles, there is not a trace in the New Testament, or in the Earliest Christian literature.

NOTE.—For PETER'S BISHOPRIC and CLEMENTINE ROMANCE see Appendix, where Dr. Carr's quotations from Harnack will be discussed.

LECTURE THIRD.

RISE OF A SACERDOTAL ORDER IN THE CHRISTIAN MINISTRY.

"He [*Jesus Christ*] is able to save to the uttermost them that draw near unto God through Him, seeing He ever liveth to make intercession for them. For such a High-priest became us—holy, guileless, undefiled, separate from sinners, and made higher than the Heavens—who needeth not daily, like those high-priests, to offer up sacrifices, first for His own sins and then for the sins of the people, *for this He did once for all when He offered up Himself.*"—Heb. vii., 25—27.

"Now, therefore, why tempt ye God, that ye should put a yoke upon the neck of the disciples which neither our fathers nor we were able to bear."—Peter, in Acts xv., 10—11.

THE CHRISTIAN FAITH.

THE New Testament Gospel centres round Christ—the Way, the Truth, the Life, the one Merciful High-priest, whose One sacrifice has for ever made an end of oblation, and has flung aside the "veil of the Temple" that hid God's presence from men. In Him all penitent men may "draw near" now to God—to offer *themselves* direct unto Him—reconciled, absolved, transformed by new forces of life, their bodies made God's living temple, because the Spirit of God dwells within them. This is the true Skekinah; and

Christ-like men are the Temple and priesthood of God. *That* is the Gospel. It has done away, forever, with all sacrificing priesthood. It calls all believers "priests unto God," a "priesthood and kinghood" in one, all of them "presenting" or "offering up" to God, from hearts of love, in Christ, the sacrifice of thanksgiving, and the service of a changed, Christ-like life. Is not it striking that Peter himself so vividly declares that all Christ's people are God's Spiritual Temple, all of them God's priests, all of them able to offer up "spiritual sacrifices?"*

From that great fact, of the one sufficient Sacrifice, offered by Christ Jesus once for all, there follow *three* things which characterize the Gospel, and the Church of the New Testament, and the New Testament Scriptures. These three things mark the unlikeness of the Gospel to all that went before it, as well as to all pagan and mediæval Priesthood.

No Order of Priesthood.

1. In the congregation or church of Jesus Christ, there is but one Atoning Priest, or High Priest, viz., Christ Himself. In Him all believing men are brought into direct relation to God.

2. There is, therefore, no special caste or order of priesthood in the Christian Church. All believing men and women, atoned and set free from condemnation in Christ, brought near to God in Him, and dwelt in "by His Spirit," are, in the New Testament, called "Priests unto God" and the Father. All of them can "offer" to God from loving, grateful hearts their only "sacrifice" on which God sets value—the living sacrifice and offering of thankful lips, and of loyal trust, and of unselfish and pure lives, respon-

---

* 1 Pet. ii., 5-9; Rom. xii., 1; Rom. i., 6.

sive to the love of God. There is no sacerdotal order in the Ministry of God's New Testament Congregation or Church—just because all God's people, in common and equally, are God's priests.* This fact fronts us all through the New Testament.† It stands out plain in the Apostle Paul's Epistles, in the Epistle to the Hebrews, in John's Epistles. It is asserted in the strongest way in the writings of St. Peter himself—that very Apostle whom, by a strange perversion of history, the Church of Rome has chosen as its legendary foundation and source. Of all believers in common Peter says:— "But ye are an elect race, a kingly priesthood." The sacrifices they offer up are no material victims, and no material bread and wine on any material altar, but the "*living* sacrifices" of the heart's love and the life's pure doing—the deeds not of darkness, but of Christ-like light.‡ That is the only priesthood, except Christ's High Priesthood, the Apostle Peter or the New Testament knows anything about, under the Gospel of Jesus Christ.

3. To the Christian Ministry—the Ministry of the New Testament Church—no sacerdotal *title is ever applied* in the New Testament, no priestly name is ever given, no priestly function is ever ascribed, except the titles and functions ascribed to all believing men—the whole company of Christians.

Now this great fact, as Lightfoot proves, is seen vividly if we examine the description of the Christian Ministry, and the titles bestowed upon it in the New Testament, *e.g.*, in the Book of Acts, or in St. Paul's Epistles, or in St. Peter's.

---

* Lightfoot, *Phil.*, pp. 181 sq. and 264-6.

† Lightfoot truly says the entire Epistle to the Hebrews would be meaningless on any other supposition.

‡ 1 Pet. ii., 9-12; Rom. xii., 1; Heb. xiii., 15, &c.

A Christian Ministry in the New Testament.

There is an order of Christian Ministry recognised clearly in the New Testament; no organisation, civil or religious, could exist without "order and government." But the "Christian Ministry," as Lightfoot, himself a great prelate, frankly said, is "no part of the *essence* of God's message to man in the Gospel," but is indispensable only for the Church's efficiency; for practical convenience; for the requirements of the spiritual growth of the members of the Christian Society or Church.

"For communicating instruction and for preserving public order, for conducting (public) religious worship, and for dispensing social charities, it became necessary to appoint special officers."*

Men of special training, understanding, and knowledge, who can devote their time to it, are necessary for this great thing—the proclaiming of the Gospel, the guiding, "upbuilding," and energising of the Church of God. But, all through the New Testament, the Christian Ministry is pictured as simply representative of all God's congregation; it is never *sacerdotal*. In the New Testament, as Lightfoot puts it—"the priestly functions and privileges of the Christian people are never regarded as transferred or even delegated to these officers. They are called stewards or messengers of God, servants or ministers of the Church and the like; but the sacerdotal title is never once conferred upon them."†

You can prove for yourselves, from your New Testament, that this is so—that no special sacerdotal function or title is given to the Christian Ministry other than those given to each and every Christian believer.

---

* *Chris. Minis. Phil.*, p. 184. Lightfoot was Professor at Cambridge when he wrote this, but up to the close of his life declared he had not altered in any way his standpoint.

† Cf. Lightfoot, *Chris. Min. Phil.*, p. 184.

Paul's Picture of the Church.

E.g., St. Paul pictures the Church—under the figure of a living *body* and its unity—Christ the one and only Head,* and all believers the members of His body, with diversity of administration. In that unity (as Lightfoot lucidly proves to us) Paul sums into two great categories the Christian Ministry. In the one category he places "apostles, prophets, &c."— those men who, in the first age of Christianity's outburst of life, had a non-local ministry of "founding," of "witnessing" to the facts of their Lord's mission and resurrection; and who had also supra-natural "charismatic" gift for the initial guidance of the entire Church. These Apostles, prophets, and inspired "teachers" went from place to place planting and "encouraging" the new Church of God. In another category St. Paul puts the *stated and local* ministry; he gives to them such titles as *these*—"pastors, help, governments."† We find them again called by St. Paul, St. Peter, and St. Luke, "presbyters" or "bishops," and "deacons."

Bishop and Presbyter in the New Testament.

I may say in a word, because the thing is no longer disputable, that by these stated ministers of the Early Church, is just meant the "presbyters or bishops" who, in each congregation, guided and taught the Christian people, and along with them the "deacons," who helped them in the administration of the Church's charities and financial requirements.‡ The "apostles

---

* 1 Cor. xii.; Eph. iv., 15, 16.
† Lightfoot, *Chris. Min. Phil.*, p. 185.
‡ This is very clearly worked out by Professor Sanday and other modern scholars. It is accepted even by Canon Gore that in the New Testament, and even in Clement of Rome, presbyters and episcopoi are the same.

and prophets and inspired teachers" necessarily passed away. From the nature of the case, and from St. Paul's description of what was necessary to constitute "Apostles," there could be no "apostolic succession"—they could (as Lightfoot shows) have no successors. But the stated and ordinary ministry remained. The "pastors" or "shepherds," with the two-fold function of oversight and of teaching, are entitled "presbyters," which is just a Greek translation of the Hebrew word meaning "elders"—those connected with the rule* of the Hebrew synagogue, or congregation. In that synagogue, as distinguished from the Temple, there was no "priesthood." St. James, the spokesman of the Jewish-Christian Church at Jerusalem, calls the Christian people, or congregation, the *sunagoge*† (synagogue), which is equivalent to *ecclesia* congregation, proving unmistakeably how, simply and necessarily, the early Christian Church, in its stated life, government, and worship, retained the shape of the Hebrew congregation. Amongst Gentile Christians and Hellenistic-Hebrew believers, another name was employed as a synonym for that word "presbyter," or elder; that name was "episcopos," overseer or superintendent, or bishop. Now I need not stay to prove that in the New Testament these words "presbyter," or elder, and "episcopos," or bishop, are quite identical in meaning. They are exact equivalents the one for the other, as equivalent, *e.g.*, as the words "Minister" and "Pastor" are in a Christian Church to-day, or as equivalent as the words "Master"

---

* The συνεδριον or Council of Elders, was attached, even for civil jurisdiction, to every synagogue. The *order* of the Society was represented there.

† Jas. ii., 2. In Heb. x., 25, the compound of this word (episunagoge) is used for the Christian congregation. St. Paul uses the *verb* for the same. 1 Cor. v., 4.

and "Warden" are in relation to Ormond and Trinity Colleges. Two passages of the New Testament, out of many (if we accept the genuineness of the New Testament writings), are enough to prove this identity. In Acts xx., 17—28, St. Paul, on his way to Jerusalem, calls at Miletus, on the coast, and there the "elders" of the Christian Church at Ephesus meet him, as time presses and he cannot go to Ephesus to visit them. Paul calls them all "bishops" (as both the Greek and the Revised have it). "Take heed to yourselves, and to all the flock in the which the Holy Spirit hath made you bishops (episcopous), to shepherd (or 'be pastor over') the congregation of God." Again, in Titus i., 5—7, elders (presbyters), in every "city" or town, are also called "bishops"—several of them in each Christian congregation or church, and each of them a bishop, needing to be "blameless as God's steward, the husband of one wife," not of several, like the heathen. So evident is this that all great scholars of these subjects in our day admit that, in the New Testament, the two names, presbyter and bishop, are identical in meaning.* The persons to whom these titles were given—and there were several such in every congregation—were just the same in function, in office, and in dignity.

---

* To deny this (as Harnack confesses) we should have to reject the genuineness of *Acts* and *St. Paul's Pastorals*. We should also have to reject 1 *Peter*. Even Gore admits the identity of "presbyter" and "episcopos" in the New Testament, and in *Clement*, at the close of the First Century. Even after the elevation of *one* presbyter, as sole *episcopos* (bishop), he was for some centuries only pastor of one congregation, or community, like our parish minister. In the *Apostolic Ordinances* it is declared that even a congregation with less than *twelve* male members may have a bishop. Cf. Sanday, &c.

No Episcopal Ordination.

The *people* "elected" their Ministry. The presbyters *ordained* them.

Then another startling fact is evident. Even an Apostle, when present for a time in a church, or district—so far as the ordinary stated government of the Church went, was simply a presbyter like the other presbyters. The act of "ordination," for example (the appointing of ministers to office), that act round which such vast mysterious jargon has gathered, as if the whole Apostolic Church of God depended on it, was performed *by the presbyters in common.* If an Apostle was present, he simply took his place as one amongst the presbyters. Two passages prove this indubitably—(1) St. Paul says that Timothy was ordained by "laying on of my hands." But, in another place, he explains that it was "*by the laying on of the hands of the presbytery*"*—all the presbyters in common—Paul himself taking his place amongst them. (2) The Apostle Peter himself writes to all his churches of Asia:—" The elders among you I exhort, who am a fellow-elder . . . Tend (shepherd) the flock of God which is among you [exercising the oversight (episcopate) thereof.†] " This utterance of Peter to the presbyters of all his churches is the more significant and pathetic, seeing that the

---

* 1 Tim. iv., 14; 2 Tim. i., 6.

† The Rheims-Douay translates "taking care of it." This word *episcopountes* is omitted in Codd. אB. It is present in the other oldest MSS. and versions. The inclusion or omission of it makes no change in the meaning of the passage, which proves incontestably that the *government* of the Church was by presbyters. In the Shepherd of Hermas (145 A.D.), says Harnack, the presbyters exercise control over the individual bishop. Lightfoot has shown that in Alexandria, as late as the middle of the third century, the bishop was nominated and ordained by the presbyters. Lightfoot *Phil.*, p. 226-229. Sanday, *Expos.*, Jan., 1887.

word "tend," or "shepherd," is just the same verb which Christ used to Peter himself, when restoring him after his shameful denial and fall—"Tend (or shepherd) my sheep" (John xxi., 16.)

This ought to be sufficient. It is absolutely certain that, according to the New Testament, in the age when the Book of Acts and 1 Peter and the later Pauline Letters were written, the words "presbyter" and "bishop" were synonymous; and the *stated ministry*, the spiritual government, of the Church was, to use Lightfoot's expression, "that of the presbyterate;" or, to use Jerome's expression, it was " by the Common Council of Presbyters," or Bishops, in each Christian centre or community. And these two words, "presbyters" and "bishops," meant just the same thing. There were no "successors of the Apostles" higher than these. Nay, even Jerome himself, the great Latin Father, on whose translation of Scripture the Roman Catholic Bible rests, declared that in Scripture and

"with the ancients, presbyters were the same as bishops; but gradually all the responsibility was transferred to a single person that the thickets of heresies might be rooted out." (Jer. *Tit.*, i. 5).

Such was the condition of the ministry in the early Christian Church. I have been at pains to set it quite clearly forth, for this one purpose—it shows that not a single priestly, or sacerdotal title was given to the ministers of that Church during all the New Testament age, and throughout the whole of the first century.

II.—Evolution of a Priesthood.

When one thinks of the shape the Church of Christ took in after ages, and of the pretensions of its clergy —great patriarchs, metropolitans, archbishops, and bishops, often making deadly war upon one another, and under them a vast order of priesthood, and what not, claiming to be a separate caste from the rest of God's people, and to have the power, by sacrifices of the mass, to open the gates of purgatory for souls imprisoned there after death, or (here in this life) to grant plenary or other "indulgences" for sins done—and then, when one looks back at the stated ministry of that early Christian Church in the first and the early part of the second centuries, one may well ask in wonder how the one ever grew out of the other?

It is a long story. I can sketch only a few of the chief stages and factors in the process. Here, to begin with, we must note that small commencings, as in a river's flow, may have vast volume by-and-bye. We must also note—what Lightfoot* draws attention to—that, unfortunately, "the word 'priest' in English, and in some other modern languages, has two different senses," which are expressed by two quite different words in the Greek and Hebrew of the Bible. Our English word "priest," in its derivation, is just the same as the word "presbyter," or elder. "It meant originally," says Lightfoot, "the minister who presides over and instructs a Christian congregation." But, by lapse of time and change of signification, it came to be "equivalent to the Latin *sacerdos*, the Greek 'ἱερεύς, the Hebrew כהן (Kohēn), the offerer of sacrifices, who also performs other mediatorial offices between God and man." Lightfoot laments the vast confusion, which has arisen in Church life, by the use of the same word to express two wholly different ideas—as, for example, in the Book of Common-Prayer, the word "priest" should only mean "presbyter." The sacerdotal idea has been "imported" into the

---

* *Philip*, p. 186. He confesses his large indebtedness to both Rothe and Ritschl.

word; it is not original.* That word, whose wholly changed meaning now bulks so large, and is used as equivalent to the Latin *sacerdos* (a mediator and absolver between God and man), meant at first only a *presbyter*, or elder, in Christ's congregation, all the members in which were equally priests to God. This term for the Christian minister was at first wholly devoid of sacerdotal meaning. The only "offerings" Christ's ministers, in the New Testament, ever "presented" to God were just the offerings presented by the whole congregation, viz., "the sacrifice of praise and prayer, giving thanks to His name,"† the bestowing of alms, and the showing of love to God by a changed and holy life. In the case of the Lord's Supper, it is specially significant that no priestly term is ever connected with it. The Lord's Supper is regarded in the New Testament as part of the ordinary service of "*thanksgiving.*" The *whole life* of the Christian was regarded as equally sacramental.‡ Present, says St. Paul, "YOUR BODIES" a *living* sacrifice, holy, acceptable to God. This is your "rational ceremonial service."—(Rom. xii., 1.) *That* was spoken in common to all God's people. And of all God's people, St. Paul (Phil. iii., 3) beautifully used the cognate verb—"who *serve* God by the spirit." As Lightfoot puts it—"We offer the true *latreia*—the service not of *external rites*, but of a spiritual worship."

EARLY FATHERS.—NO SACERDOTALISM.

Now, up to the closing years of the first century, as we can prove, two great facts are prominent—(1) that no sacerdotal function and no sacerdotal title were as yet given to the Christian Ministry; (2) that, after the death of the Apostles, the presbyters were the

---

* Lightfoot, *Phil.*, pp. 245 et 186. † *Id.*, p. 265, sq.
‡ *Id.*, pp. 262-266 ; notes.

highest order of the abiding ministry in the Christian Church. No one presbyter had as yet (at least outside "Asia Minor") lifted himself up, as a special and single bishop or presbyter, above the others. The modern Episcopate, as Lightfoot says, has arisen by evolution out of the presbytery. Naturally, as an Episcopalian, he would like to find that evolution as early as possible, and to join it on to Apostolic times. He adopts the theory of the eminent German Presbyterian scholar Rothe, viz., that the first appearance of incipient episcopacy was in John's Churches in Asia Minor. But he confesses he cannot get proof of *that*. At the close of the first century we can find no trace of a separate Episcopacy—no trace of *one* single "bishop"—*in Rome*, or in Corinth, or in Greece, or in Italy, or in any city or land of Europe.

Clement of Rome.—No Priesthood.

Of that we have the clearest proof. We have in our hands the letter of Clement of Rome at the close of the first century (96 A.D.), after all the Apostles were dead. But *that letter has not a trace either of Episcopacy or of a Sacerdotal* order. Archbishop Carr rashly (as it seems to me) appealed to that letter, and to the later writings of Ignatius and of Hermas.* Here they are in our hand. In Clement (cap. xlii., xliv., xlvii., lvii.) we find that in Corinth there were a good many bishops at one and the same time in the church or congregation there. All of them Clement calls "presbyters" and also "bishops." He knows of no higher office in the Christian Ministry than that of "pres-

---

* Professor Sanday, of Oxford, inclines to agree with Ritschl that the writing of Hermas (145) in the middle of the second century, in its assertion of the rights of the presbyters, "marks the time when the Presbyterian form of government was passing into the episcopal."

byters"—and he calls their office ἐπισκοπή (bishopric).*
He knows of no single Bishop of Corinth, and no single
Bishop of Rome, much less Pope of Rome. He knows
of no sacerdotal functions belonging to presbyters or
bishops. In Clement, Jesus Christ is the only
"High-priest of our souls," and "High-priest of our
offerings" (C. 61, 36). The "sacrifice" is offered by
all the people. It is "the sacrifice of *praise*" (C. 35).
And again, "sacrifice unto God is a contrite spirit"
(C. 18). The only *orders* of priesthood known to
Clement—"high-prist, priest, levite"—are those of
the *Old Testament*, done away in Christ (C. 32, 40,
16). (See Lightfoot on cap. 40; also *Phil.*, p. 249.)
If we had Clement now as the Creed of the
Church (barring that wild story he tells about the
Phœnix living 500 years, and at its death giving origin
to a new bird from its own decay†), why, we might
have the "re-union" of Christendom to-morrow.
There would be no "historic Episcopate," and no
sacerdotalism, and no sacrifice of the mass, and no
prelacy, and no purgatory, and no invocation of
Saints, and no Mariolatry, and no monkhood, to bar
the way. We should have just the Religion of the
New Testament.

ROMANIST MISTRANSLATION OF CLEMENT, &C.

Before passing from the *first* century into the
second, it is necessary to glance at a characteristic
instance of the maltreatment these "Fathers" have
received in the interests of Sacerdotalism. Thus in
the 57th paragraph, or brief "chapter," of Clement's

---

* Lightfoot, *S. Clem.*, vol. ii., p. 127 sq.

† *Clem.*, cap. xxv. See Lightfoot's valuable note. The most intelligent of the pagans believed this; also Tertullian, Ambrose, &c., also the Jewish Rabbis.

letter, the faction-makers in the Christian community in Corinth are urged:—

"Ye therefore that laid the foundation of the sedition, submit yourselves to the *presbyters* (*presbuterois*). . . . For it is better for you to be found small and esteemed in the flock of Christ than to be had in exceeding honour, and yet be cast out from the *hope* of Him." (Cf. Lightfoot's, with Roberts' and Donaldson's renderings.)

But Archbishop Carr rendered it to the public:— "Submit yourselves to *your priests*!" And Clement's word ἐλπίδος (*elpidos*) *hope* he rendered "*fold*;" and Clement's beautiful word "*flock*" he rendered "sheepfold!" And this is all the worse, because that Greek word ποίμνιον (flock) is the direct translation of Hebrew words in the Old Testament which mean "flock." In the New Testament it is applied, as Thayer's Grimm or any competent modern Lexicon could have told him, to "bodies of Christians (churches) presided over by Elders. Acts xx. 28, 1 Pet. v. 3." How "Romanist" it all sounds as Dr. Carr speaks it! How Christlike, and universal in its simple beauty, it is, as Clement spoke it:—"flock" of Christ, and "hope" of Christ, and "presbyters" of Christ's Congregatian. Poor Clement, to have his beautiful words so mishandled as to back up the un-Christian notion of a great, palisaded, uniform, autocratic Church, with priests and pontiff, whose anathemas cast men out of the "Fold!" But, as Dr. Stacey Chapman has dealt with that instance lucidly, we need not dwell on it further.*

Archbishop Carr, however, answers that he relied upon "Allnatt's *Cathedra Petri*." I am aware of that! That is the cause of the trouble—Allnatt, and the Rev. Luke Rivington, and the Rev. Father Ryder, and all these handbooks of "Catholic

---

* *Alleged Papal Supremacy*, pp. 15-17.

Controversy," written in defence of the *Cathedra Petri*, and drawn up for the militant forward movement of the "Catholic Campaign." This is but one instance out of the many. When we come to Ignatius and the rest, the handbooks are kin in quality.

One could not wish a better service done to Protestantism and Christianity than to have Clement's letter widely printed and read. In cap. xlvii. he urges the Corinthians to read the Epistle of "Paul the Apostle"—

"Of a truth he (Paul) charged you, in the Spirit, concerning *himself, and Cephas, and Apollos*, because that even then ye had made parties. Yet *that* making of parties brought less sin upon you, for ye were partisans of Apostles that were highly reputed, and of a man approved in their sight."

This alone would be sufficient proof of the baselessness of the Romanist claim for a supremacy for Peter, or for Rome. Clement puts Paul in front of Peter—"himself (Paul), Cephas, and Apollos." He calls the two—"Apostles that were highly reputed." He says not a word of Rome having "Apostolic" authority as descending from any one of them. On the contrary, he says those who made faction then, as partisans of the more distinguished Apostles, were less culpable than those who make factions now, when Apostles no longer exist.

I have already sufficiently pointed out, that in cap. xlii., xliv., &c., Clement makes it clear that "*presbyters*" and "bishops" are the same, and that in every Christian congregation there were several of these. And these "presbyters" were then the *highest order in the Christian Ministry*. There is no trace in Clement of ANY ONE BISHOP IN ANY CHURCH ANYWHERE. And *there is no trace of sacerdotalism.*

SECOND CENTURY.—THE "THICKETS OF HERESIES."

The second century brings us into the midst of an altered and tragic spectacle. It is what Jerome, later on, called "the thickets of heresies." The Christian faith had spread widely amongst the Gentile peoples; but it got interwoven thick and deep with the peculiar notions of the pagan cults, and theosophic speculations. It was the era known by the general term "gnosticism." It was the age also of successive harassing persecutions. The Church was torn and distracted by endless "heresies," distorting the faith into a hundred diverse shapes, and breaking into countless factions the Church's unity. It was necessary to the existence of the faith, and of a Church of God at all, that it should be consolidated, centralised, and should have rapid inter-correspondence between its chief centres. To this movement, as all great modern scholars on this subject are agreed, was due the first development, of what is called "monarchical episcopacy"—the lifting of one presbyter or bishop, in each congregation, or place, or Christian community, above other presbyters, to voice the faith and common fellowship in Christ, in the unity of the Church's hope, as that faith had come down from the Apostles of Christ. It was not at all the unity of *shape* they were concerned about, but the unity of the gospel. This fact is admitted in the frankest and clearest way by Jerome, the great Latin Father:—

"Before factions were introduced into religion by the promptings of the devil," says Jerome, "the Churches were governed by a common council of presbyters" (elders*). When afterwards one presbyter was elected that he might be placed over the rest, this was done as a remedy against schism, that

---

* Jer., *Tit.* i., 5.

each man might not drag to himself, and thus break up, the Church of Christ."*

Or, as Bishop Lightfoot says :—

"To the dissensions of Jew and Gentile converts, and to the disputes of gnostic false teachers, the development of episcopacy may be mainly traced."†

Origin of Bishop.

There was another reason for the lifting of *one* presbyter, or bishop, above the other presbyters. In fact, the tendency is seen in every committee or society when it needs an effective "voice" as its president or chairman. In those times of persecution and of varied perplexities, it was needful that the various Christian Churches should have communication with one another. This could be done, as we see already in Clement's letter, only by the Church in one city writing to the Church of another city through the hand of its best-known presbyter, and by sending, where possible, delegates. Especially was this done when the Christian community in a wealthy city, like Rome or Alexandria, felt impelled to send aid to some poorer Christian community. The eloquent preaching-presbyter who was wont to "conduct the thanksgiving worship," which culminated in the Lord's supper with its "Love-feast" (Agapé) and its "giving of alms," became, in association with the deacons, specially identified with this loving duty, the correspondence between the Churches, and the "communication," to beneficence.‡ This tendency was further necessitaed

---

* Epist. cxlvi., *ad Evang.* See on this *Alford*, Acts xx.; Sanday, *Expos.*, Jan. 1887.

† *Phil.* 206-229, sq.; also Creighton's *Hist. of Papacy*, p. 4.

‡ This is the main element of truth, it seems to me, in the Hatch-Harnack theory, which traces the development of the *sole-episcopus* to the congregational *worship* and its *alms-giving*, which alms were distributed by the "bishop" through the "deacons."

when times of persecution set in. The civil law compelled the Christian society in each city to be *registered*, and accountable to the civil authorities, in the name of some *one* presbyter who was thus known to them by the Gentile name "*episcopos*," else the Christian society would have been deprived even of common burial rights.*

The Ignatian Letters.

In the middle of the second century, from such various causes, we can trace this tendency to let *one* presbyter, called definitely "*episcopos*" (bishop), speak in the name of the church, or congregation, in each town or city. It is significant, also, that this is first heard of just in *those* districts where the *gnostic heresies* first sprang up into power, viz., in the region of Syria and Asia Minor.† It is first articulately presented in the Letters of Ignatius of Antioch in his journey along the border of Asia Minor—those strange letters over whose spuriousness or genuineness the heavy cloud of doubt will always hang. For *they stand alone in the first half of the second century.*

This "Saint Ignatius," on his way to Rome to be martyred, shed round him letters broadcast, to various cities as he passed, urging the Christian congregation in each place to be united and steadfast in the faith, honouring their "*episcopos (bishop) with the presbytery and deacons.*" He uses very wild and whirling words, and he is interesting, as every vivid personality is, but chiefly as the earliest man who speaks of a distinction (in the stated Ministry) between the *presbyters as*

---

* This is brought out vividly by Prof. Ramsay.

† Lightfoot points out, also, that the spurious Clementine *Homilies* show us one of the earliest assertions of *episcopacy*.

a whole, and *one* presbyter called "*episcopos.*"* These letters Harnack places about 140 A.D., Lightfoot earlier (and I think wrongly) about 118. [I fancy scholarly opinion will swing round again to reject all these letters as spurious.]

But what I draw attention to, in the whole matter, is this—the one letter which Ignatius wrote to Rome— is just the only letter which he wrote to a Church *outside Asia Minor.* And it makes not the slightest reference to a bishop in Rome. It is addressed simply to the church—" which hath the presidency in the place of the region of the Romans."†

OTHER FATHERS IN SECOND CENTURY.

Later still, in *Hermas,* we have it declared of the Christian community in Rome that it is "*the presbyters who preside over the Church.*" In keeping with this is the light thrown by the recently-discovered *Didache* (or Teaching of the Twelve Apostles), which shows us still existing in the second century *two* (not three) "*orders,*" or "functions," *in the Christian Ministry,* viz., *elders or bishops,* and *deacons.* And it is *the people* who elect or appoint these presbyters.

---

* These writings have, as all confess, been greatly forged and interpolated. They are extant in three main forms:—(1) the shortest, or Syriac (three letters); (2) the Short Greek, or Vossian (seven letters); (3) the Longer Greek, and Latin (thirteen writings). The Short Greek is the only form that can be genuine. Many great scholars regard all as spurious. Zahn, the eminent Presbyterian scholar, vindicated ably the genuineness of the short Greek letters. In this he has been followed by Harnack and by Lightfoot. Harnack's main reasons for regarding these letters as *possible* in the first half of the second century are:—"(1) Their author does not name the bishops as successors of the Apostles—it is Irenaeus who first invents that; (2) he says nothing about an institution of bishops by the Apostles; (3) he deems the bishop, as representative of the truth of God and the faith of Christ, to be the head of only one particular congregation or community."

† Ign. *ad Rom.* 1.

"Appoint, therefore, for yourselves *bishops and deacons* worthy of the Lord; men that are meek and not covetous, and truthful, and approved, for they also perform for you the service (or *minister the ministry*) of the Prophets and Teachers." —*Did.*,* c. xv.†

Do you think, had there been any Bishop of Rome, not to say Pope of Rome, in 142-145, Hermas could have written *that* way?

First Trace of Bishop of Rome.

That is remarkable! The process of change to "episcopacy" was slower in Europe than in the East. But, when it set in, it came with a rush. There were special reasons for the uprising of a single bishop in Rome. *Rome* was then the metropolis of the world,—centre of wealth and influence. It was the Imperial city—the city of the Emperor's court and palace. Many members of the Roman Church had relations soon with the Emperor's household. Before the close of the first century some of the Emperor's near relatives were Christians. Every Church that was impoverished by famine or persecution sent an appeal to the wealthy Church at Rome. The prominent martyrs were sent to suffer at Rome. The Christian traders gravitated towards Rome.

In the closing years of the second century we find "episcopacy" almost everywhere. But what was that "episcopacy?" Certainly not anything like diocesan episcopacy. The "episcopos," as Sanday shows, corresponded to a modern parish minister or the

---

* Prof. Sanday says that the discovery of the *Didache* has dissipated the doubt expressed by Lightfoot whether the rulers in Hermas might not mean "bishops" in the later sense. Harnack says Hermas is proof that "episcopacy" had not yet arisen in Rome.

† cf. Sanday, *Expos.*, Jan., 1887. The inexpensive book, *Church of Sub-Apostolic Age*, by Prof. Heron, of Belfast, deals lucidly with this.

incumbent of a town church, or (shall I say?) a Wesleyan circuit leader, with his presbyter-helpers, and his deacons or stewards round him. There was, as yet, no sacerdotal caste, and nothing like diocesan episcopacy, or any separate ordination for "presbyters" and for "bishops."*

THE MESSAGE OF PEACE BETWEEN THE CHURCHES.

We are, as Sanday says, alas, "slaves of words." The metaphorical Old Testament language about "High-priest, Priest, and Levite" has dominated, as Lightfoot vividly shows, our Christian imagination. Similarly the word "bishop," with its mediæval pompous sound, has led our historical reason captive. For the "bishop" of the close of the second century was a very limited and humble personage.† Sanday says truly:—

"Every town of any size had its bishop; the whole position of the bishop was very similar to that of the incumbent of the parish church in one of our smaller towns."

He says further, and beautifully:—

"The Christian Church consisted of a number of scattered congregations islanded, as it were, amongst the masses of an alien population."

Further still he declares:—

"In some respects the Non-conformist communities of our own time furnish a closer parallel to the primitive state of things than an Established Church can possibly do. Christianity itself was an instance of non-conformity."

That is fine, as coming from a scholar who himself prefers the modern Episcopal system, when reformed. And I, who was born within an "Established and

---

* The distinction is not clearly drawn, Lightfoot shows, till the *fourth* century.

† *Expos.*, Feb. 1887. Cf. Lightfoot, *Phil.* 231 *et Ignat.* i. 397.

Presbyterian Church," heartily endorse it. And this is still finer:—speaking of the Church's earliest stages, when the Christian communities first got dotted down, here and there, and then gradually came to be cared for by presbyters, he says:—

"The Church passed through a congregational stage, and . . . it also passed through a presbyterian stage."

The hearty recognition of these facts, he declares, ought "to result in an eirenicon between the Churches."

Earliest Traces of a Priestly Caste.

Towards the close of the second century we come upon three new features. It is significant that they occur simultaneously: (1) the earliest assertion that "bishops," as distinct from "presbyters," are successors of the Apostles; (2) the earliest distinct assertion of special priestly titles as belonging to the Christian Ministry; (3) the first distinct claim made by the Roman Church to precedence, and to a kind of more authoritative voice than other Churches. This meant the atmosphere and mood of Roman, pagan Imperialism, invading the Congregation or Church of Jesus. Irenaeus is the first to voice the first of these notions, viz., that "bishops" are successors of the Apostles. Ignatius, fifty years earlier, with all his whirling rhetoric, had never uttered this. The original identity of bishops and presbyters as presiding over the Church is still visible, even in *him*. Thus, in *his* vehemence for the Church's faith and harmony, he speaks of the bishop as—

"Presiding in the place of (or, after the likeness of) God, and your *presbyters as in the place of* (or, after the likeness of) *the assembly of the Apostles.*"[*]

---

[*] Ign. *ad Magnes.*, cap. vi., *Trall.* 2, 3, *Smyr.* 8.

"But be ye obedient to the Presbytery as to the Apostles of Jesus Christ, our Hope." And, again, he urges respect for "the presbyters as the Council of God, and as the College of Apostles."

"The presbyters, not the bishops," says Lightfoot (*Ignat.* vol. i., p. 397), "are here the representatives of the Apostles."

So that if there is any external "Apostolic succession" it would inhere in the *Presbyters!* That is certainly the *one* order of the *stated Ministry* which has continued all through, from the earliest hours of the Christian Church and down till to-day. By the law of "the survival of the fittest" the order of presbyters will, apparently, continue after bishops shall have passed away. For, as a witty friend of mine in the Old Land said :—"According to John's Apocalypse, in the Vision of the Church perfected, the presbyters (or elders) have a large and honoured place. But there is no mention whatever of bishops!" If any Church can claim *external* "continuity," those Churches which have the Presbyterial system can surely claim it. But, let us all thank God, "succession" and "continuity" depend on a factor more certain than any externalisms of human appointment, or of men's hands resting on heads, whether the hands be bishops' hands or those of presbyters, viz., on the abidingness of Christ's truth and gospel, and of God's redeeming grace, on the never-failing presence of Christ's living Spirit in the hearts of men, who make confession and thanksgiving together before God, in the unity of the love of their common King and Saviour. This is the Kingdom of God. This is the Congregation, or Church, of Jesus. Let us honour it, and its ministry, in all its forms, however simple, however stately, if only it be true, in living love and in unselfish beauty of the life, to the Spirit and the presence of Jesus.

Priesthood Born in North Africa.

It is well that this has been shown by a great and learned prelate, viz., Bishop Lightfoot, so there can be no charge of bias. The first time we find the name "hiereus" (sacerdos) "priest" applied to Christian ministers is by a heathen writer.* The first Christian Father "to assert direct sacerdotal claims on behalf of the Christian Ministry" is Tertullian, of Carthage, in North Africa, and of Rome. He calls the bishop the chief priest, "summus sacerdos," and says that the right of baptism belongs to him.† That is the first clear note of Sacerdotalism in Christian history, more than 160 years after *Christ* died. And yet he modifies this thought greatly by saying that Christian laymen also are priests, and where no clergy are at hand, laymen "present the eucharistic offerings, and baptize, and are (their own) sole priests. For where three are, a Church is, though they be laymen."

It is the same Tertullian, as I showed in last lecture, who said that Peter was baptising in the river Tiber, at Rome, and that St. John was plunged in a caldron of oil at Rome, and yet came forth unhurt.

At the same epoch Victor became Bishop of Rome, the first man of Latin birth who ever held that office. A Roman, accustomed to the Roman mood, of dominating all the rest of the world, and having "relations with the Roman Imperial Court," he attempted to assert a specially decisive voice amongst the Churches, on a question of Church order. But his claims were at once forcibly and bluntly repudiated. Irenaeus, of Gaul, who had hitherto flattered the Roman bishop, at once strongly protested. Tertullian, of Carthage, the very Father

---

* *Lucian*, see Lightfoot. † Light., *Phil.*, p. 255.

who had asserted a sacerdotal order as belonging to the Christian Ministry, and who had enlarged the story of Peter's preaching at Rome, stood against this growing arrogance of the Roman bishop.

"The Chief Pontiff, forsooth, has issued his commands!"† laughs Tertullian, a little later. Little dreamt Tertullian that this very name "Chief Pontiff," the name of the highest pagan priest, would by and bye "be claimed for, and granted to, a later and far more ambitious Bishop of Rome!"

These things belong, however, to our concluding lecture.

Seeing what Rome was, the *spirit* of the Papacy was born so soon as the assertion of a separate priestly caste, in the Ministry of the Church of God, was once accepted. The *form* of the Papacy was not yet born, for many a day.

Spirit of Papacy Born.

Its *spirit* was born, at any rate, from the third century, and onward, from the time Cyprian made the bishops to be successors of the Apostles, and specially inspired of God. Lightfoot proves that the priesthood in the Christian Ministry first arose from *heathen influences*. But, so soon as the episcopate and the presbyterate got looked upon as distinct orders, so soon as men began to dream of a threefold order of bishops, presbyters (or *priests*), and deacons, then the Old Testament notion of *high-priest, priest, and levite* came to be regarded as the type of the Christian Ministry. In *that* lay germs of the hierarchy and the Roman Papacy.‡

---

* It is probable that it was of the baleful Callistus Tertullian thus spoke. Others say Victor, or Zephyrinus.

† Lightfoot, *Phil.*, p. 262, sq.

In the beginning of the third century:—

"The solitary bishop represented the solitary high priest; the principal acts of Christian sacrifice were performed by the presbyters as the principal acts of Jewish sacrifice by the priests; and the attendant ministrations were assigned in the one case to the deacon, as in the other (case) to the levite."*

Thus the analogy seemed complete. Bishop, presbyter, deacon was made to run—high priest, priest, levite.

The Analogy Disloyal to Christ.

"To this correspondence," however, as Lightfoot points out—

"There was one grave impediment. The only High Priest under the Gospel recognised by the Apostolic writings is our Lord Himself."

But the growing spirit of ecclesiasticism soon pushed that scriptural and spiritual "scruple" aside. And, with a growing external pomp and "observation," a hierarchy of priestly rank above rank rose. It took the place of that Kingdom of Christ and of Heaven, of whose secret and spirit Christ, who brought it, said— "The Kingdom of God cometh *not with observation*; neither shall they say 'lo, here! or, there;' for lo, the Kingdom of God is within you." Amidst the din of Cyprian and Novatian† contending about the validity of the ordination of Cornelius as Roman bishop, and of Stephen, Bishop of Rome, contending with a greater than himself, Cyprian of North Africa (who was called by the Roman Church "Papa"— Pope) about the re-baptism of "the lapsed"—amidst the far fiercer contendings of the Councils, which followed, regarding hair-splittings of doctrinal pro-

---

* Light. *Phil.*, p. 263.
† Cf. Harnack's masterly paper in *Herzog u. Plitt.*

positions—there was lost out of sight what the Master had said, what even Tertullian had reaffirmed—" *Where two or three are gathered together in My name, there am I in the midst of them.*"

Dr. Carr on Altar, &c., in Ignatius.

Note.—Dr. Carr's attempt to deal with the startling fact that, in the New Testament, no special sacerdotal titles or functions are ascribed to the Christian ministry, or to the Lord's Supper, and that even in the Earlier "Fathers" up to Tertullian's day, the "presbyters," and stated ministers of the Church generally, are not regarded as priests, save just as all believers are "priests to God," is surely flimsy. He tries to take refuge in High-Anglican Blunt and his suggestion that "it was the object of the Apostles to wean the mind of the Jew from the external associations of his ancient faith." Is this meant as humour? The fact is that the whole New Testament is full of Apostolic reference to "the external associations of the ancient faith," and to priesthood too. And all Christians are called "priests," and Christ is called High-Priest, and all this is contrasted sharply with the "ancient faith." But no special priesthood is ascribed to the Christian minister. And there is no external "altar" of any kind in the Apostolic and sub-Apostolic Church.

Dr. Carr does not, himself, think much, evidently, of poor Blunt's desperate exegesis. So he tries for himself. He says that to argue from

"the mere absence of the word *hiereus* (priest) from the Apostolic and sub-Apostolic writers betrays a manifest unfamiliarity with their teaching. For instance, in the works of St. Ignatius, who was bishop in the lifetime of the Beloved Disciple, the term *hiereus* does not occur," &c.

But Dr. Carr goes on to argue that

"*Power over the natural body of Christ, in which the essence of the Christian priesthood consists,*"—

is actually "clearly expressed" by Ignatius. Also, says Dr. Carr, "the term *thusiasterion* or sacrificial altar is frequently found in his works." And Dr. Carr proceeds to quote a passage from Ignatius "*To the Philadelphians,*" which (with precise reference and loyal translation) I will set here :—

"If any man walketh in strange doctrine he hath no fellowship with the passion.* Be ye careful, therefore, to observe one eucharist [eucharistia=thanksgiving] (for there is one flesh of our Lord Jesus Christ and one cup unto union in His blood ; there is one altar, as there is one bishop [episcopos] together with the presbytery and deacons, my fellow servants) that, whatsoever ye do, ye may do it after [the will of] God." (*Philad.* iii., iv., Lightfoot's trans. See, also, Roberts and Donaldson).

---

* *I.e.*, the suffering of Christ.

Dr. Carr translates:—"*One chalice which unites us to His blood.*" And his foot-reference is, "*See Lightfoot, Apostolic Fathers, part ii., p. 257-8.*" (This is better than a great many of the foot-references in his book, but none, save a student who had made this whole subject a special study, would in the least know what that reference may possibly mean. And the actual passage of Lightfoot, when looked up, is in direct contradiction to Dr. Carr's exegesis). Also, when Dr. Carr goes on to quote Harnack about this matter of "priesthood," he is again equally remote from what is relevant or exact.

Now, briefly, let me answer:—(1) The word *hiereus* (priest) *does* occur in Ignatius. Nay, more, it occurs in the very letter from which Dr. Carr undertook to quote. Thus:—"*The priests*, likewise, were good; but better is the *High-priest*, to whom is committed the holy of holies."—*Philad.* ix.

Lightfoot here explains (what is surely scarcely necessary), that "the contrast here is between the Levitical priesthood and the Great High-priest of the Gospel," viz., Christ. He also shows how, in a later century, *the interpolator* of Ignatius *had altered the passage so as to make a reference to the three orders of the Christian Ministry.*" And this has misled Roman Catholic writers (Lightfoot *Apos. Fath* part ii.; *S. Ignat. et S. Polyc.*, vol. ii., pp. 273-4).

(2) Wherever *thusiasterion* (θυσιαστηριον) occurs in Ignatius, it *never refers to the Lord's table*, or to any *material altar* in the Christian Church. No such "altar" existed anywhere in that age. Thus Lightfoot (on the very pages to which I suppose Dr. Carr's foot reference points) says:—

"It would be an anachronism to suppose that Ignatius, by 'the altar,' here means 'the Lord's table.' Even in Irenaeus, though he is distinctly speaking of the Eucharist in the context, . . . yet only *a spiritual altar is recognised.*"

Lightfoot, also on that page, says, "The 'one flesh' here is the one Eucharistic loaf, betokening the union of the one body of Christ." (*ut supra*, p. 258). Lightfoot also *proves* that by "*altar*," where God's people are gathered, is meant, in Ignatius, "the congregation gathered together" in Christ's salvation, corresponding to the "court of the altar," or "court of the congregation," where God's people assembled in Old Testament times. Even the collected "body of widows" was called "God's altar" (Lightfoot *id.*; Ignat. *ad Eph.* v., *ad Trall.* viii.). Again, very strikingly, in his letter *to the Roman* Christians, Ignatius calls the *amphitheatre* at Rome, where he will have to *suffer before the assembled people*, "*the altar.*"

"That I be poured out a libation to God, while there is still *an altar* ready." (*Ignat. ad Rom.* i.)

3. In all this, as scholars have shown long ago, *Ignatius* is full of *Pauline* thoughts and metaphors. Paul's thought of his own approaching martyrdom as *a libation* "poured out on the sacrifice

and service" of the Church's faith is in Ignatius' mind. The thought of Heb. xiii., 10—13, is also all through his letters—the thought of Christ's faithful ones " going forth without the camp" where Christ suffered, bearing His reproach and partaking, in spiritual fellowship, of the "altar" of His cross, where He suffered and so gave life and strength to us. Surely Dr. Carr knows that great Roman Catholic interpreters like Thomas Aquinas and Estius, as well as great Protestant ones—Bengel, Bleek, de Wette, Delitzsch, Lightfoot, Alford, A. B. Davidson, &c.—have declared that *thusiasterion* there means not the Lord's Supper, but *the Cross of Christ*, through which redemption comes to all believers, uniting them as God's people into one; one in faith, service, and suffering.

As to Harnack on Cyprian, of course, "in the second half of *the third century*," in North Africa, there is *priesthood* strongly developed. That is just what I say. And yet, even in that third century, Origen and others have to reply to the pagan taunt that "the Christians *have no altar, and no temple.*" Origen's noble answer is that "*every good man's spirit*" is "an altar from which arises an incense," spiritual and true, viz., prayer and the offering of the gifts of loving character and of unselfish life. For Christ is there. And all Christians are "*living stones*" in a "spiritual temple." They are all "a holy priesthood." (Orig. adv. Cels. Bk. viii., 17, 18, 19.)

But, in the earlier age, Harnack shows clearly that the *whole life* of the Christian was regarded as *sacrificial.* "It was a fixed principle that only a *spiritual* worship is well pleasing to God, and that all ceremonies are abolished. . . . The Christian worship of God was set forth under the *aspect of the spiritual sacrifice.*" Though the language of Ignatius might, at first sight, seem "realistic," yet "many passages show that he *was far from such a conception.*" Thus, "in *Trall.* 8, *faith* is described by him as the flesh, and *love* as the blood of Christ." And so in many passages. With Ignatius, as with John, "the concept 'flesh of Christ' is a *spiritual one.* (Harnack : *Hist. of Dogm.*, Eng. ed., vol. i., pp. 204, 211-12.) Of course I doubt not we shall see tiny fragments of Harnack figuring in books of Catholic controversy in favour of sacerdotalism. But "*take, read!*" (May I explain that Lightfoot's great work, *Apostolic Fathers*, Part II.—*S. Ignatius, S. Polycarp*—is in three big volumes. The pages to which Dr. Carr's reference should point are in *vol. ii.*, pp. 257-8.) I need not stay to scatter the legend that Ignatius was the disciple of the "Beloved Disciple," John. There was no end to the legends about Ignatius and his martyrdom, or about Peter.

LECTURE FOURTH.

EVOLUTION OF THE PAPACY: ITS EARLY STAGES.

"The Kingdom of God cometh not with observation for, lo, the Kingdom of God is within you."—S. Luke xvii., 20—21.

"Jesus answered—'My Kingdom is not of this world; if My Kingdom were of this world then would my servants fight."—St. John xix., 36.

AT the end of the first century, when Clement of Rome wrote to Corinth, it was *the congregation*, the church* that spoke through its presbyters. There was no hint then of any "Bishop of Rome." When Hermas wrote, later than the year 140 A.D., even then in Rome it is *the presbyters* who preside over the Church.†

"The later Roman theory supposes" (says Lightfoot) "that the Church of Rome derives all its authority from the bishop of Rome, as the successor of St. Peter. History inverts this relation, and shows that as a matter of fact, the power of the bishop of Rome *was built upon the power of the church of Rome*. It was originally a primacy not of the episcopate, but of the church."‡

---

* This form was continued for a good time, as Lightfoot shows.

† Hermas, cap. IV. Harnack *Dogm. Gesch.*, cap. iii., § 7, &c., Sanday *Expos.* Jan. 1887, p. 3.

‡ *S. Clem.*, vol. i., p. 70.

The Christian community in the central metropolis of the Empire, naturally, lent special importance to its representative presbyter. The Early Church was, to use Professor Sanday's phrase, "essentially urban." It existed mainly in cities and large towns. The dwellers in the country and villages (pagani) were as yet untouched, a fact vividly evidenced by the word "pagan" (a "villager") which we still apply to non-Christian people. And of all cities Rome had the *principatus*—" the first place " the "pre-eminence." It is in keeping with human nature that, first, the Christian *Church* in Rome should think itself entitled to the *principatus;* and, secondly, that its "*bishop*" should by degrees come to think *himself* entitled to the *principatus* also. Hence all this trouble about "*the Primacy*!" Hence the huge ambition, reached up to after the lapse of centuries, of clutching, and forcing to unheard of new meanings, Christ's figurative words to Peter about the Rock on which His Church should rest! It is earth's way, and Time's, the way of the Kingdoms of the world, that "come with observation," with external show of power :—

"For why? Because the good old rule
Sufficeth *them*, the simple plan
That they should take who have the power,
And they should keep who can."

The odd thing is—but this is human nature too—that those who do " take," and keep for a while, get to think that it has been so arranged by God and by the fiat and inspiration of His Spirit. This is the secret of all " Toryism" and of all " Clericalism," in State and in Church. The holders of "*the power*" come, quite sincerely, to believe that it was God who made them a special " caste;" they conveniently forget (till some Luther or some Puritan age roughly shakes them into honest examination of *facts* and of God's truth) that "the power" was gained, in part by accident and misconception and weight of circumstance, in part by strong, selfish exercise of force. They forget, above all, that *Christ* said, in opposition to all these (for His Church at least): "My kingdom is not of this world, else would my servants use force."

First Note of Roman Assumption.

Several things conspired to the assumption of superior influence, on the part of the Christian congregation in Rome. The forceful do, usually, find things "conspiring" towards their purposes. The need to centralise and consolidate the Christian communities, during that second century as against "the thickets of heresies"* was one great factor. The new distinction in the Christian Ministry of "bishop" in each congregation or town, as distinguished from his fellow-presbyters or bishops (so that there should now be sounded forth the ear-filling triad of titles—"bishop, presbyter, deacon"),—this distinction, first heard of in gnostic-vexed Asia Minor, invaded the Church everywhere. And it helped towards the uplifting of the bishop in each great city, and of a priestly gradation of "orders." These things sweep the field rapidly. "Anglo-Catholicism," for example, has, more swiftly than this, changed, in two generations, the face of the modern Church of England. And the second century was an age of rapid fermentation of all kinds—"apocryphal writings," manifold "martyr legends," Apostolic "journeyings," leaders of "heretic schools," countless new shapes of blended Christian truth and non-Christian speculation. Words of *metaphor* in the Old Testament, or in the Apostles'

---

* Jerome.

writings, were grasped at, and twisted into a new *literalism* of meaning. Above all, that new distinction in the local Christian Ministry in its stated congregational worship—"bishop, presbyter, deacon"—was made to chime with the Old Testament notions—"high-priest, priest, Levite."* The step from *that* was swift to another distinction, which arose not as (what Archbishop Carr unhappily calls) "the irresistible outcome of the facts of history," but as the half unconscious outcome of human ambition and self-assertion—viz., the lifting of the Church in a great city into importance as above the Church in a smaller city, and, by-and-by, the lifting of the bishop of the Church in a wealthy and powerful city above the bishop of a Church in a city that was remote and unimportant. If, in the second century, the distinction grew in—"bishop, presbyter, deacon,"—just as inevitably the bigger distinction would grow in, during later centuries—"Archbishop, bishop, presbyter, deacon." Finally, over the "Archbishop" or "Metropolitan," a "Patriarch"† would be lifted up. Finally, at top of all, the bishop of the greatest City of the West would claim to be Prince of all bishops and of all archbishops, and even of apostles. He could even claim to speak with the voice of Peter,—Simon of Galilee, transformed into the Church's foundation-rock, and vice-gerent of Christ in one! That was the tendency and method of it!

THE CROW TURNS EAGLE.

George Washington's simple "coat of arms"—three wooden bars of a fence, and one crow perched apologetically on the topmost bar—within less than a century, expanded and evoluted into a great, forceful,

---

* This has been vividly worked out by Lightfoot, cf. *Phil.*, pp. 261-3. † Schaff, *Nic. and Post-Nic. Chris.*, vol. i., p. 271.

screaming eagle on the top of endless "stripes," and surrounded by all the "stars" of the universe, claiming, under spell of some mystic "Monroe doctrine," sole primacy over a whole "American Continent." *That* is *political* assumption of power, and is tolerable. It yields to its citizens large freedom of thought. The Roman assumption is vastly more startling; the tragedy and self-contradiction of it are—not only that it comes with anathemas—but that its claim to rule is in the *spiritual* sphere. It is in antagonism to the very principles and spirit of Christ, in constituting His Kingdom.

It was an unusual junction of what appealed to man's spiritual nature, with the Externalism of centralised wealth and political power that gave the special impetus to the Roman Church. In Rome, the first memorable martyrdom on a vast scale had been endured. That curious legend, which arose in the second century, and blended together Peter and Paul, making them found the Church of Rome in company and then die as martyrs in company, appealed to the pious imagination, in an age when men (as we see in Ignatius) forced themselves upon martyrdom as a glorious gateway towards Heaven. Ignatius himself, though the more sober narrative of his martyrdom makes him die at Rome, torn by the beasts of the Amphitheatre, as on a rough altar-cross, is represented as transported soon to Antioch. The legend makes *him*, finally, get buried in his own Antioch, all the bones and parts of him quite intact.* Such was the mood of the time. John was plunged into boiling oil at Rome; but the legend-weavers could not get rid of the fact that, in the Apocalypse

---

* Lightfoot, who has done his wonderful best to set up a genuine Ignatius, scouts this part of the legend.

and other Scripture writings, his main career was found at Ephesus and on Patmos. So John is made to escape unhurt from that unique ordeal at Rome, and "is relegated to an island." But Peter and Paul lived not so long. And no Scripture had told the closing scenes of the life of Peter. Legend could work on these two Apostles. It worked *this* as the result. They, both of them, founded the Church of Rome; and they, both of them, fell there in heroic martyrdom.

Now, at the close of the second century—when all the Apostolic facts and realities lay far away in the background of the past—all these various growths meet and intertwine together in Rome. Just then we hear, for the first time, Irenaeus of Gaul propounding the theory that the bishops of congregations are "successors of the Apostles."* Just then we hear, and for the first time, the notion, suggested by Tertullian of Rome and of North Africa, that the Christian minister (presbyter) is a priest and the bishop a chief priest, "*summus sacerdos*." Just then we hear, for the first time, from Dionysius and Tertullian and Irenaeus that Peter had been in Rome, and that, with various modifications, both Peter and Paul had joined together in founding the Church in Rome, and glorifying it by conjoint martyr-death. And, just then, arose the first strong man of actual, undoubted Roman birth, and speech, and predilections. The Roman dominant mood is upon him—the mood of uniform government, and of a certain indifference to the feelings, and freedoms, and rights of other cities, and of distant provinces. That man was Victor, first Latin bishop of Rome. We shall hear *from* him and *of* him.

---

* Harnack, *ut sup*.

Till his day, the Christian Church in Rome had been Greek in speech, and in sympathy with the East. The Latin Church had been centred in Carthage of North Africa, in Southern Gaul, and in North Italy, and Spain. Now the Latin *régime* has begun in Rome. Its Greek epoch is closed. Henceforth we shall find it purely Latin and Roman in its temper, its genius, its sympathies. Tertullian soon finds himself rebuffed, affronted by the arrogant, dominant ways of the Roman clergy, and revolted into Montanism by their conduct; Tertullian, the forceful, pure-minded, lonely-hearted genius, whose mood did so much to mould the Latin Church, whose words the later Cyprian read every day, and whose memory the still later Jerome loved, so that he waxed wroth thinking of those jealous clerics of arrogant Rome. What a story it is!—men like Zephyrinus and Callistus to be the Latin "successors" of the strong-willed but true Latin bishop, Victor. And what figures they all are, to be regarded by a later age, through the hallowing mists of time, as infallible vicars of the merciful and holy Christ on this vext and oddly-arranged earth! We honour Irenaeus of Gaul (despite his tendency to the fabulous) for resisting bravely the first note of Roman assumption, sounded by the first Latin bishop of Rome, Victor,—backed though Victor was by the potent female influence of the pagan Imperial palace.* The softening haze of distance causes us to invest those early ages of the Church's existence, after the Apostles and the Apostolic men were past, with a sanctity, both of faith and of conduct, they did not at all possess. Our imagination ascribes to them a uniformity and amity foreign

---

* See the striking details in Hippolytus, *Haer.* ix., 7; Lightfoot, *Philipp.*, pp. 223-4. It gives us a surprised peep into the then state of Roman Christianity and the Roman Court.

to their actual condition. Rome, that was fed by all streams and influences and peoples, from west and east, received into her Christian community all the contending and heretic elements which were the wonder and trouble of that second century.

Lightfoot of England, and Harnack of Germany, following up the investigation of Ritschl and others, have, indeed, done much to disprove the theory of the Tübingen school, that the vexed internal history of the early Roman Church was due to its being predominantly "Ebionite" or Judaistic, and so thrown into antagonism against the message and spirit of the Gospel brought by the Apostle Paul. It was not *mainly* "Ebionite" heresy, or Jewish heresy of any kind, but *Gentile* heresy and rival personal influences which distracted that Church. "Her early history, indeed," says Lightfoot, "is wrapt in obscurity." "Most of the great heresiarchs . . . taught in Rome." And again he declares:—

"As late pagan Rome had been the sink of all pagan superstitions, so early Christian Rome was the meeting-point of all heretical creeds and philosophies."*

The Church of Rome, during part of the second and of the third centuries, was so torn by internal conflict that many eminent modern scholars hold that there must have been two or more separate Christian communities in the early stages of the Christian movement in Rome, "each with its own separate government." Professor Sanday, in common with many distinguished students of the question, holds that this, in part, explains what Lightfoot calls "the marvellous discrepancies in the lists of the early bishops, which perhaps point to a double succession"

---

* *Galat.*, pp. 336-7, 344-5.

of *presbyters* or *episcopi*.* Akin to that is the startling fact that the "bishop" of the second century, even after his elevation over the presbyters, was but the head of a Christian congregation. He was a presbyter still, as *primus inter pares*, first amongst his equals, *Moderator*, † one says, amongst the rest. In keeping with this is the other startling fact, vividly proven by Hatch, Sanday, and others, that up to the time of the Council of Nicaea (325 A.D.)‡ there might be two "bishops" in one place, and that, for example in Africa, Phrygia, &c., there were apparently as many "bishops" as there were congregations.§ In the earlier half of the third century Hippolytus and Callistus (both of them "saints" now) were bishops in Rome and bitter enemies; the one was Puritan, the other lax. A little later, in the middle of the century, Novatian and Cornelius (A.D. 251) are both bishops, and rivals in Rome. Cyprian, Bishop in Carthage (the most influential Christian leader then in the west), was appealed to in their rivalry. Apparently for the first time, he (the father of the genuine "episcopal succession" theory) enunciated the doctrine which, though as yet in its incipient stage, was the basis of modern episcopacy, viz., that, "when once a bishop has been appointed and approved by the testimony and judgment of his colleagues and of the people, another bishop cannot be set up."‡ But still, there was as yet no such thing as "diocesan episcopacy."

---

* Lightfoot in his *Galatians* also held this view. In his *Clem.* he does not think it necessary, but he has not convinced the greatest scholars, even of his own school, *e.g.*, Sanday.
† Lightfoot calls Clement this, but even this distinction had not yet been made.
‡ Canon viii.
§ Sanday, *Expos.*, Ser. iii., xlvii.; cf. Lightfoot, *Phil.*, pp. 224-5.
‡ *Ep.* 44 (41) 3; Döllinger, *Hippol. and Callist.* (E.T.), pp. 67-93; Sanday, *ut sup.*

Roman Church: Middle and End of Second Century.

The Roman Church had welcomed the Clementine and other Ebionite legends of Peter and of Paul, and soon profited by them. But it shook itself free, *as other Churches did*, from the special "Ebionite" *doctrine*, with its low view of Christ's Messiahhood. It was *Gentile* influence that swept specially upon the Roman Christian community rather than Jewish influence. Lightfoot paints the situation from the middle of that century onward, with its wealth of "romance" about Peter and other eminent Apostles:—

"The religious romance seems to have been a favourite style of composition with the Essene Ebionites, and in the lack of authentic information relating to the Apostles, catholic* writers eagerly and unsuspiciously *gathered incidents from writings* of which they *repudiated the doctrines.*†

The Forged Decretals.

A startling illustration of this, in a much later age, is the fact made vivid by Lightfoot that on the basis of this same (apocryphal) Clementine romance regarding Peter and his "journeys" was built up, in the ninth century, the gigantic fraud of the forged "decretals of Isidore," by which the papacy got its vastest impulse towards power. To quote Lightfoot's strong words in his latest writing:—

"Thus the Clementine romance of the second century was

---

* By "catholic" in its early signification, and as scholars like Lightfoot and Harnack use it, is meant what pertained to the *whole* Church in all places, as holding the teaching handed down from the Apostles, as contrasted with a *local* Church. This term Ignatius first uses:—"where Jesus Christ is there is the Catholic Church."

† Cf. *Appendix.—Clementine Romance.* Lightfoot, *Gal.*, p. 367. Harnack, *Hist. of Dogma*, Eng. ed., p. 315, &c.

the direct progenitor of the forged Papal Letters of the ninth —a monstrous parent of a monstrous brood."*

But what concerns us now is the state of the Church in Rome at this *early* date, when the second century merges into the third. That I may not be accused of exaggerating, let me put it again in Lightfoot's words:—

"The gleams of light which break in upon the internal history of the Roman Church, at the close of the second and beginning of the third century, exhibit her assailed by rival heresies, compromised by the weakness and worldliness of her rulers, altogether distracted and unsteady, but in no way Ebionite. One bishop, whose name is not given, first dallies with the fanatical spiritualism of Montanus; then, suddenly turning round, surrenders himself to the patripassian speculations of Praxeas.† Later than this, two successive bishops, Zephyrinus and Callistus (A.D. 202-223), are stated by no friendly critic indeed, but yet a contemporary writer, the one from stupidity and avarice, the other from craft and ambition, to have listened favourably to the heresies of Noetus and Sabellius."‡

Indeed, to all that age as to the age which preceded it, with the strange oppositions and factions through which the Apostolic witness to Christ had to make its way, we may well apply this great scholar's startling but helpful words, reminding us that the divisions of opinion in the modern Churches are far less than those in early ages, which we ignorantly glorify. The pompous talk of "Apostolic Ages" and "Fathers," and of their uniformity, is proven curiously unmeaning when we look at the reality.

"However great may be the theological differences and religious animosities of our own time, they are far surpassed in magnitude by the distractions of an age, which, closing our eyes to facts, we are apt to invest with an ideal excellence. In the Early Church was fulfilled, in its inward dissensions no less than in its outward sufferings, the Master's sad warning that He came not to send peace on earth, but a sword!"

---

* *S. Clem.*, vol. i., p. 102, *et* pp. 414-415.
† Lightfoot *Gal.*, p. 344, Tert. *adv. Prax.* 1.
‡ It is St. Hippolytus who says this (*Haer.* ix., 7 seq.)

Irenaeus Resisting Victor of Rome.

The earliest distinct step to anything like a claim of special authority for the Church in Rome, amongst the other churches, was taken when Victor, bishop at Rome in the close of the second century (*cir*. 190-202), attempted to sever communion with the Churches of Ephesus and Asia—the Churches which held the tradition of the Apostle John—as to the date of the observance of "the Lord's Passover." John's Churches made it chime with the 14th day of Nisan (whatever day of the week it might be). Not *day*, but *date*, they said. *That* was the date of the Jewish passover. Rome, as the Church of the Gentiles (with the Lord's day as the centre of the year), rejected this. And Victor, the first bishop of Roman blood and of Western partialities, finding his flock distracted on this question, attempted to compel uniformity, and arrogantly to sunder all Christian fellowship with the Churches of Asia.

Some thirty years earlier, when Anicetus was the leading presbyter or bishop in Rome, the aged Polycarp, of Smyrna—"a disciple of the Apostle John"—visited Rome. There was then the same difference on this matter. Polycarp, true to the custom of John's Churches, observed Easter so as to make its date coincide with the Jewish passover. Anicetus observed it differently. And neither would yield to the other. But, instead of the thought dawning upon them that either of them could excommunicate the other, they, in a true Pauline spirit, agreed to differ on this matter; and Anicetus permitted Polycarp "to celebrate the Eucharist (Lord's Supper) in his stead."*

---

* Lightfoot, *Gal.*, p. 343; Euseb., H.E., v. 23, 24. Schaff, *Ante Nic. Chris.*, i. 210 seq.

Victor, in the close of that second century, was of another mood. He was a Roman. Had he lived later, he would have made a model Laudian or Star Chamber bishop, in the ill-starred time of the Stuarts. In answer to his arrogant assertion that there should be *uniformity* of practice, Polycrates, "bishop" in Ephesus, at that time the most venerable Christian figure in the East, and backed by all the "bishops" of Asia,* protested and held to his own way. "Words of theirs are extant sharply rebuking Victor," says Eusebius.† *That* sounds unlike language used to a "Pope," a lineal descendant of an infallible Peter, Prince of all Apostles and Vice-gerent of God! Doesn't it?

The Asian Churches Quote Peter Against Rome.

The words of Polycrates sent to "Victor and the Church of Rome," whom he (Polycrates) significantly addresses as "Brethren," are noble in their dignity and firmness. He tells Victor that the Roman observance was *not* the observance of the Apostles—not that of the Apostle Philip; not that of the Apostle John; not that of the Holy Spirit who guided the noblest martyrs; not that of "*the rule of faith.*"‡ Polycrates adds these emphatic words:—

"I, therefore, brethren, who have lived sixty-five years in the Lord, and have met with the brethren throughout the world, and *have gone through every Holy Scripture, am not affrighted by terrifying words.* For those greater than I have said—'*We ought to obey God rather than man.*'"§

That is what Polycrates wrote to the Church in Rome and its truculent high-tempered bishop-presbyter

---

* Euseb., H E., v., 24.   † Euseb., *id.*, cap. xxiv., 10.
‡ *Id.*, cap. xxiv., 6.   § Acts v., 29.

Victor. *I like Polycrates*, and his straightforward scriptural method of argument. It was a hard knock, but a true knock he gave to Victor! He flung at him not only the names of the Apostles Philip and John, but especially the "Holy Scripture." And then, most cruel of all, he quoted to him what *Peter* had said in presence of the Jewish *Sanhedrin*, in the face of that authoritative council of the ancient priestly Church. It just means *this*:—"*You are only fallible men; we ought to obey God rather than men.*"* There is in those words of Polycrates† a genuine ring of the Christian Gospel—*a genuine Protestant ring.* And the oddest thing of all is that Polycrates is quite ignorant of any Romish notion about Peter being the head of the Apostles, or about the Bishops of Rome being his successors.

Now, when Victor, in Latin Rome, received and read those words from Greek Ephesus, he was in a very un-Christlike temper. And he flamed out into a threat, and immediately attempted, as Eusebius says, to cut off all communion with the Churches of Asia.

Irenaeus Admonishes Victor.

Now, just as the members of the Christian Church in Rome were closely related to those in Corinth (for Corinth was a Roman military city, and this is the reason, as Lightfoot shows, why Clement of Rome wrote to Corinth a century earlier) so the Churches in the south of Gaul were descendants of Asian Greek emigrants. Irenaeus, now their leading man, was himself from "John's Churches" in Asia. Irenaeus now stands up on behalf of the liberties of the Churches, as against an iron uniformity, and a centralized authority. "He fittingly admonishes Victor," says

---

* Acts v., 29, also iv., 19.   † Euseb., H.E., Bk. v., cap. xxiv., 6, 7, 8.

Eusebius. Irenaeus was willing, for himself, to observe the Roman and Western mode. But he reminds Victor of—

"*The presbyters before Soter, who presided over the Church which now thou rulest.* We mean Anicetus, and Pius, and Hyginus, and Telesphorus, and Xystus."

Yes, *that* is significant. It is a clear reminiscence of the time when it was *Presbyters who presided over the Church of Rome.* He tells Victor further that all these had not attempted to impose their mode upon the Christians from Greek Asia, who came to Rome (as great numbers of them did on business) from their cities of Asia. "None of them were ever cast out on account of this form"—says Irenaeus. He reminds him, also, of Polycarp and Anicetus. He also, in that "fitting admonishment" he gave to Victor, tells him the startling fact that the Roman custom is different from that which Polycarp "*had always observed with John, the disciple of our Lord, and the other Apostles with whom he had associated.*"* Truly that was a sore blow to come from the most learned bishop and Saint of the West against the bishop of Rome, who, according to the modern Romish creed, is infallible in pronouncing doctrine, and is the head of all the Apostles. Irenaeus tells him that his teaching and pronouncement are wrong, and contrary to the Apostles; that there are certain things on which difference should be allowed, and that the faith is better for want of uniformity in these indifferent matters.† That is a dash of Protestantism from an unexpected quarter, and Victor, bishop of Rome, had to yield.

---

* Euseb. H.E , v., 24.
† The forty days of "Lent" were then unknown. Irenaeus says —"Some thought they should fast one day, others two, and others more."

In fact the sentence with which Eusebius closes the narrative of this whole matter is, of itself, enough. He says of Irenaeus—

"And he conferred by letter about this mooted question, not only with Victor, but also with most of *the other rulers of the Churches*."*

Think of that. Both by Irenaeus, on the verge of the third century, and by Eusebius, the Emperor Constantine's friend, in the fourth century, Victor, bishop in Rome, is regarded simply as head of the Christian community in that Italian city, and on a par with "the other rulers of the Churches." All and each of the others have a right to be consulted just as much as Victor.

Mistranslation of Irenaeus' Words.

We come now to a passage of Irenaeus, very simple in itself, but which Romanist advocates have made famous, or notorious. Archbishop Carr's second lecture is wholly given up to Irenaeus, and at least fifteen pages are taken up with the one passage to which I shall now refer. I will not spend much time upon it, for to translate it accurately, and then look at its simple meaning, is quite enough. Does it not seem evident that if there were any truth in the Romanist position, if Christ's Church and man's salvation depended on Rome and its bishops, this would have been made so clear, in the revelation from God given in Scripture, that Romanists would not be under this painful necessity of casting about for forced and unnatural renderings of fragmentary passages, in

---

* Schaff, Wace, and M'Giffert's rendering. Euseb., H.E., Bk. v., c. xxiv., 18. To Professor Macdonald's fine sense for books, and to his recent visit to the Old Lands, our College library, already well-stocked with "the Fathers," owes this beautiful edition.

"fathers," here and there, on the verge of the third and in the fourth and fifth centuries?

Now Rome, in Italy, was nigh to Lyons, in Southern Gaul; nigh also to Carthage, in North Africa, across the narrow belt of the Mediterranean. With the wealth of its members, and its proximity to the Imperial Palace, its Christian Church had frequent opportunities of benefiting the less powerful Churches in the west. It was the Central or "Mother Church," from which, probably, most of the Churches in Gaul, North Africa, and Spain had been first evangelised and "founded."*

Had the Roman Church been modest, this influence would have been helpful and beautiful. It would have had, as Lightfoot finely puts it, "a presidency of love." And that it had, *despite the heretic factions which vexed it*, retained, in common with all the Churches east and west, "the traditions" of the faith held in common by the Apostles, Irenaeus gladly acknowledged. To that tradition of the common faith, preserved in all the Churches by the teaching of the successive presbyters and episcopi, Irenaeus appeals, in his conflict with the chief leaders of "heresies," as shown in his greatest work, *Against Heresies*. Irenaeus is the first "Father" to ignore, or forget, the fact that presbyters and bishops were in the New Testament identical.† Along with this (as Harnack shows), he was the first to

---

* The position of independence affirmed, however, each for itself, by even the Western and Latin-speaking Churches, such as N. Africa, Gaul, and North Italy, is very significant. Thus, the Church of Milan (cf. Schaff) claimed to have been founded by the Apostle Barnabas, and, till the end of the sixth century, had no contact with the Roman Pope. So also Aquileia stood quite independent.

† Alford thinks he was "disingenuous" in this. Lightfoot holds that he and other "Fathers" were beginning to *forget* the fact (as so many "High Anglicans" conveniently forget it now, and *rapidly*). When Jerome, in a later age, began exact Bible study, the fact was again brought to light.

affirm "the *successions*" of these congregational or local "bishops" *from the Apostles.*

In truth it is not a *succession* of bishops Irenaeus is caring about, but the succession or endurance of the *faith*, the faith in God and in the actual Christ, the faith which the Apostles proclaimed, and which "the heresies" were striving to alter and undo. That this faith is one and the same, says Irenaeus, is proven by the fact that it has been handed down and retained in *all* the Churches, as evidenced in "the successions of all the Churches."*

This could be proven, he says, by "contemplating" *any* and all of the Churches in the teaching of its successive bishops. But it would be very tedious to go over them all. I will take one example, he therefore says, one that is "*universally known*," the case, viz., of the metropolitan city, Rome. This is the simple and unforced meaning of the argument in Irenaeus from which "the famous passage," · so daringly mishandled by most Roman Catholic advocates, is taken. I say "most," for, to the honour of a few Roman Catholic scholars, they have translated it quite differently.

Archbishop Carr says he has been "charged with mistranslation regarding this particular passage of St. Irenaeus," viz., by his "Anglican" critics.

I do not charge him simply with *that*; for any man may make occasionally "a mistranslation," innocent of any thought of misleading. Even a few Protestant scholars, ere now, have blundered over this passage. My charge is that Dr. Carr, if fit at all to speak on subjects of this kind, must know that there is a quite different translation; and, further, that, in the opinion of the best and latest scholars on this question, the translation given by him is clean

---

* *Haer.*, Bk. iii., cap. iii., 2.

against the sense. Yet he gives no hint of that. Nay, further, I am sorry to say, he asserts, regarding Protestant scholars on this matter, what the facts directly disprove.

The Passage from Irenaeus.

Irenaeus begins his statement in Bk. iii., cap. iii., 1, thus :—

"It is within the power of all, therefore, in *every Church*, who may wish to see the truth, to contemplate clearly the *tradition of the Apostles manifested throughout the whole world*," &c.

In the next paragraph, or section 2, he points out that this testing of all the Churches severally would be "very tedious."

"Since, however, it would be very tedious, in such a volume as this, *to reckon up the successions of all the Churches*, we do put to confusion all those who, in whatever manner, whether by an evil self-pleasing, by vain glory, or by blindness and perverse opinion, assemble in unauthorised meetings, by indicating that tradition, derived from the Apostles, of the very great, the very ancient and universally known Church,* founded and organised at Rome by the two most glorious Apostles, Peter and Paul, as also the faith preached to men which comes down to our time through the successions of the bishops."†

---

* The original Greek text of Irenaeus has mainly perished. It is represented to us by a Latin text, into which, of course, very many corruptions may have been introduced. Here is Lightfoot's translation of the latter part of the above (and it makes a startling difference):—
"The greatest and most ancient *Churches*, well-known to all men, the *Churches* of Rome founded and established by the two most glorious Apostles, Peter and Paul [hand down] announced to mankind that tradition and faith, which it has from the Apostles, reaching to our own day through its successions of bishops." (*Clement of Rome*, vol. ii., p. 495.) Is not this an instance of "Homer nodding?"

† Iren. *Haer.*, cap. iii., 2. Bishop Coxe's Revision of Roberts and Donaldson. I have taken care to give the translation of another, so that no charge of bias can be made.

Then follows immediately "the famous passage," round which ranges such war of words. I will translate it as it is translated by a candid Roman Catholic scholar, and then contrast that with Archbishop Carr's rendering—

"For to this Church, on account of more potent principality, it is necessary that every Church (that is, those who are on every side faithful) *resort*; in which Church ever, *by those who are on every side*, has been preserved that tradition which is from the Apostles."†

Now the meaning of that, when looked at frankly, seems simple enough. The only drawback to that Roman Catholic translation is that *undique* does not mean "*everywhere*, or on every side," but "*from all quarters, from* every side." Irenaeus is arguing against those (makers of "heresies,") who, he declares, "consent neither to Scripture nor to tradition."*
Not to be "tedious," he takes Rome, the central city of the west, as one illustration of the "tradition" of the faith handed down from the Apostles, and preserved in all the Churches. To this Church, viz., of Rome, on account of the more important eminence ‡ [of that *City*; or, is it, of that *Church?*] it is a matter of necessity that Christian believers from every Church, far and near, should *resort* (*convenire ad= come together*), for Rome was the centre of the world's traffic and business. So we say of *London*, that *Scotsmen gather there* from *every side.* And, I know, it is

---

* Berington and Kirk, vol. i., p. 252. † Cap. ii., 2.

‡ The whole passage in the Latin is:—Ad hanc enim ecclesiam propter *potiorem* [or *potentiorem*] principalitatem necesse est omnem *convenire* ecclesiam, hoc est eos qui sunt undique fideles, in quâ semper ab his qui sunt *undique*, conservata est ea quae est ab apostolis traditio. There are two readings, *potiorem* principalitatem and *potentiorem* principalitatem. It is of no consequence which is right. *Principalitas* is defined in Lewis and Short's Edit. of *Freund's Latin Dictionary* as "the first place, superiority, *pre-eminence*, excellence."

said of the Presbyterian Church in London that its faith and tradition are preserved by outside Presbyterian people who come together to it *from all quarters.* So, says Irenaeus, with his Eastern and Gallic sympathies,—"*By those who are from every quarter (ab his qui sunt undique)*—has been preserved in Rome the tradition of the faith, which is from the Apostles." If the Latin of this passage means anything, it means that, not chiefly by Rome herself, but by the many Christian *strangers*, who are always coming to Rome from every Christian Church outside, is preserved the pure Apostolic faith—the faith which is the unity of the Church, "the tradition of the Apostles manifested throughout the whole world." iii., III., 1. [See note in Appendix.]

Archbishop Carr Against Himself.

I am quite sorry to spend time on this, but the Archbishop has made it the principal thing in his Lectures. Look at the use he makes of this. It is, according to him, a "testimony" to the "Primacy of the Roman See." And that "Primacy" he had defined as absolute *sovereignty*, "an authority to teach, to rule, and to correct," a "primacy of jurisdiction over the whole Church," "promised immediately and directly to the blessed Peter the Apostle, and conferred upon him."*

Here, then, is how Irenaeus is shaped so as, if possible, to fit. "So saturated is he (Irenaeus) with Roman doctrine," according to Archbishop Carr, that one wonders he cannot get some *better* passages. He translates him thus:—

"For *with* this Church, on account of *its superior principate*, it

---

* Carr, pp. 48-49, *et* p. 8.

is necessary that every Church agree ;* that is, the faithful everywhere (every Church), in which by the (faithful) everywhere the Apostolic tradition is preserved." †

That does not seem to make "sense;" and it is certainly not a correct translation. But the wonder increases when we turn to the *Advocate* (28th March) and read the "*in extenso* report" of Dr. Carr's Second Lecture as he delivered it to the mixed audience. There the translation is:—

"For *to* (or with) this Church, on account of its superior principate, it is necessary that every Church should *come together* (or agree), that is, the faithful who are everywhere." That is at least more accurate, and it gives the truer translation foremost. *Now*, in "the book form," that truer translation is cut wholly out. The words *convenire ad*, which simply mean "*to come together to*," are made to mean to "*agree with*." The word *undique*, "from all quarters," is translated as if it were *ubique*, "everywhere;" and *the words* "on account of the more important eminence" (or, as the Roman Catholic scholars say, "on account of more potent principality") are translated "on account of *its* superior principate," making it refer, not to the *City* of Rome as metropolis, but necessarily to the *Church* of Rome.

But, oddest of all, in his *Replies*,‡ published a year ago, Archbishop Carr had left out that translation "agree with" altogether, and had translated thus:

"For to *this* Church, on account of its superior principate, it is necessary that every Church should *come together*, that is, the

---

* The only excuse I can see for this strange translation, viz., to make *convenire ad* mean "agree with," is that "the Protestant translators" in Clark's Series so render it. But, then, what do they say below? As to this and Bright, &c., see note in Appendix.

† Carr, *Primacy*, p. 49 ; In Dr. Chapman's *Papal Supremacy*, pp. 23-25, this matter is lucidly dealt with.

‡ P. 34.

faithful who are everywhere, for in this Church the tradition, which is from the Apostles, has been preserved by those who are everywhere."

This "chopping and changing," to use Browning's phrase, is not the worst of it. Archbishop Carr was bound, I think, in fairness to give some hint that the majority of recent scholars are quite against his latest rendering, and that the meanings "agree with" and "everywhere," forced by him upon Latin words, are quite erroneous.

[To make this matter worse still, Dr. Carr declares:

"Thus, to mention a few out of the many distinguished names, Canon Bright, Regius Professor of Oxford, and Gieseler, admit that the words *convenire ad* mean *to agree* with."*

This strange assertion I meet simply by quoting Canon Bright's own words, which affirm the exact opposite:

"For *convenire ad* would be a strange Latin equivalent for 'agree with.' And, further, *the ensuing words would have lost their point if 'agreement with the Roman Church' had been the idea."* †

What are we to say regarding these assertions of Archbishop Carr? And what are we to say of an "infallible Church" that needs such unnatural and constantly shifting translations, from fragments of "Fathers" in the end of the second and later centuries?]

Third Century.

At the close of the second century we have seen Irenaeus resisting Victor, bishop of Rome, in his effort

---

* Carr, *Primacy*, p. 56.
† Bright, *Roman See*, p. 33. Bright has had to "heckle" the Rev. Luke Rivington for similar assertions. Rivington tries to make it "sovereignty," and to refer it to the Roman Church. "Mr. Rivington, who relies a good deal on sheer *iteration*, renders it 'sovereignty' five times within four pages." Bright: *id.*

to dictate to the Asian Christians who visited Rome. We have seen, also, Tertullian, of North Africa, denouncing the bishop of Rome, at once, for arrogance and laxity.* Of course, it is answered that Tertullian had now been driven into Montanism. Yes, Jerome says, *by the arrogance of the Roman clergy*; other historians say by their laxity, as is evident from his his own pages.

St. Hippolytus' Picture of Roman Bishops.

St. Hippolytus, at any rate, was not a Montanist; but a great "Father" of the third century, and bishop at Rome.† He is a "Saint" besides. Hippolytus was the most learned Father of the west. His great writing, *The Refutation of all Heresies*, re-discovered in 1842, and published in 1851, casts surprising light on the state of the Church in Rome in the early part of the third century. Hippolytus joined, says Lightfoot, the learning of the east with the practical energy of the west. Hippolytus had been Victor's friend.

He gives us a dreadful picture of the two successive bishops in Rome who followed Victor, viz., Zephyrinus and Callistus (202-223). Especially is the latter startling. He had been a slave, a peculator of widows' money, had been on the tread-mill, had been banished as a convict to the mines of Sardinia, had by his

---

* Tert. *de Pudic.*, 1. Lightfoot thinks the bishop denounced was "either Victor or Zephyrinus;" others Zephyrinus; others again Callistus.

† Döllinger makes him anti-bishop. Sanday and many others regard him, similarly, as bishop of one Christian party, the purer community then in Rome. Lightfoot thinks he was bishop to the *Strangers* at the port of Rome.
Schaff's Herzog-Tertullian.

financial skill got into the household of Zephyrinus, then succeeded him as bishop.* He leant to both the Patripassian and Sabellian heresies. Let us hope that picture is overdrawn.† But the fact which stands out indubitable from it is—that here you have at Rome two bishops in the third century. He who, in the Roman lists, is called Bishop of Rome, Callistus, is declared by a fellow bishop to be both loose in doctrine and loose and blackened in life, and yet the one bishop cannot depose the other. A curious illustration of "the successors of the Apostles," and also of Rome's claim that the Bishop of Rome is the Supreme Vicar of Christ on earth, and alone carries "Peter's keys" to open the Kingdom of Heaven, and to declare and pronounce the Church's doctrine and practice. Callistus, bishop of Rome, if we are to trust Hippolytus, believed and pronounced heresy, and his practice was not even good Paganism. Hippolytus, another bishop at Rome, at that same time, whom Archbishop Carr has honoured as "St. Hippolytus," who calls himself also "High-priest" and successor of Apostles, declares all this, and denounces Callistus as a heresiarch. Where is there to be found in that third century the notion of the Supremacy of the Bishop of Rome?

---

* Hippol. *Haer.*, Book ix., c. vii. The most impressive fact of all is that when Victor, through Marcia, had the Christian Martyrs (confessors) in the mines liberated, he did not give the name of Callistus. Here is Hippolytus's startling description:—"Marcia, a concubine of Commodus (the pagan emperor), who was a God-loving female and desirous of performing some good work, invited into her presence the blessed Victor, who was at that time *a bishop of the Church*, and inquired of him what martyrs were in Sardinia. And he delivered to her the names of all, but did not give that of Callistus, knowing the acts he had ventured upon."—Hippol. ix., 7.

† Döllinger thinks so; but Hippolytus was one of the best of the "Fathers," and not likely to lie.

" Pope Cyprian" of Carthage : And the Bishop of Rome.

The next stage is reached, when, in the middle of that same Century, Cyprian, the energetic and versatile Bishop in Carthage, of North Africa, the student of Tertullian, had vigorous relations with Cornelius Bishop in Rome (*cir.* 251), and afterwards with a much more aggressive Roman Bishop, Stephen (253-257). Cyprian I have already spoken of, and I shall rapidly sketch the two aspects of his influence which have relation to our question.

Now Cyprian entertained very extreme and high notions of the independence, equality, and "unity of all bishops." The notion of the priestly function and order, which we find first rhetorically imaged in Tertullian, the notion of the *episcopi* as successors of the Apostles,* first hinted by Irenaeus, now got further developed by the autocratic mood of Carthage and Rome. It got blended with the Montanist notion of *direct inspiration.* So, in Cyprian, all the "bishops" then existing, and they were as numerous in North Africa as the larger congregations,† were regarded as recipients of the

---

* The after thought of Liddon and Canon Gore, viz., that, though the presbyters and episcopi of the stated ministry, in Apostolic times, were the same, and though the Apostles in their special ministry had no successors, yet the *wandering* "prophets" and "evangelists" (such as they imagine Timothy and Titus to have been) got gradually *fixed* and *localised* as the first "bishops," is scouted by both Lightfoot and Sanday, as well as by German scholars. Sanday dismisses it as "irrelevant." Lightfoot shows that this fantastic notion was entirely unknown in the Early Church.

† In a council, convoked by Cyprian, there were 87 North African "bishops." In an earlier Council, 90 "bishops." "The enormous number of African 'bishops' a few centuries later," says Lightfoot, "would seem incredible were it not reported on the best authority." There were 690 North African "sees," or bishops' centres of teaching. In fact, any Presbyterian clergyman, or incumbent of a church, or Congregationalist or Wesleyan minister of a church, has a large "primacy" as contrasted with all these. What a fantastic theory that of "Apostolic" succession in "bishops" is!

Apostolic gift, and of direct inspiration by God, the recipients specially of the Holy Spirit.* In keeping with this bold and sweeping notion is that famous declaration of Cyprian, to which I drew attention in an earlier lecture, viz., that what Christ said to Peter He said to him for all the Apostles equally. Thus there is both perfect equality and also a symbol of unity.

"Assuredly the rest of the Apostles were also the same as was Peter, endowed with an equal partnership both of honour and power; but the beginning proceeds from unity."

This statement, as Lightfoot says,† "was very unsatisfactory to a later age;" therefore Rome interpolated such words as—"And the primacy is given to Peter," &c., which contradict Cyprian's whole meaning, and which all scholars have cut away as spurious. Now, with this strong clean-cut notion of the equality of all bishops in the unity of the Church of Christ, which Cyprian calls "the root and matrix of the catholic church," he was ready for action. So, when the "Novatian Schism" occurred at Rome, on the appointment of Cornelius (251 A.D.), Cyprian in Carthage, over the sea, hesitates about co-operating with him in this equal participation of the episcopate. He will not acknowledge him as brother-bishop, or "colleague"—until he inquires.‡ Then, when he finds "through his colleagues," who were sent to inquire, proof that Cornelius has been *legitimately* appointed, he writes him—"Cyprian to Cornelius, his brother, greeting," telling him—

"Having received letters lately from both parties, we read your letters, and intimated your ordination to the episcopate in the ears of everyone."§

---

* Cyp., *Ep.* 66, &c. See also Lightfoot, *Phil.*, p. 240-2.
† *Clem. of Rome*, vol. ii, p. 485. Bright, *Rom. See*, p. 42
‡ Cyp. *Epp.*, xl., xli. § *Ep.* xli.

A little later he writes Cornelius, in similar terms, that "lest a schism made in the city should confuse the minds of the absent," he had decided—

"having got a greater authority for the proof of your ordination"—

that letters should be sent to Cornelius by all of Cyprian's colleagues in North Africa, "approving and maintaining both you and your fellowship."* So the unity of the catholic Church, and its charity would be preserved. That is odd language to use to "a Pontiff." It is language which any senior and respected Congregational minister in Melbourne, and his colleagues in the ministry of Churches, might send to a newly-appointed "brother" minister of an important Church in "pre-eminent" Sydney or London, "approving and upholding both him and his fellowship." How "we are slaves of words," with the modern vision of a Lord-Bishop in lawn sleeves, or a Cardinal with his hat, haunting and bestriding us, when we read the letters of these "urban bishops" of the third century! Cyprian speaks of "our mother, the catholic Church."† I hope we will all speak just so of the one universal spiritual Church of Jesus Christ—"the Jerusalem which is from above" (as Paul has it) which is "the *mother of us all.*"

But never a word speaks he of the Bishop of Rome as *superior* to other bishops on account of any special descent from Peter.

Cyprian's Conflict with Stephen of Rome.

A little later (*cir.* 253-7) Cyprian found in Stephen (a new Bishop of Rome) a man fiercer in temper and as autocratic as himself. It was the age of the terrible Decian persecution, the first universal and persistent

---

* Ep. xliv. † Ep. xlii.

attempt to suppress Christianity within the Roman Empire. The edict was specially against the bishops. Cyprian, a man of elegance and wealth, fled, though in a later persecution he stood firm and died in martyrdom at Carthage. It was in part from his hiding-place he fought his own deacon and others who disputed his right to be bishop, and contended with them about the restoration of the "lapsed." After his return to Carthage, when that particular persecution was past, the Church fell into disputation over the amazing subject whether baptism performed by heretics and schismatics is valid. Stephen said "Yes." Cyprian, the older and more revered man, said "No." And he and other bishops, east and west, such as Firmilian of Cæsarea, knew so little of "Peter's supremacy," or of the Bishop of Rome's supremacy as representing Peter, that they flung at Stephen's head the example of *Paul* as if *that* should settle the matter.*

Now, here are two things which may astonish us. On the one hand, there is that curious contradiction in practice which still prevails in the Romanist Church in an extreme shape, viz., that "in case of need," baptism can be performed by orthodox or heretic, cleric or non-cleric. Yet it is a "sacrament" as solemn as the Lord's Supper. On the other hand, there is the odd fact that these "bishops" who, according to the Cyprianite and Anglo-Catholic and Roman Catholic notions are "successors of the Apostles," and have "received the Holy Ghost," illumining them above other men, yet took *such opposite views of truth and practice*, and fought, and excommunicated one the other." This theory of Apostolic succession in "bishops" is so droll, so fantastic!

Stephen, indeed, made repeated blunders, as arrogant men do in all Churches. Certain Spanish bishops, who had been removed from their " sees" by the neighbouring clergy and people for unworthy conduct, induced Stephen to recognise them as in communion, and possessing the status of bishops. The Spanish Churches appealed to Cyprian, the most trusted bishop of the west. Cyprian* held a council which " struck strongly, and one stroke." They declared that the unworthy and deposed bishops had "deceived Stephen, our colleague, placed at a distance, and ignorant of what had been done, and of the truth."
So it was also in the case of the dispute about *Baptism*. Cyprian held successive councils. Asia Minor and Spain sided with him.† At a council in 256, Cyprian, in his address of welcome, smites thus at the new pretensions of the Bishop of Rome:—

"None of *us* sets himself up as a bishop of bishops, or seeks to constrain his colleagues by the terror which tyranny can inspire."‡

Apparently Stephen sundered all communion with all the Churches which sided with Cyprian, and treated them as heretics. But look at this state of things: " St. Cyprian" is the "greatest Father" of the Catholic west in the third century. He died, also, with the " stroke of the sword" in martyrdom, saying, nobly enough, when sentenced to death,—"*Deo gratias!*" He is a " Saint." Yet he considers Stephen, Bishop of Rome, only as one of his "colleagues." He condemns him also for " pride, severity, obstinacy."§ He resists and defeats for that age his attempt at *uniformity*, in

---

* Ep., 67. 5.
† Lightfoot *Phil.*, p. 242 sq. [Bright *Rom. See*, pp. 50-51.]
‡ This is apparently the third of Cyprian's Councils on the Baptism question, and his sixth Council in all. Hefele. Counc., Clark's Edit., p. 96.
§ Cyp. Epp., 73, 74.

keeping with the Roman mode. And Stephen impotently tries to revenge himself by cutting off all fellowship with most of the Churches in the west and east.* Truly this is an odd kind of "sovereignty of jurisdiction" possessed by Bishops of Rome in the third century! And is there anything more grotesquely *unlike* the guidance of the Holy Spirit than these squabbling bishops, fighting about "goats' wool," such as the question of "the rebaptism of the lapsed," and the validity of heretic baptism? Truly an un-Apostolic "team" of "successors of the Apostles!"

Fourth Century: First Christian Emperor.

It was the *laity, not the Bishops*, that saved Christendom. Such is the startling verdict from a quite unexpected quarter—John Henry Newman, writing on the struggles of the fourth century! I will return to this a little later.

The fourth century was momentous for good and ill. It saw the arrival of the first avowedly Christian Emperor, Constantine, and the stoppage of persecutions, and the founding of the New Rome (Constantinople) in the East, and the removal to it of the principal Imperial Court, and the practical splitting of the empire into two halves, with its weaker half in the west. Thus there came a chance to the Bishop of Rome, for stronger action and larger influence. For Rome was the only *great* city in all the west that claimed to be an "*Apostolic* See," and it was still the ancient Imperial City, while the cities that claimed to be "Apostolic" Sees in the east—Antioch, Ephesus, Alexandria, and the

---

* Neudecker, *Stephen*, in *Herzog* u. *Plitt*. Schaff, *Ant. Nic. Chris.*, vol. i., 263-5.

rest were fiercely jealous of one another as neighbours, and that, too, Greek neighbours are wont to be. None of these cities was the Central or Imperial city. They were too much on a par, and so rivals. Had Constantine fixed his centre of government in Alexandria, it is certain that Alexandria would have been the centre of Christendom, despite the fact that her Church had only St. Mark, an "Apostolical" man, as her traditional "Apostle founder." Milan, in North Italy, had got hold of Barnabas somehow as her traditional founder, and for centuries stood out independent of Rome. But Rome, by that rare twofold legend of Paul and Peter founding the Roman Church, had got hold of two actual martyred Apostles; and in her yellow Tiber—a quite odd place—Peter had baptised, and within her borders John had resisted boiling, and had been relegated to an island. And now, when the Christian Emperor removed his curbing presence far away eastward, the Roman Bishop, with Rome's backing of wealth, and of autocratic temper, and of legendary glamour, got her opportunity. She had another advantage. The Greek mind was subtle, metaphysic, litigious. The fierce disputes over fine, theoretic, theologic distinctions were mainly carried on in the East. They kept the energies of the great Greek bishops distracted and antagonistic. Rome had no intellectual troubles of this kind. Her mood is—believe and obey! She had what served better than intelluctual thought in a long struggle for power. She had the Western organising, drilling, practical, administrative, wealth-gathering power. She seized hold of, and adapted to herself persistently, the theology and the monastic system which the Christian Greek mind thought out and fought out. She clothed them with more imperious sanctions; she gave them the coherence of her own forceful mood—"*command! obey!*"

Cardinal Newman truly says:—*

"The See of Rome possessed no great mind in the whole period of persecution. Afterwards, for a long time, it had not a single 'doctor' to show. The great luminary of the western world is St. Augustin; he, no infallible teacher, has formed the intellect of Europe."

And Augustin was not a Roman. But Rome had forceful sagacity—she could "divide and conquer." And she could *keep*.

THE COUNCIL OF NICE: AND ROME.

The Fourth Century saw the assembling of the first of those "great Councils" at which the bishops met, and debated, and were violent, and schemed both for the formulation of the Church's faith and for their own individual supremacy.

The first great Council,* called by Constantine at Nicaea, in Bithynia (325 A.D.), for his new capital (Constantinople) on the Bosphorus was not built till five years later, gives no hint of any Primacy of jurisdiction belonging to the Bishop of Rome.

The object for which the Emperor summoned this first representative Council of all Christendom—east and west—was to decide what is known as "the Arian conflict." The question involved was the true

---

* I do not stay here to discuss the Western Council of *Arles* (in Gaul) which Constantine previously summoned (314) on an appeal by the Donatists against the decision of a small Council in Rome under its bishop, Miltiades (Melchiades). Romanist advocates try to represent this as somehow supporting the notion of Papal Supremacy, because Marinus, the Bishop of Arles, who *presided* at that Council, and other members reported to the Bishop of Rome, Sylvester (who had "succeeded" that year), the Council's *decisions*, that they might be *announced* in the metropolis, as in other places. Funny kind of argument to make an appeal from a decision in Rome to a Council of Bishops in Gaul a proof of Rome's infallible Supremacy!

Divinity of Christ, the Son of God. The question vexed Christendom for many an age. All the other main questions regarding Christ's person, with which the Councils of the fourth and fifth centuries were vehemently agitated, are inter-related with this one. The conflict had begun in Alexandria, between its bishop, Alexander, and the forceful Arius, who represented the tendency of Antioch. Behind Alexander stood his gifted deacon, Athanasius, afterwards his successor as Bishop of Alexandria.

It is no part of the purpose of these lectures to discuss theology. It is enough to say that the decision of that Council emphatically excluded Arianism. Our *present* duty is simply to trace the successive early steps of the advance of a claim made for the superiority, and finally the "supremacy," of the bishopric of Rome.

The bishops and presbyters, who gathered at Nicaea, were of all sorts. Some had come from great distances. Some bore on their bodies the scars of sore mutilations, endured by them in Pagan persecutions. But they had retained not only life, but a vast vitality of the old Adamite temper. That is inseparable from politics of all kinds, profane and sacred. The Bishop of Rome, Sylvester, was not present. He was represented by two presbyters.*

When the Emperor, handsome, tall, slim, splendidly attired, yet with reverent mien, entered the Council, a master, and shrewd judge of men, he made a great impression. He was welcomed in the name of the Council, probably by Eustathius, Bishop of Antioch, the "oldest Christian see," the earliest so-called " See of Peter."†

---

* Vito and Vincentius. Of the whole "Nicaeno-Constantinopolitan Creed," the ordinary English reader will get a succinct account (by Harnack) in Schaff's *Herzog* ; or Schaff's *History*. [On the Romanist arguments regarding this Council see Bright *Roman See*, p. 66 sq.]

† So Theodoret. Others think it was Eusebius himself.

Romanist writers try to make out that the President of that Council was Hosius of Cordova, in Spain. Then they try to paint Hosius as "the Pope's representative." Others, with much more reasonableness, hold that there were two or three " Presidents," such as Eustathius of Antioch, and Alexander of Alexandria (who, as backed by his brilliant supporter, Athanasius, was a principal figure in the Council). The Emperor, when present, was President. But he was a shrewd manipulator of men, this Constantine. He delivered the assembly over to the Presidents ($\pi\rho o\acute{\epsilon}\delta\rho o\iota s$).* It is, I think, probable enough that the aged Hosius, "the Father of the West," and the special friend of the Emperor, *sometimes* presided, taking his place in turn with the bishops of Alexandria and of Antioch.† Hosius had already gone, at the request of the Emperor, to Alexandria to attempt to heal the dispute. If he presided at all, it was as the Emperor's old and closest personal friend.

---

* Hefele, the Roman Catholic historian, argues laboriously that Hosius presided. . . . Then, with Roman audacity, at a later point he assumes and asserts that Hosius "presided at the assembly *as Papal legate* in union with the two Roman priests, Vito and Vincentius." (Hef. *Councils*. Clark, 2nd edit., vol. i., pp. 37-42, 260, 281.) This is bold, and quite contrary to the facts. Schroeckh., Ernesti, Hinschius, and other investigators, such as Tillemont, the eminent Roman Catholic and Jansenist historian, have shown that the attempt to represent Hosius as the Pope's legate rests on the notorious falsifications of Gelasius of Cyzicus in the latter part of the *fifth century*! On his falsification of facts, see *Dict. Chris. Biog.* ii., 620. [One could not have a better example of Romanist advocacy than by first reading Hefele (one of the most moderate of R.C. advocates) on this subject, and then reading the criticism of it in Prof. Bright, *Roman See*, p. 71 seq., and foot-notes. Bright thinks Hosius presided as the Emperor's trusted friend. Against this the plural "presidents," used by Eusebius, seems conclusive. It is not probable, is it, that a Council meeting in the East, composed of Greek bishops and presbyters, with only eight Westerns, would be presided over by *Westerns* alone?]

† So Schaff, &c.

The canons of that Council prove the Romanist claim to supremacy to have been quite undreamt of in that fourth century. They assign to the Bishop of Rome, as was natural on account of Rome's political position in the West, spiritual jurisdiction—*i.e.*, the right to ordain bishops—over Middle and Lower Italy, with the Islands of Sicily, Sardinia, and Corsica, *on an equality with** the bishop of Alexandria, who had spiritual jurisdiction—*i.e.*, the right to ordain all the bishops—over Egypt, Libya, and the wide Pentapolis. The arrangement was just according to divisions of the Empire and its great cities. No thought of the bishop of Rome as Bishop of Bishops, and wielding Supremacy over Christendom, had as yet dawned upon men.†

---

* Even Hefele confesses:—"The Council of Nicaea points out that the Bishop of Rome has also rights analogous to those which it acknowledges for the Bishop of Alexandria and for the Bishop of Ephesus." On Hefele's amusing effort to get out of this absolute disproof of the Roman claim see the whole passage.—Vol. i., pp. 394—399. (Bright, *Roman See*, p. 75 seq.) Archbishop Carr has ventured to accuse me of "a quibble" regarding Renan. How one sees his own reflection! For, if ever pitiable quibble was written, surely it is Dr. Carr's attempt (p. 202) to get out of the facts about Nicaea. He says, trying to follow Hefele—"The subject of the Primacy was not mentioned at the Council." Quite true! For there was no such thing then in existence. The Roman bishop is simply called "the bishop *in* Rome."

† For a luminous, brief statement of the gradual elevation of the *city* bishop above the *rural* bishop, then the elevation of the "metropolitans" above the ordinary city bishops, then of "the five patriarchs," the "oligarchical summit," above the metropolitans, and of the relation of this to the divisions of the Roman Empire, read Schaff, *Nicene and Post Nic. Christianity*, vol. i., pp 263—274. The Patriarchs were the bishops of "the four great capitals of the empire"—Rome, Alexandria, Antioch, Constantinople. To these was added, as honorary patriarch, the Bishop of Jerusalem. This development of the Patriarchs was, of course, later than Nicaea. Constantinople was founded 330 A.D., five years later than the Council of Nicaea, and then began a conflict for precedence between the Bishops of Rome, Constantinople (the new imperial capital), and Alexandria.

Hosius Recants: The Pope Turns Heretic.

The epoch succeeding the Council of Nicaea presents a singular spectacle. Alexandria, with its Athanasius, was the centre of orthodoxy. If a "See" means rightly a "chair" of teaching, and if the Nicene Faith be true, then to Alexandria—not Rome at that time—belonged "the Apostolic Chair" and the "Primacy."

In Julius I., who became Bishop of Rome about the time of Constantine's death, Athanasius had found a hearty supporter. The two sons of Constantine took different sides. Constans, in the west, backed Athanasius; Constantius, in the east, Arius. Constantine, alas, had allowed the beginning of a new thing—*persecution*, the use of force by Christians against those who did not conform.* Both Orthodox and Arian used this new weapon pitilessly.

At a Council summoned at Sardica (343), the Eastern bishops withdrew and held an opposition Council. The rest, in the interests of Athanasius, who had been deposed by Constantius, resolved that a deposed bishop may "appeal to the Roman bishop Julius." This expedient of battle against Antioch and the East failed. That "Council" was never accepted as œcumenical. The Emperor refused any sanction. Christendom rejected it.

But the Sardican move was answered in a rougher and tragic way. Constantius, now sole Emperor, and siding with the "Eusebians and semi-Arians," attempted to compel uniformity. The aged Hosius, who had been severe upon the Arians, was flung into prison, and summoned before the Synod at Sirmium. Alas, alas!—But, indeed, we will not tell it ourselves.

---

* At first it was confined to scourging and banishment. After Theodosius, and in the age of the great Councils, the death penalty was also enacted.

We will let John Henry Newman and others mainly tell it. Hosius, who had presided at Sardica, (who, the Roman Catholic writers argue, presided at Nicaea), recanted under torture, and by the Synod of Sirmium, though he would not sign the condemnation of Athanasius, was induced to accept and subscribe a formulary which forbade the mention of the "*homoousion*," and thus "virtually condemned the creed of Nicaea,* and countenanced the Arian proceedings." Yes; he subscribed a creed forbidding it to be said that Christ is of the same substance with the Father. He retracted again at Corduba.†

"And Liberius"—the Pope!—Peter's successor? He began as a vehement opponent of Arianism. But he now joined in condemning Athanasius, rejected the Nicene creed, joined in church fellowship with the Arians; and, in fact, poor Newman has to quote Jerome's striking sentence, in the Latin of it—"Liberius, conquered by the weariness of exile, and subscribing to the heretic pravity, had entered Rome as a conqueror."‡ Newman uses the strong word "apostasy."

I do not want to dwell on these sad things at all. Only when Archbishop Carr is so severe in speech on Cranmer, might not he feel a touch of ruth in presence of these tragic facts that fill the foreground of Roman Church History?

Cranmer also was old. More than any other

---

* Müller in *Herzog u. Plitt.* Schaff, 635 f. Newman (425, 448) calls it Hosius' "blasphemy" and "fall."

† Newman's *Arians of the Fourth Century*, p. 323, *et seq.* See also Note v., p. 445. Is there anything in literature more striking than the practical condemnation, shown in all that note, of the theory that the Church of God depends on Papalism, or on Episcopacy, or Externalism. Yet he attempts to argue out of this position.

‡ Newman, *id.*, p. 449. The case of Felix ii.; afterwards "sainted" was still worse.

Protestant, he shuddered at the thought of the agony of slow burning in the flame, like Ridley. Yet at the last, as Tennyson paints him:—

> "Then Cranmer lifted his left hand to Heaven,
> And thrust his right into the bitter flame;
> And, crying in his deep voice more than once—
> 'This hath offended—this unworthy hand!'
> So held it till it all was burn'd, before
> The flame had reached his body; I stood near—
> Marked him—he never uttered moan of pain;
> He never stirr'd or writhed."

He never deemed himself *infallible*. And the other Protestants whom no terrors could make recant, and whose names have sunk undyingly into the memories of British men—*they* did not deem themselves and their Church *infallible*. God and His Gospel alone they deemed *in*fallible. But not even Cranmer could have been got, for all Earth's pain, to subscribe denial of the Essential Divinity of Our Lord, like Hosius and " Peter's Successor" Liberius. I do not want to speak any severe word about these men at all. I tell these things with all reluctance, and with a shudder of shame at all these councils and men, because they show the huge unreality of this whole notion that the Church of the living God depends on the stability of a line of Roman bishops, or of any bishops, as depositories of infallible truth, and as Rock of the faith, and as recipients of the Holy Ghost.

> "The episcopate, whose action was so prompt and concordant at Nicaea, on the rise of Arianism, did not, as a class or order of men, play a good part in the troubles consequent upon the Council, and the laity did. The Catholic people in the length and breadth of Christendom were the obstinate champions of Catholic truth, and the bishops were not."

So says Newman.* Rome and the Pope were not then *a Rock!*

---

* *Arians of Fourth Century*, p. 445, also 461, 465.

Rome and Leo.—Fifth Century.

We reach the hour when the Papacy was born. Leo, deacon of Celestine, Bishop of Rome (422-432), and himself Bishop of Rome (440-461), was the father of the Papacy. Amid the anguish of the dying Empire of the West, intensified by the agony of the Nestorian controversy, the ecclesiastic Papacy was born. Its "temporal power" was born much later.

Celestine (with whom, for his own purposes, Cyril, of Alexandria, inheritor and intensifier of the orthodoxy of Athanasius, but making it repellant by his haughty sacerdotalism, joined hands) was strenuous and forceful. Leo was a greater, more intellectual Celestine. The diaconate and bishopric of this energetic ruler of men have the stir and thrill of a great romance or tragedy. Leo was cradled amid the noises of battle, the falling of World-powers. From the beginning of that century the Goths and other heathen peoples of the north had been pressing down, from all sides, upon the fated Greek-Roman Empire. Alaric, the Goth, had in the beginning of the century sacked Rome. The feeble Emperor of the West fled and entrenched himself amidst the marshes of Ravenna.* The Church of God alone stood firm. It was the heroic hour of Rome's Episcopate. By its power, its resources, its state-craft, the awe it inspired in the minds of even heathen leaders, especially by the influence it exerted over them through intermarriage with its Christian womanhood, the bishop's seat at Rome became the rallying point of a new political confidence. The Bishop of Rome proved himself the most important secular voice in the West. Leo, with great skill, at once took advantage of the state of things to further his extreme sacerdotal views, and to

---

* Hence came *Romagna*, a *new Rome*.

make Rome ecclesiastically supreme. When the Bishops of Gaul* resisted his dictation, Leo induced the young weakling Emperor in the West, Valentinian III., to issue (445) a rescript declaring that none henceforth should venture to resist the primacy of the Pope, which the Lord himself had instituted! This rescript was, of course, never acknowledged by the patriarchs and Churches of the East. The Latin Churches of North Africa, also, had stubbornly refused to acknowledge anything but a "primacy of honour." Those of North Italy and Aquileia steadily, and till much later, maintained their independence.†

Leo was the first to formulate the Romish notion of a priestly and ecclesiastic monarchy ‡ under the headship of Peter, as Prince of the Apostles. That whole figment rests on "two propositions:"—(1) Peter's primacy of jurisdiction amongst the Apostles, so that all pastors of God's Church are under Peter's authority (Serm. iv. 2). (2) That Peter's authority and supremacy were transferred to his only successors, the bishops of Rome; so, whenever the Bishop of Rome speaks, Peter himself speaks (Serm. iii. 2). Leo added to these a third equally startling proposition:— That to revolt against this primacy of the Roman Bishop is to precipitate yourself into hell (Ep. 10). § There was a charming directness about Leo. He had a quite swift and even sulphureous way of disposing of his antagonists that was most serviceable to Rome's advancement in power.

Another thing that uplifted Leo was the inroad into Italy of Attila the Hun, when, amid the terror, Leo had to manipulate his retirement, and arrange about his demand of a vast sum of money, and the woful

---

* Hilarius of Arles, &c.

† Schaff, *ut supra*, p. 293.   ‡ K. Müller in *Herzog u. Plitt*,

§ K. Müller, *id.*

bargain of giving up to the great savage leader Honoria, the delicately-nurtured sister of Valentinian, the Emperor. But it was by the theological troubles in that fifth century that Rome's ecclesiastical influence, as over against the divided and distracted East, got for the time a decided advance. *This*, too, stands out quite clear,—just in proportion as the power of the Imperial house is weak, or disunited, or the Eastern patriarchs are found at variance, in like proportion does the solid Roman bulk advance its front; just in proportion as the East presents a strong Emperor, and a united Church, does the Roman bishop's ascendancy dwindle and fall back. For centuries after Leo, no Pope presents so truculent a front, or claim, as did he.

Cyril and His Monks.

The troubles which now vexed the Eastern Church concerned the doctrine of the Person of Christ. Nestorius, Patriarch of Constantinople, which was now rival of both Rome and Alexandria, emphasised the tendency of the Christian school of Antioch, laying stress upon the two natures—human and divine —in Christ. He especially objected to the expression, "Mother of God,"* given to the Virgin Mary, and urged the name, "Mother of Christ," instead. His forceful adversary, Cyril of Alexandria, emphasised the Alexandrian tendency, and laid stress on the Divine Nature. Cyril accused Nestorius of resolving Christ into two. Nestorius accused Cyril of making the Divine transmuted into the human, so blotting out the distinctions of nature. And, as Möller says, each was unfair to the other. Döllinger has emphatically said, when we go to the writings of Nestorius himself

---

* Theotókos in Greek.

we get a quite different view of him from what his foes at Alexandria and at Rome ascribed to him.

Had these men, in simple loyalty to Christ and His New Testament Gospel, been able to meet together as friends, and to speak their views in quiet, with no rival pride of Alexandria and of Rome, and of the new rival Rome (Constantinople) and its ally Antioch to egg them on, or had there been then a strong Emperor and an undivided Imperial Court, the shame and tragedy of those battling Councils could never have been.

The Emperor* at Constantinople was a weakling. His wife, the gifted and beautiful Eudocia, had a deadly foe in Pulcheria, the Emperor's elder sister, and erewhile dictatress. Cyril had Pulcheria as his fellow-plotter. Celestine, Pope in Rome, and Cyril, Patriarch in Alexandria, clasped hands, and used the divided Imperial Court to effect their ends.

At the Council, summoned to Ephesus by the Emperor (431), Cyril and the Alexandrians arrived before John of Antioch and the Syrian bishops could get forward. Cyril, who came with a powerful body of Egyptian bishops, slaves, and armed seamen, opened the so-called Council, and presided; Celestine's legates from Rome being present. Nestorius would not attend, the other bishops not having arrived. The proceedings were summary. Despite the protest of the Imperial Commissioner, Nestorius was anathematized. John of Antioch and the Syrians arrived to hold another Council, which deposed Cyril of Alexandria, and his henchman Memnon of Ephesus.†

This miserable scene was followed by a scene more miserable. Cyril, Pulcheria, and Celestine had effected

---

* Thodosius II.

† Schaff, *id.*, p. 723, seq. Milman, &c., pass the severest judgment on these councils. Gregory Nazianzen called them "assemblies of cranes and geese."

the destruction of Nestorius. But Cyril's policy outwitted itself and outwitted Rome also. It was Constantinople that was aggrandized.

Cyril is that relentless and potent personality whose features are limned so graphically in Kingsley's *Hypatia*, and whose monks, "the hounds of Cyril," tore the beautiful and gifted Hypatia limb from limb, with shouts of "God and the Mother of God." His policy, too, lived after him, but with the unlooked for result of elevating the Patriarchate of the Eastern metropolis, Constantinople, rather than Alexandria or Rome.

The "Robber Council."

Eutyches, the head of a cloister of three hundred monks at Constantinople, was kin in sentiment and mood to the monks of Alexandria. He was incensed at the compromise which Theodoret,* of "the Antioch school," had got arranged, viz., affirming *two natures* in our Lord's one Person after the incarnation.† Eutyches fiercely denounced this. And, when deposed by a local synod of Constantinople (448), held by Flavian, its Patriarch, he called to his aid Alexandria. Cyril was dead.‡ His archdeacon, Dioscuros—a more vehement, less intellectual Cyril—sat in his chair. Dioscuros and others demanded of the Emperor a new General Council. But Leo, now Patriarch, or Pope, in

---

* Of Cyros. He was of the school of Antioch, pupil of the famous Diodorus and Theodorus. He was one of John of Antioch's synod which "deposed" Cyril at Ephesus in 431. He was himself deposed by the "Robber Council" of Ephesus, 449, but restored by the Council of Chalcedon.

† Schaff holds that it was just "moderate Nestorianism," as drawn by Theodoret, which actually obtained the victory, by the help of the Bishop of Rome (Leo), at the Council of Chalcedon. And when Protestantism rejects the dreadful title "Mother of God" from the Chalcedon formulary, you have that victory complete. ‡ In 444 A.D.

Rome, recognised that Flavian's theology in Constantinople was the same as his own. Leo was the first theologian the Roman Church had produced. His masterly letters to Flavian, defining the Faith, are but an exposition of what had been thought out by successive Greek minds like Athanasius and Theodoret.

But the Alexandrians did at Ephesus in the Council of 449 what Cyril had done in 431. Alexandria and Ephesus again coalesced. Dioscuros of Alexandria presided. Eutyches was restored; Theodoret, Flavian, and Leo of Rome were deposed and excommunicated. The three delegates from Leo, Bishop of Rome, did not even venture to read Leo's letter. In the fierce *melée* Flavian was so sorely wounded by the monks that he died a few days later. That Council, though denounced by Leo as "the Council of Robbers,"* was as genuine an Ecumenical Council as that which crushed Nestorius; and had much more claim to be so than the Western Council of Trent, or that of the Vatican which decreed the infallibility of the Pope.

From that "robber Council" the bishops and monks swayed out into the streets, where, in torchlight processions, the mob made the night hideous with the battle-cry of the Alexandrian monks—"God, and the Mother of God!"

Chalcedon; and Leo of Rome.

The Emperor died in 450, not without sore suspicions as to the accident which caused his death. With Pulcheria, his strong-willed sister, now on the throne, and Eudocia banished, Leo's plans seemed prosperous. But Marcian, the Empire's general, whom

---

* In a letter to Pulcheria. See the details in Schaff, *ut sup.*, vol. ii., and in Neander, Hefele, Milman, &c.

Pulcheria chose for her husband, had, as Emperor, a will of his own. He used Rome, and let it lead that he might lead. At the new Council, summoned at Chalcedon, nigh to Constantinople (451), the emperor and empress were present. For the first time the legates from Rome were the spiritual presidents. They sat on the left of the imperial commissioners. This Council anathematised both "Nestorianism" and Eutycheanism. The Epistle of Leo and the Synodal letters of Cyril were laid before the Council, and received with cries of: "That is the faith of the Fathers! That is the faith of the Apostles. Through Leo, Peter has thus spoken; even so did Cyril teach. This is the true faith." That Council reduced the substance of those letters, and the substance of Theodoret's statement, into a complete setting forth of the Nicene Creed,* with the awful title given to Mary, and embodied in the Church's creed for the first time—"Mother of God."† The Council, at "the solemn ratification of this Confession, in the Emperor's presence, burst into loud cries in eulogy of this weather-wise general:

"Thou art both Priest and King; victor in war; teacher of the Faith."‡

This Council had been almost as tumultuous as "the Robber Synod." The imperial officers had to intervene repeatedly between the passionate disputants.

When Leo read the decisions of the Council, and heard the incidents of it, and of its cries placing—"Thus Cyril did teach"§ on an equality with his own formula, "Through Leo Peter has spoken," he was enraged well-nigh as much as by the previous de-

---

* "Nicaeno-Constantinopolitan."
† "This was the real turning-point in the devolopment of Mariolatry."—Stcitz.
‡ A good account is given in Schaff.
§ Archbishop Carr drops this out, p. 214.

cision of "The Robber Synod" of Ephesus. He found that he had been given only a primacy of honour, and that the patriarch of Constantinople, the Emperor's new and non-apostolic city, had equal powers with the Bishop of Rome, having jurisdiction over Asia, Pontus, and Thrace.* In all these arrangements it is clear that precedence went just by the importance of the provinces and cities of the Empire.

The Epoch of Shame.

For a century after *Leo* there followed what has been called "the Epoch of Shame." The Popes of Rome were successively the subjects, or puppets, of the barbarian kings, or of the reviving power of the Greek-Roman Empire at Constantinople. The weakness and the worthlessness of these Popes chime together. One of these Popes, Gelasius I. (492-496), who struggled hard against the rival claims of Constantinople, lets a gleam of light ray out. He condemns the sacrilege of withholding the cup from the laity. His successor, apparently one of the best of these Popes, but who was more friendly towards Constantinople, is the Pope whom Dante puts in hell,† an odd place for an inspired successor of St. Peter, and of that Leo who consigned to hell those who did not receive the Pope as Peter's successor. Under the mighty sway of the great Emperor Justinian the Popedom of Rome fell lower still, till his puppet Pope Vigilius (537-555), retracted and withdrew that very condemnation of Eutycheanism, formulated so solemnly by the Council of Chalcedon, on the basis of the letter of Leo.

---

*Schaff, p. 279 ff.
†Anastasius II. Even Baronius explains his sudden death as God's manifest judgment.

Gregory the Great.

But in the close of the sixth century (590—604) there arose, in the person of Gregory I.—named "the Great"—another Roman Patriarch, kin in spirit to Leo. An eminent historian calls him "the greatest, most capable, noblest, most pious, and most superstitious in the whole 'long series of Popes.' "* Another takes his influence as marking the transition from "the patriarchal system into the strict Papacy of the Middle Ages."†

As with Leo and the Goths and Huns, so with Gregory and the ruthless Longobards (Lombards), whose descent upon Italy has left their name stamped still upon one of the fairest and strongest of Italian provinces. Amid the misery, Gregory's great wealth, drawn from wide lands and other possessions—"the Patrimony of Peter"—in mid-Italy and the islands, gave him a sort of royal power. His character and vigour lent this power nobler sanction. An ex-monk himself, Gregory reorganised the monkhood; he also imposed upon his clergy several characteristics of the monastic life he strongly favoured.‡ His main interest for us British people is his scheme of pushing missionaries northward and westward into the Teuton lands. Hitherto it had been the Eastern, and, indeed, the Arian missions that had won the Gothic and northern peoples. That "mission" sent out by Gregory had been forestalled also by a Christian movement amongst the *Celtic* peoples of Scotland and Ireland—a movement which, from its centre in the Scoto-Irish Churches, spread into North England, and across as far as Germany and Switzerland, and

---

* Kurtz.   † Zoepffel, in *Herzog u. Plitt*.
‡ Schaff, &c.   Creighton, *Hist. of Papacy*, vol. i., p. 8.

finally came into determined conflict with the advancing movement from Rome.*

The sore thorn in Gregory's side was the rival imperial new Rome in the East, the Emperor's city (Constantinople), with its potent patriarch. To that patriarch the Emperor Justinian had already given the title of Universal (Ecumenical) Bishop. Now, John the Faster,† Patriarch of Constantinople, adopted, with special emphasis, this title, higher than the Roman Pope's title. Gregory, in vain, endeavoured to induce the Emperor Mauritius to compel John to forego this title of "Ecumenical Bishop." When the Patriarch of Alexandria, to checkmate Constantinople, addressed Gregory as "*Universalis Papa*" (Universal Pope), Gregory, in his reply, refused such a title, and admitted for the sees of Antioch and Alexandria rank equal with that of Rome. He also likened John of Constantinople to Lucifer, and branded as an anti-Christ every Bishop who would raise himself above his fellow-bishops.*

The two indelible blots which stain this great Pope's memory indicate the means by which a special recognition for the Roman Bishop was gradually and persistently furthered. The Frankish Fury, Brunhilda, "the New Jezebel" of the West, stained with the worst of crimes, he loaded with flatteries, receiving gratefully her promises to support the English mission, to promote celibacy, and to foster monasteries throughout her realm.

In the same way, when the brutal rebel Phocas mounted to the Imperial throne in Constantinople by the murder of the noble Emperor Mauritius,

---

* See Green's *Short Hist. of the Eng. People*, pp. 17, 28, 29.
† John Jejunator.
* Schaff, Kurtz, Zoepffel, &c. On the subtle distinction by which Bellarmine and other Roman Catholic writers attempt to meet this, see Schaff, *id.*, p. 329.

his hands reddened to a deeper dye by the ruthless execution of the Empress and the five sons and three daughters of the slaughtered monarch, Gregory, with the most fulsome laudation, welcomed the despot's advent. In his congratulation he "makes all the angelic choirs in heaven and all tongues on earth break forth in jubilees."*

These actions on the part of one of the best Popes illustrate the mode in which the Bishops of Rome pushed, through every possible avenue of worldly and political influence, their path towards predominance.† A little later, and the East, in its terrible struggle with Mohammedanism, and in the splendid effort made by the great Emperor Leo to cast image-worship out of the Church, as giving to Mohammedans their main argument against Christianity, was pitilessly deserted and resisted by the Popes of Rome. This disregard on the part of the Western Papacy to the life and death struggle of Eastern Christendom is deemed, by some great historians, as *one* of the indelible crimes of the Roman Popedom. As the Mohammedan advance weakened Jerusalem, Antioch, and Constantinople, so Rome, in the West, thrust forward her claim to solitary power. Against her arrogance, at last, the East rose up in disdain, and there took place that vast separa-

---

* Kurtz, *id.*, p. 274. Schaff, Kurtz, Zoepffel, as well as other historians of the period, regard it as probable, in each case, that Gregory *did not know* the *facts* or the character of either Brunehild or Phocas. Of course, if so, it raises odd questions as to the "inspiration" a Pope is supposed to possess. But *how* he could be ignorant that *Phocas* could not have gained the throne in any good way it is hard to see.

† It was Phocas who, in gratitude, first called "the chair of Peter" at Rome *caput omnium ecclesiarum*—"head of all Churches." This title of honour was, of course, not recognised by his successors, or by the Churches.

tion which has cloven the older Christian East and the Latin West, with its Popedom, for ever asunder.*

From all this survey of the early stages of the Roman claim, two facts stand out clear.

First, each step of the advance of this claim to ecclesiastical and worldly dominance has been closely identified with the weakness, or the perfidy, or the power of some World-kingdom, or ruler, or with the political contendings of rival patriarchs and bishops.

Secondly, all this looks tragically unlike, in shape and spirit, to the mission of that Paul who wrote from Corinth to Rome :—" I am ready to preach the gospel to you also that are in Rome." It flatly contradicts Peter's injunction :—" Be not lords over God's heritage." It seems strangely foreign to that Christ who said, at the judgment-bar of Rome's Magistrate, " My Kingdom is not of this World."

THE END.

---

* E. A. Freeman; Creighton, *Hist. of Papacy*, vol. i., pp. 8, 9.

APPENDIX.

With regret I have had to crush out of this Appendix much which I had planned to insert. In particular, I should have liked to publish (anonymously) a few of the letters received by me from leading laymen in Victoria. One of these, from a distinguished Medical man, evinces a surprising grasp of the whole situation, and livingness of interest in the issues involved in the modern assertion of Sacerdotal Clericalism (as betokened at once by the "Anglo-Catholic" movement, and by the renewed activity of the "Roman Catholic Campaign.") Indications of this kind are encouraging. So long as the educated and intellectual laity continues to take a wide-awake and genuine personal interest in our common heritage of Christian Faith and Freedom, all is well.

I.

ARCHBISHOP CARR'S "PROTESTANT TESTIMONY."

Here is an illustrative specimen of the Archbishop's favourite method of "proof." He seeks by a promiscuous array of *names* to prove that Peter visited Rome—a proposition we have no objection to see proven, if only any actual proof were forthcoming. Says Archbishop Carr:—

"Further Protestant testimony in proof of St. Peter's residence in Rome would be wholly superfluous. If required, it may be abundantly found in the works of Hammond, Usher, Whitby, Blondell, Schaff, Scaliger, Le Clerc. We may, therefore, on exclusively Protestant testimony, put aside the assertion that St. Peter never was in Rome." Now, that is a comfortable mode of "proving" theories if there is nobody near to challenge your premises, or to ask the awkward question—Is *that* what you call "*proof*?" The Roman Catholic mind—may I say it without offence?—seems impressed by a non-chronological array of *names*, marshalled as "authorities." The Protestant mind asks for *facts*.

Moreover, here be names, as Shakspere would say, "sorted and consorted"—very ill. How Schaff, the modern scholar, got jammed in amongst that array is the odd thing. And these names are followed by Bramhall, and preceded by Neale and Whiston. If the Archbishop had but explained to his auditory who these men were!

Now, let me take these names *seriatim*—

(1.) "Neale" should really *not* be quoted as "Protestant testimony," or as *historical* testimony of any kind. He was one of the extremest advocates of "High Catholic" views, and of the Romanizing tendency. As such he was inhibited by his bishop for fourteen years. "His sympathies," says Professor Bird, his most appreciative critic, "seem rather Roman than Protestant, and dubious legends were accepted by him with unquestioning belief." It is his hymnody alone for which he should be quoted.

(2.) "Whiston," Archbishop Carr's next "Protestant testimony," broadens the smile. I take for granted that the Archbishop has not read the life-story of the "cranks and freaks of fancy and of religious and chronological vagaries," through which this eccentric and lovable individual passed. Born 1667, died 1752, he placed the Millenium in 1776. Amongst other achievements he made out for himself an Arian "Primitive New Testament." And both it and his views on Primitive Christian history would startle hugely Archbishop Carr, and be consigned to an awful "*Index Expurgatorius*." Why does Archbishop Carr quote from this extremely "Rationalist" and also antiquated writer, as representative Protestant "proof?" The value of Whiston's views on Primitive Church history may be judged from the facts that his scheme of Old and New Testament chronology is now found quite erroneous, and that he declared that Arianism was the original and dominant faith in the first two centuries in Rome and all over Christendom, and that the apocryphal book called "*Apostolical Constitutions*" was "the most sacred of the canonical books of the New Testament."

(3.) Dr. Carr's next "Protestant testimony" is Hammond. When I say that Hammond (born 1605, died 1660), a personally estimable gentleman, was the favourite chaplain of Charles I., and that his writings were included by Pusey and his compeers in the *Library of Anglo-Catholic Theology*, Oxford, the public will estimate the value of his opinion on a question of modern historical criticism such as "*Did Peter Visit Rome?*"

(4.) Usher (1581—1656) comes next. Of him I shall speak last.

(5.) Whitby comes next. Our wonder grows. What a man he was to be quoted as an exponent of "Protestant testimony" and "proof" that Peter visited Rome! "Dr. Daniel Whitby" (1638—1726), says Professor Christlieb, who made a special study of the phases of Doubt in England, "is best remembered for his striking theological changes"—first, extreme Protestant, and having his book publicly burnt in Charles II.'s time at Oxford; then making humble confession of his "heresies" to the wrathful High-Church Bishop of Salisbury; then writing a book in reconcilement of all differences, and commanding all non-conformists to return into the Stuart High-Anglican fold; then extreme Arminian; then finally retracting all his former expositions, and ending as extreme Arian, declaring the Trinitarian dogma to be a tissue of absurdities—such was Dr. Daniel Whitby.

And, of course, it is quite appropriate that Archbishop Carr should quote him as an important representative of "Protestant testimony" in the same lecture in which he similarly quotes Renan. Only, what is the value of it all? And would not this array of names produce on Dr. Carr's hearers an impression quite other than a frank examination of facts warrants? They would think—surely these names are of weighty authority in modern scholarship when the Archbishop so impressively quotes them as Protestant "testimony" and "proof."

(6) Blondel (1591-1655) is the next name. And we have to go back again to get at this fine French Protestant scholar, who, in his masterly writings against Rome, mainly took his master, Calvin's position on this question. Here is a quite odd thing:—Dr. Carr names Blondel as affirming Peter's residence in Rome. Schaff quotes him as denying it! The notion that Peter was ever founder of the Roman Church, or bishop of Rome, or head of the Apostles, he regarded as contrary to Scripture and history.

(7) Schaff, who comes next, was an eminent historical scholar of our day, quite recently deceased. He held the opinion that Peter had visited Rome for a brief time, and also that "no personage in all history has been so much magnified, misrepresented, and misused for doctrinal and hierarchical ends, as the plain fisherman of Galilee." The only other person who has, to anything like the same degree, "undergone a similar transformation," according to Schaff, is the Virgin Mary. And both results, he says, are due to the same cause, viz.: "the work of fiction," which "began among the Judaizing heretical sects of the second and third centuries, but was modified and carried forward by the Catholic, especially the Roman Church, in the third and fourth centuries." As no hint of anything like this from Schaff is to be found in Dr. Carr's lectures, I set this little bit of it here. How Schaff came to be "slumped" in the midst of those Laudian and other ancient clerical persons of past centuries, in defiance of that historical proportion he himself so dearly valued, is "unexplained." The notion of Peter's "Primacy," or bishopric at Rome, Schaff, in common with modern scholars, rejects. Let me give another bit from Schaff:—"The weaknesses even more than the virtues of the natural Peter, his boldness and presumption, his love for secular glory, his use of the sword, his sleepiness in Gethsemane, are faithfully reproduced in the history of the Papacy; while the addresses and the epistles of the converted and inspired Peter contain the most emphatic protest against the hierarchical pretensions and worldly vices of the Papacy."

(8.) Scaliger (1540-1609), a man of vast learning in his day, made out a scheme of sacred Chronology, which, like the many similar schemes of that day, is now quite antiquated; it is proven by modern research to be erroneous.

(9.) Le Clerc (Clericus) (1657-1736), a Frenchman "of wide learning and excessive vanity," as has been said by the critics, swung away from his Huguenot faith, and went over to the Remonstrants of Holland. He is the editor of Hammond, Charles I.'s chaplain.

(10.) Then comes "Bramhall, Archbishop of Armagh," frequently referred to by Archbishop Carr, and who averred that "St. Peter had a fixed chair at Antioch, and after that at Rome." It is a very awkward testimony from a very awkward man. For it puts Antioch before Rome. But the "testimony" is worth just nothing. I am sure the Archbishop's audience did not know that Bramhall (1593-1663) was one of the most extreme of the Laudian bishops in the *Stuart* epoch, and was called "the Laud of Ireland." It was Bramhall's writings that deeply influenced Pusey and his compeers in "their Romeward movement." Bramhall, also, was one of those impeached by England's Parliament, along with Strafford, for their scheme to crush Protestant England by the Catholic Irish army, in support of Charles I.'s Stuart despotism. He is not a very valuable "Protestant testimony."

Then, finally, as to Archbishop Usher (1581-1656), we will all gladly agree that he was one of the greatest and saintliest Anglo-Irishmen. He was a great scholar in his day, also ; and, if his plan for a modified Episcopacy and the recognition of Presbyterian ordination, as the true scriptural mode, with bishops as superintendents of districts, had been carried, there would have been an end soon of the cleavage of the great Protestant Churches.

But, then, Ussher had his drawbacks. His great scheme of chronology is now seen to be impossible. Besides, why should Archbishop Carr, of all men, quote Ussher as " proof." Has not he, in former lectures, wholly rejected Ussher's views as to the coming of Christianity to Britain? Why, then, does he attach value to the same Ussher's views as to the coming of Peter to Rome? I am sure also that Archbishop Carr *does not* accept Ussher's historical view that the expiry of "the thousand years," during which Satan was to be bound, took place when Hildebrand, Gregory VII., became Pope, and then Satan came forth in the Roman Papacy "to deceive the nations" (Rev. xx., 7, 8). I do not agree with Ussher's historical view as to this. But it is just as valuable as his historical view regarding a probable visit paid by Peter to Rome. This illustrates a great mass of the names adduced by Archbishop Carr as "proof" for historical matters.

II.
ARCHBISHOP CARR ON LEIBNITZ.

Equally irrelevant are the quotations from Grotius and from Leibnitz. The one was born 1583, died 1645; the other was born 1646, died 1716. Archbishop Carr fills six pages of his Lecture I. with long passages from these gentlemen. I will take briefly Leibnitz as an *illustration* of his method of giving "Protestant testimony." Leibnitz, "for keenness of intellect and vast and varied learning, has probably no equal amongst Protestant writers." So Archbishop Carr assures his people. Then two pages and a-half are occupied with passages from Leibnitz in support of what Archbishop Carr calls "the Sacrament of Orders" and the "Sovereign Pontiff." Now Leibnitz was in his day an eminent name in the history of philosophy and of mathematical discovery, not an eminent name as a student of history. He was the founder of a now discarded school of pre-Kantian philosophy. To anyone who knows the story of Leibnitz's life it must seem a brilliant joke to quote from his *Systema Theologicum*, as Archbishop Carr does, as a specimen of "Protestant testimony."

A few facts will be sufficient. Leibnitz had been the tutor of the powerful Baron von Boineburg, a Protestant pervert to Romanism. The Thirty Years' War, with its long horrors, had closed. It had made men tired with the ghastly tragedy of Rome's conflict with Protestantism. Bossuet and others, on behalf of Rome, made conciliatory overtures for reunion. This had been already powerfully urged by the Baron von Boineburg, Leibnitz's patron. It was taken up eagerly by Leopold, the Romanist Emperor of Germany, and was urged by him upon the attention of Duke Ernst August of Hannover, Leibnitz's then master. Leibnitz acted as negotiator for Duke Ernst, and the negotiations made a prolonged flutter of expectation and inter-communication between Vienna, Hannover, and Rome. Leibnitz, during this epoch, drew up his *Systema Theologicum* as a tentative treatise of suggested agreement between Roman Catholicism and Protestantism. It "made," as Professor Eucken says, "the genuineness of his Protestant faith suspected by many." That it does not express his own opinions seems proven by the fact that when he found the authority of the Council of Trent, and its claim to be an Ecumenical council, insisted upon by the Romanist negotiators, he at once cancelled all schemes for union, and absolutely rejected the authority of the Romish Council. Now, really, doesn't it seem too absurd of Archbishop Carr to quote from the *Systema Theologicum*, as if this were a striking example of Protestant "testimony," and the result of Leibnitz's profound investigation!

III.

CANON BERRY'S LETTER.

The following letter from the Rev. Canon Berry, M.A., examining Chaplain to the Bishop of Melbourne, appeared in the *Argus* of 22nd May. Its expression of personal regard I value. But it has a wider significance. Its standpoint as to the facts of the Early Christian Church indicates the true historic attitude of the Reformed Church of England in her best and purest days. It has also been the standpoint of her greatest and most cultured minds. Canon Berry is none the less, but all the more, a loyal son of the Church of England, that, as a scholar, he recognises the facts of history, and also the common fellowship of the historic Churches of God in Christ. His words are emphasised by the impress of his own personal character. The only possible path towards ultimate reunion of Reformed Christendom—"the Eirenicon between the Churches"—seems indicated in the spirit and attitude of Canon Berry's letter.

"THE SACERDOTAL ORDER.

"*To the Editor of the Argus.*

"SIR,—Will you allow me space to thank Professor Rentoul for his three* masterly lectures. I have not found in them one word to which a moderate Episcopalian would object. And on the subject of 'presbyter' and 'bishop,' they are in entire agreement with the remarks of Canon Spence on the same subject in his treatise on the recently recovered *Teaching of the Apostles*, the earliest Christian manual extant. How Archbishop Carr can be satisfied with them is mysterious, but that is not my affair. I am, &c.,

"D. M. BERRY."

IV.

ST. AUGUSTINE ON PETER AND "THE ROCK."

Archbishop Carr, like other R.C. advocates, is very sensitive over the fact that Augustine, the greatest "Doctor" of the whole Latin Church, declares, as his final and mature judgment, that "it was not said to him (Peter) 'Thou art *Petra*' (the rock), but 'Thou art *Petrus* (Peter). The rock, on the contrary, was Christ (*Petra autem erat Christus.*" Dr. Carr ventures the hazardous assertion that "St. Augustine's private opinion on the literal meaning of the text of St. Matthew counts for very little, as he was ignorant of Hebrew or Syro-Chaldaic." Now, a Roman Catholic must be hard driven when he says that. Here are two odd things—

1. If Augustine's "private judgment," which was his true and final judgment, "counts for very little," why has Archbishop Carr

---

* My third lecture had just been reported.

cumbered his lectures by piling together such an indiscriminate mass of "private judgments" and odds and ends of "testimony" from all sorts and conditions of men, so-called "Protestants," Romanists, and what not? It seems to come to this, that any "judgment" is good if it can be made to look favourable for Rome; but if it be unfavourable, then, though it came from Augustine, or even St. Paul, it "counts for very little." This fantastic distinction Rome seeks to draw between "private judgment" and other judgment has an unreal ring. Had Augustine been Pope, then this "private judgment" would have been an "infallible judgment." It is all so grotesque!

2. To state that Augustine said so because "he was ignorant of Hebrew or Syro-Chaldaic," puts Dr. Carr on thin ice. And the thin ice quite gives way under him when he adds that "the language in which our Lord spoke and St. Matthew wrote his Gospel," was (as is implied) "Hebrew or Syro-Chaldaic." For (1) some of the very greatest of modern Hebraists have endorsed Augustine's view, which was, as I have shown, held by other great Fathers. (2) That our Gospel of Matthew, in its present complete form, was not written in "Hebrew or Syro-Chaldaic," though a certain "source" of it may have been written in Aramaic, is affirmed in opposition to Dr. Carr by the main weight of modern critical, and linguistic scholarship. The Douay Bible, *suo more*, asserts what Dr. Carr says, and also that it was written "about six years after our Lord's ascension!" (3) The assertion as to the language in which our Lord spoke at Cæsarea Philippi is hazardous in the extreme. It *may* have been Aramaic ("Syro-Chaldaic"), as Romanist and some Protestant scholars hold. Also, it may very well not have been. The fact is now accepted by modern scholars that the people of Palestine—at least in Galilee—in Our Lord's day were *bilingual*. "The evidence that Greek was spoken commonly in the towns bordering on the Sea of Galilee, and that St. Peter must, therefore, have been well acquainted with it, is ample."* The Galileans spoke both Aramaic and Greek, just as, along the borderland of Wales and parts of Scotland and Ireland, the people speak both Celtic and English. That Our Lord and His Apostles spoke Greek, as well as Aramaic, is quite certain.

I am not concerned to defend Augustine's linguistic scholarship, which, though scant, was vastly greater than that of most of the Popes. Of the first "infallible" Pope, viz., the late *Pio Nono*, Döllinger, the most learned man the Roman Church possessed, said he was a man " of astonishing ignorance."

I simply wish to point to two facts. Dr. Carr's argument is this: Christ spoke in Hebrew or Syro-Chaldaic. He would thus say to Simon: "Thou art *Kepha*, and on this *Kepha* I will build My Church." And some Protestant scholars have said so, too. (It

---

* Lightfoot, *Clem.*, vol. ii., 494.

could not be Hebrew, of course, for Hebrew was then a dead language. In Hebrew, also, the form Kepha does not occur. Keph would be the Hebrew, but it is found only in the plural. The word for Rock—Isa. xxviii.—is quite different in Hebrew.)

Now, the assertion that our Lord said Kepha, where Matthew says Petros, is perilous at best, for Matthew's Greek is the only shape in which the sentence is preserved; and it indicates the sense in which the early Apostles understood it. The name, when applied to Simon, is always used in a Graëcised form, *Cephas*, or *Petros* = man of stone, or man of rock; or, shall we call it by his own translation, "living stone?"

Now, when Augustine's ignorance is insisted on, let us hear what one of the greatest of all Hebraists says—viz., the elder Lightfoot:—"'*Thou art Peter*, &c.' There is nothing either in the dialect of the nation, or, in reason, forbids us to think that our Saviour used this very same Greek word, since such Graëcisings were not unusual in that nation."

Then he goes on to say that if, to avoid controversy, it be "granted that He used the Syriac word, yet I deny that He used that very word כיפא (*Kepha*), but he pronounced it *Kephas*, after the Greek manner; or He spoke it כיפאי (*Kephai*) in the adjective sense, according to the Syriac formation." That is said by the great Cambridge scholar, whom Schaff calls "one of the greatest Hebrew scholars in history," who "enjoys to-day a universal fame," with learning and insight such as "to make his books imperishable." Now take the (probably) greatest Hebraist of our own day—Delitzsch. It is significant that in his translation of the New Testament into Hebrew he does not translate "Peter" and "Rock" by the same word at all, but "Graëcises," just as Lightfoot had said Christ did. He translates:—" And I say unto thee that *thou art* [פטרוס ועל הסלעהזה] (*Petros* we'al has-*Sela'* hazzeh)] *Peter, and upon the Rock, this (Rock) will I build my Assembly.*" Seeing, then, that the greatest Shemitic scholar of the seventeenth century, and the, probably, greatest of the nineteenth have translated as Augustine and some of the greatest Fathers did, it will scarcely do to say that the interpretation arises from ignorance of Hebrew.

V.

BINDING AND LOOSING.

When Archbishop Carr called Meyer "probably the most eminent New Testament scholar" and quoted a dislocated fragment of him in favour of the reference of the word "rock" to Peter, might he not have kindly hinted that Meyer shows, quoting the elder Lightfoot, that "to bind and to loose are to be traced to the use so current among the Jews of *àsar* and *hithir* in the sense of to *forbid* and to *allow*." Also, Meyer shows that the "idea of forgiving *sins* is a pure importation." I have shown that Tertullian, very early, says the same. Meyer also "testifies" in the strongest way against the Romish notion of Peter's primacy. Dr. Carr quotes the *context* of *that*. But he makes no reference to *that*. "It is ever thus!" Meyer is good, also, on "the *evasive interpretation* of Catholic expositors" regarding Peter and "Get thee behind me, Satan!" The elder Lightfoot, as Morison also reminds us, had proven by very many examples that to "bind and to loose" was simply a term amongst the Jews for *forbidding and permitting*. Thus Rabbi Meir "*loosed*," *i.e.*, permitted the mixing of wine and water on the Sabbath to a sick man. But he "bound" it (*i.e.*), forbade it to all others. In the discipline necessary to guide Christ's new society, Peter and the Apostles would, under the spiritual leading of the Father in Heaven, have wisdom and courage to distinguish what should be forbidden and what permitted. And their wise guidance and rule of Christ's congregation would be a transcript on the Earth of God's gracious and righteous rule in the Heaven. This is the simple meaning. The history of the Early Church shows that this was true. Peter, John, and the rest, guided and shepherded the Church well. If the Church is a society at all, it must have the power of discipline and self-government.

VI.

"GATES OF HADES."

The meaning is vividly brought out in King Hezekiah's Song of Thanksgiving—"When he had been sick unto *death*, and was recovered of his sickness."—(Isa., xxxviii., 1, 9-10.) Looking back at the "sickness" out of which he had just arisen into new hope (the power shattered, the strength getting spent, as when a "house is broken up," or as when the threads of the warp in the loom get shorter, and finally they are broken off, and the web is rolled up and put away in darkness), the King pictures his own sad thinkings when death and the breaking up of Earth's Kingdom stared him in the face:—"I said—'In the noontide of my days I must depart into the *Gates of Hades*.'"

No forces of death or decay or ruin, Christ means—no "Gates of Hades"—shall prevail against the spiritual Messiah Kingdom built upon the Rock.

VII.

"PILLAR" AND "LIVING STONES."

I have often thought that St. Paul, in calling (not without a slight touch of humour) "James, Cephas, and John," those "who are reputed to be pillars" supporting the edifice of the Jewish

Christian Church, and St. Peter, in calling all believers "living stones" built upon the Rock laid in Zion, are the best interpreters of Matthew xvi., 18. Peter was certainly a strong buttress and stay (in the early years he was eminently a buttress) of the young Christian Society, Christ's Kingdom in the world. By-and-bye, he and Paul call every believer a "living stone," forming part of the building's strength. St. Paul calls *all believers* in their unity " the pillar and ground of the Truth." So freely is this metaphor of Rock,' and stone, and pillar used, but always with the same central thought, viz., that *Christ is foundation and basis of all, and that all who grasp Him, in the great truth and faith which Peter so clearly confessed, become joined to Him, and in Him are each a living element and supporting "stone"* in His Kingdom's living structure !

Alford, Bruce (*Training of the Twelve*, cap. xi.), and Briggs (*Messiah of the Apostles*, 1895) each in his special way put this strikingly. Plumptre and Morison put the argument that by the PETRA is meant Christ only, very powerfully.

Lightfoot shows both the *fact* and the *brevity* of Peter's "primacy of historical inauguration." He, as the most forceful member of the early band, guided, along with the other Apostles, the Church's first steps. In the faith of his confession of Christ he, but never acting alone, opens the Church's door to Jew, and then partially to Gentile. *Then his primacy is completed.* " He vanishes suddenly out of sight." Paul, the wise master-builder, takes his place. "Peter retains the first place as Missionary Evangelist to the Hebrew Christians, but nothing more."—Lightfoot, *S. Clem.*, vol. ii., 487-490.

VIII.

CANON POTTER'S ERROR AS TO KEPHA.

I have spoken elsewhere of the ability displayed by Canon Potter in a Lecture on the Roman Primacy, in his treatment of Our Lord's Words to Simon (Matt. xvi., 18). I hinted, however, that in some respects there was a serious drawback. I feel it necessary to point out a remarkable error into which Canon Potter has fallen. In this respect he is, oddly enough, quite too "ultra-Protestant," and I greatly fear that, in the next controversial onset, his statement will be taken advantage of, as if it were representative of Protestant scholarship on this question. He says (*Argus*, 13th April) :—

"Further, there was the authority of Syrian scholars that the words 'Peter and Rock' in the Syrian language, although spelt alike, were not the same in gender. One took the masculine article and the other the feminine; and in the most ancient Syrian version of the Greek St. Matthew, this distinction was actually made."

This statement discloses such a non-acquaintance with the simplest rudiments of Shemitic languages and of the grammar of Syriac and Biblical "Chaldee," with its law of the "definite" or "emphatic state" of the noun, that I wish to make no comments of my own upon it.

It is, altogether, so astonishing a statement that I have asked Professor Harper, whose words as a Shemitic scholar will carry authoritative weight, and who has had no part in this controversy, to write a brief sentence regarding it. Professor Harper says:—
"There is no article, strictly speaking, in Syriac. The *status emphaticus* takes its place, and is the same for both genders. In Matt. xvi., 18, in the *Syriac Version*, the word in both clauses is כיפא (Kipho), and there is no distinction between them in any respect. In the second occurrence of the word in this passage [on this Rock] the demonstrative is feminine, because that is the ordinary gender of the word 'rock' in Syriac."

If our Lord spoke in Aramaic it would be the South-western, or Syro-Chaldaic, in which the word would be masculine in both clauses, unless He "Graecicised," as the elder Lightfoot says.

We have no need of any heroic violence done to linguistic laws. Notice with what strength and care the elder Lightfoot puts this matter. There is no reason forbidding us to think that our Lord used this very same Greek word *Petros*; and if he used a Syriac word, it would be not Kepha, but the adjective form Kephai, "according to the Syriac formation"—"rock-like." The Syriac Version is simply the translation of a later century, and throws no real light either way upon the subject. The one fact that stands out certain is that in Matthew's Greek the words Petros and Petra are quite distinct, and that the after language of the Apostles and of the New Testament never speaks of Peter as the Rock, but only as a "living stone," or "a pillar" in common with many other "pillars" or stones—all Christians, or all Apostles.

I regret, also, that Canon Potter, in the interests this time of his "Anglo-Catholicism," should affirm the antiquated date 107 for Ignatius, and the fantastic theory that Timothy and Titus were "successors" of the Apostles, and the "continuers" of a line of bishops. Both these theories are due to "stress of weather." They are shown to be impossible by modern scholars such as Lightfoot, Harnack, and Sanday.

IX.

PETER AND "THE CLEMENTINE ROMANCE."

It seems to me an exaggeration on Renan's part to ascribe the fiction of Peter's "episcopate" in Rome *wholly* to the Clementine legend. I have expressed my conviction that the fiction was the result of *two* streams of growing legend. The first was the imagination of the Early Christian Churches working upon St. Paul's words to the *Corinthians*, about the UNITY of himself with Cephas and Apollos. Then, later, the mention by Clement of Rome (in his letter to the Corinthians) of the two Chief Apostles' names as united in constancy and suffering gave further impulse. It is significant that it is in Corinth and in Rome that this notion of Paul and Peter as *co-founders* first appears. Dionysius of Corinth first speaks it, and he says Peter and Paul were co-founders in Corinth, and then proceeded together as co-founders into Italy. Here are all the marks of genuine imaginative legend, through the misconception of Paul's and Clement's words.

Then, secondly, in connection with Clement's name (through the similar misconception that he was Clement the high-born martyr*), the Judaeo-Christians had put forth their legend of "Peter's Journeys" and "Preaching." The two streams blended together. "The religious romance," as Lightfoot well says (*St. Paul and The Three*, Gal., p. 367), "seems to have been a favourite style of composition with the Essene Ebionites; and in the lack of authentic information relating to the Apostles, Catholic writers eagerly and unsuspiciously gathered incidents from writings of which they repudiated the doctrines." (See also Bright, *Roman See*.)

Now, Dr. Carr is very angry at Dr. Salmon, of Dublin, who says that the real inventor of the story of Peter's Roman episcopate was an editor of the Clementine Romance. But Dr. Salmon is not the only "sinner" in this respect. Our Bishop Moorhouse, of Manchester, has been saying that the "inclusion of Peter in the episcopal list" makes "such a divergence from the older Roman tradition as 'the Clementine fiction' alone can account for." Dr. Carr has called this "a modern and widely-accepted Anglican theory." He spends over seven pages on it (pp. 152-159). His only substantial attempt at answer is two quotations from Harnack (Eng. trans. of his *Hist. of Dogma*, p. 311). One of Harnack's long footnotes is transferred bodily into Dr. Carr's pages; it looks impressive and scholarly there. Unlike "Bramhall," "Whiston," &c., it is *modern*. It is also *irrelevant*. For what Harnack is speaking of is the "*Recognitions and Homilies in the form in which we have them.*" It is this latest and now "*redacted*" form of them he is discussing as "the pseudo Clementine writings." If some of these writings could be shown to be, in their latest form, a little later than the second century (as I think parts of them certainly are), it would not improve the case for Dr. Carr, for these writings rest upon *earlier and undeniably second century apocryphal writings which they quote and work up* into new shapes.

It is not an Anglican theory, merely, Dr. Carr has to contend with. It is the conviction held substantially, in one shape or other, by the foremost scholars of our time. Thus, Lipsius holds that to

---

* cf. Lightfoot.

the Peter legend, embedded in the oldest form of these spurious "Clementines," was due not only the fiction of Peter's bishopric, but also the other fiction of his visit to Rome. Hilgenfeld, in his great work, held that these writings rest on a Jewish-Christian spurious writing, "the Preaching of Peter," which originated in Rome. Ulhorn, who has probably made the profoundest investigation, and who, like Lightfoot, puts the *Homilies* as the earliest of these writings now extant, says they all go back to some old writing "not now extant." Renan says—"A vast Ebionite legend arose in Rome." He points back to its original shape. "Under the name of 'the Preaching (Kerugma) or the Journeys of Peter,' it took a fixed shape about the year 130 A.D." Several times he explains this legend and its conflict of Peter against Paul, as *Simon Magus*, being gradually toned down into a fiction of Peter and Paul together resisting *Simon Magus*, and founding together the Church in Rome. In Harnack's note 3, just above the long note Dr. Carr quotes, he distinctly says—"The theory of the genesis, contents, and aim of the pseudo-Clementine writings, unfolded by Renan, is essentially identical with that of German scholars." Just two pages later he says—"It cannot be made out with certainty *how far back the first sources* of the pseudo-Clementines date, or what their original form and tendency were." And just below he says—"*I do not mean to deny* that the contents of the Jewish-Christian histories of the Apostles *contributed materially to the formation of the ecclesiastical legends about Peter.*" (Harnack *Hist. of Dogma*, p. 315). Further back (p. 308) he had told us that the "journeys of Peter," which got connected with the name of Clement and the "*Ascents of James*," and other early apocryphal writings were dear to the extreme Judæo-Christian sects. In many of his writings he tells us that the Clementine writings, in their present form, are only "redactions" of earlier spurious writings. And, in his special treatment of Peter, he distinctly says of the early apocryphal writings—"The Preaching of Peter," and the "Journeys of Peter,"—that "*Both works underlie the Clementine Recognitions and Homilies.*" In view of all these facts, Dr. Carr's assertion that all this is an "Anglican theory," and his boulder of a big footnote from Harnack about the latest form of the pseudo-Clementine writings," seem to have lost their proper bearings.

Again and again Lightfoot, in various works, has dated the romance in the middle of the second century or soon after. Thus he places the writing "about the middle of the second century" (*St. Clem.* vol. i., p. 100); and, again, he tells us that the Clementine romance "must have been written soon after the middle of the second century" (p. 55). Again, speaking of what is, in its present form, the latest portion of the romance, viz., *the letter to James* of Jerusalem as head of all the Apostles, giving an account of Peter's appointing Clement as Peter's own successor in Rome, Lightfoot says its date can hardly be earlier than the middle of the second century, or much later than the beginning of the third.

That fragment of those spurious writings, and the whole vast

Clementine Romance, have played a tragic part in the evolution of the Papacy. The early shape of it gave impetus to, if it did not wholly create, the fiction that Peter had been bishop of Rome. In a later age, the Clementine Epistle to James, as Lightfoot says, was "made the starting point of the most momentous and gigantic of mediæval forgeries, the Isidorian Decretals." See, on this, Lightfoot, *St. Clem.*, vol. i., pp. 414-419.)

But, says Dr. Carr, following Mr. Rivington, the Clementine Romance "had an Eastern and not a Roman origin." Now, this is just one of the points on which great scholars have *not*, as yet, decided. But, suppose it had an *Eastern origin*. Does that prevent Rome from having seized upon it and adopted it? It is an odd argument for a Roman Catholic. Had not Christianity itself "an Eastern origin?" Yet Romanists claim that Rome appropriated Christianity and its "rock" and "keys" and its supremacy as early as the year 39 or 42. Had not Peter an "Eastern origin?" Yet Rome appropriated Peter. Is not it a fact that nearly every special Roman Catholic feature "had an Eastern origin"—"image-worship," "mariolatry," "purgatory," "dogma," and all the rest of it? Then Rome seized upon it, shaped it to her own ends, adapted it to Rome, made it imperious and imperative.

Take what Dr. Carr calls the earliest list of the "bishops of Rome"—the Irenaean list, which he and others assert, rests on an earlier list made by St. Hegesippus after the middle of the second century. Dr. Carr is even very angry at Dr. Salmon for ignoring "the list of St. Hegesippus," though it is no longer extant. Now, *who was St. Hegesippus?* Had not *he* "an Eastern origin?" Yet Rome and all Roman Catholicism have been hanging on to his Eastern tails (tales) from a very early time. Hegesippus, Lightfoot thinks, was a Jewish Christian; and he certainly came from *the East* to Rome. You will get the most favourable picture of him in Lightfoot (*Gal.* and elsewhere). Hegesippus tells about the multitudinous heresies—" the league of godless error"—which had worked underground and then broke out at the close of the first century. Apocryphal writings, claiming Apostles' names, abounded. It is, indeed, putting it mildly for Lightfoot to say that Hegesippus "has interwoven many fabulous details." Alas! he has, credulously, swallowed the very writings which make part of "the Clementine Romance," *e.g.*, "the *Ascent of James*." Thus he tells that James at Jerusalem "never used the bath;" also that he alone was allowed to enter into the holy place of the Temple; also that his knees, from constant kneeling in prayer on the Temple floor, got horny, like a camel's knees, and so forth, and so forward! Truly an appropriate man to draw up a list of early bishops of Rome, or of the "Anglo-Catholic" Apostolic succession! But does not Archbishop Carr know that there is the gravest doubt whether St. Hegesippus ever *did* draw up any such list, and whether the Greek means *that?* And, if he did, I just want to say that a list of so-called "bishops" drawn up by a Father like St. Hegesippus or St. Irenaeus is worth just as much as the accounts St. Hegesippus gives of the camel-like knees of "James the Just," or the statement Irenaeus gives of our Lord's ministry lasting for nearly twenty years, and of His living till He was an old man.

This fact stares us in the face. In the close of the second century there is a Pauline tradition in Rome which says that Linus was the first presbyter-bishop. There is also another Petrine tradition, at the same time, which affirms that Clement was first presbyter-bishop. And Irenaeus joins the two together, and says Linus was first bishop and Clement third bishop, with another unfortunate bishop sandwiched between, who gets sadly tossed about in the after lists, and finally gets fixed down as *two bishops* —one called Cletus, and another Anacletus. No wonder these things perplexed poor Rufinus, Epiphanius, and Augustine in ages when they came to believe an "Episcopal succession" to be necessary to the Church.

X.

"THE FAMOUS PASSAGE IN IRENAEUS."

(See Lecture IV.)

Haer., iii., 3, 2.

There are only three questions of any importance to be asked about this passage—1. To what does the word *"principalitas"* ("eminence" or "pre-eminence") refer? Is it to the *City* of Rome or to the *Church* in Rome? I myself do not care to which it refers. It is plain that the City of Rome, the Emperor's capital, was the wealthy and eminent city. It is plain also that the Christian community in that city, in the close of the second century, was the most influential and wealthy Christian Church. But I want simply to point out that some of the greatest of recent scholars who have studied this matter most carefully hold that what is meant must be the *City* of Rome itself. So Prof. Salmon, Fr. Puller, and Bishop Coxe, whose special labours on Irenaeus make his opinion of great value. To the honour of the R.C. scholars (Berington and Kirk), their translation is so loyal to the Latin text—"*on account of more potent principality*"—that it may mean either the *City* of Rome or the *Church* there. In Cyprian (Ep. 48) there seems striking corroboration of the view that the eminence of the *City* is referred to. He writes:—"Since Rome, *from her greatness*, plainly ought to take precedence of Carthage, he (Novatus) there committed still greater and graver crimes." It is the *greatness* of the *City* that gives the Roman Church its importance.

Some other scholars, *e.g.*, Wordsworth, take the term as referring to the *Church* in Rome. In either case it has not the slightest reference to any "primacy" or control over other Churches.

(2.) The only other questions are:—(2) What is meant by "those who are *from every side*?"

(3.) And what is meant by *resorting to the Roman Church*? These questions recent scholarship has settled, by pointing out the exactly parallel passage in the Antiochian canons which are deemed to be a quotation from this passage of Irenaeus (Coxe *Elucidat.*; *Fath.* i., p. 460) [cf. Bright, *Rom. See*, p. 33]:—"Because that in the metropolis there resort together (lit. run together, or come together συντρέχειν) from every side, all those having business to transact." The Greek of "from every side" is πανταχόθεν (pantachothen) = Latin *undique*, the very word used here. And Liddell and Scott translate this Greek word as follows:—"From all places, from all quarters, from every side, Latin *undique*." Nay more (to complete the proof) fortunately a fragment of the Greek of Irenaeus is extant in Bk. iii., 11, 8, and there the word is this same word, viz.—*from all* quarters.' Cf. Coxe, Iren., *Haer.*, iii., 3, 2. [Bright, in his recently-published work, confirms this—"The word *undique* must be noted; it is not *ubique*, and πανταχόθεν (from all sides) refers to the idea of winds blowing *from all quarters.*"]

The meaning, then, of this passage, so tortured by Roman Catholic advocates, seems simple. Irenaeus, writing in the West in defence of the Christian faith against the leaders of "heresies," shows that it is the same faith and the same Lord Jesus in all the Churches. It would be "very tedious," he says, to go over all the Churches, so as to show that in each the same faith has been handed down. So it is enough to take the Church in Rome, for it was known everywhere. For to it, as Rome was the centre of all trade, Christians had to come from all sides. And, by these—"the faithful from all quarters"—the "Apostolical tradition" common to all the Churches had been preserved.

[Bright puts it clearly thus:—"It is inevitable, St. Irenaeus means, that Christians from *all other parts* of the Empire should, from time to time for various reasons, visit the Church in the great centre of the Empire. This is a process which is always going on—which cannot but go on."—*Roman See*, p. 32-3.]

Archbishop Carr may plead that Roberts and Rambaut have translated as he does in his latest, making *convenire ad* mean "*agree with*," and *undique* mean "*everywhere.*" But, then, those translators confess distinctly that they "are far from sure that the rendering given above [by them] is correct," and Coxe and every other later editor of standing have shown that it is incorrect.

XI.

THE DOUAY CHRONOLOGY AND PETER.

It is remarkable that in the chronology attached to the Douay version not a word is said about Peter having visited Rome until the year 68, after Paul's first Roman imprisonment. The startling thing is that not until the very last year of Peter's life (which is set as 68) is any hint given of Peter having gone to Rome. Also, his "Second Epistle," according to this Chronological Index, is set down prior to the statement that he came to Rome. His First Epistle is set down in the year 48, but has no indicated connection with Rome. All that is said of Peter prior to 68 is connected with the East, apparently. Then, for 68 A.D. it is said :—"St. Peter about this time wrote his Second Epistle. About this time St. Peter and St. Paul came to Rome. See Tillemont, &c. Not long after they were both put in prison and suffered martyrdom."

How all this, with the surprising reference to the Jansenist scholar Tillemont, can be made to square with those marvellous lists relied on by Dr. Carr—"The Armenian Version" of Eusebius' Chronicle, and its affirmation that St. Peter "stays there [in Rome] as prelate of the Church for twenty years," or with Jerome's statement that Peter preached the Gospel for twenty-five years in Rome—it is difficult to see. But then it is all in the region of cloudland.

XII.

THE "TROPHIES" OF PETER AND PAUL.

Gaius, the Roman presbyter, contemporary of Hippolytus in the early part of the third century, vehemently opposes the Montanist assertion that *women* might speak God's message, and "prophesy." The Montanists had a good deal to say for themselves, and quoted the example of the daughters of Philip the Evangelist, who actually "prophesied" (Acts xxi., 8, 9). Such audacious and independent young female persons were altogether perilous to the Roman spirit of repression. So Gaius, round whose personality much mist hangs, seeks to suppress such views by the authority of a Church which actually had had two Apostles, Peter and Paul, at the founding of it. "We have got their 'trophies' (as Harnack says, whatever *that* may mean) actually in Rome," says Gaius. Protestant archæologists (Lipsius, Erbes, Von Schultze, &c.) think this meant two *trees*. Roman Catholic advocates make it mean "tombs." Let us listen to Gavazzi, himself a man of Bologna and Rome. In the famous debate* in Rome (1872) between three Roman Catholic clerical

---

* Edited by the late Dr. William Arthur, the Wesleyan divine.

champions and three Italian Protestants, Gavazzi in his wonderful address thus dealt with these "trophies" and Gaius :—

"Here it is said is his tomb . . . or his trophy, or his martyr memorial, and therefore St. Peter was martyred in Rome! By no means. . . . There was a martyr-memorial of Laurence at Ravenna, and Laurence was not martyred at Ravenna. There was a martyr memorial of Stephen in Ancona, and Stephen was not martyred in Ancona. There were twelve martyr memorials in honour of the twelve Apostles in Constantinople in the time of St. Sophia; and the twelve Apostles were not martyred in Constantinople. . . . But his (Peter's) relics? Softly with those relics, gentlemen! . . . In Rome, I am told, there is the body of St. Stephen in one of your basilicas. Remember, I am *told* it. I do not guarantee it. But, because the "relics of St. Stephen are found in Rome, perhaps St. Stephen suffered his martyrdom in Rome!"

XIII.

BISHOP MOORHOUSE ON THE COUNCIL OF CHALCEDON.

Just as the last proof-sheet leaves me, a copy of the Bishop of Manchester's Replies to Bishop Bilsborrow and Father Vaughan on *The Roman Claims* has come into my hands. I beg to direct the readers of it to pp. 37-42, bearing on the secret influence of Cyril with the ladies of the Imperial Court in the Nestorian conflict, and on the 28th Canon of the Council of Chalcedon—that awkward disproof of the whole Romanist theory.

THE END.

XIV.

CORRESPONDENCE BETWEEN ARCHBISHOP CARR AND DR. RENTOUL.

As preface to these letters, I desire simply to point out that in the book form of his Lectures Dr. Carr has significantly broken the connection of his "quotations" from "Protestant writers" and from "exclusively Protestant testimony," as published *in extenso* in the *Advocate* of the 14th and 21st March, and to which he himself appealed as the full and authoritative shape of his utterances. The correspondence is conditioned by *that*. In that *Advocate in extenso* transcript of his Lecture I., the quotation from "Nevin" ended with the words—"beyond which no memory of man to the contrary then reached." Then the words immediately followed :—
"Neander testifies to the antiquity of the Papal claims to a Primacy of jurisdiction," &c. Then came Renan, ushered in by the declaration that we must regard such writers' "admissions in favour of the Roman Primacy as the irresistible outcome of the facts of history."

But, now, in the book form of Dr. Carr's Lectures (pp. 21, 22) a new passage is introduced, adding nothing whatever to his argument, but breaking the original connection of "Protestant testimony." The new *passage*, occupying about a page, *breaks in after* "*Nevin's*" words *with a quite new connection* thus :—

"*A Catholic could hardly express with greater clearness the universal belief of ages in the doctrine of the Roman Supremacy than does a non-Catholic writer in the Union Review.*" Then, after the quotation from the *Review*, "Canon Everest" is quoted, and then our Laudian acquaintance, "Archbishop Bramhall." Then, after this curious break, Neander, on Dr. Carr's original string of "Protestant testimony," is here resumed (part of p. 22). And then follows Renan !!

Archbishop Carr says mysteriously :—" Renan, like Presbyterian writers, dates the radical change in the primitive form of Church government from a very early period. He is, accordingly, quoted by Presbyterian writers with much approval" (p. 226). What may be the sense of this mysterious language I do not know. I need scarcely say that " Presbyterian writers, ' if they permitted any bias in the matter, would "date the radical change in the primitive form of Church government" not "from a very early period" (as the Archbishop strangely says), but from *as late a period as possible.* When the Archbishop ventures to say that Renan "is accordingly quoted by Presbyterian writers with much approval," he ought to reflect that it was he himself who projected Renan and his "Protestant testimony" into the discussion of this question. Had he not done so, and had he not misquoted in doing so, no Presbyterian and no Protestant of any kind would have named Renan's name. In his lectures of 1893 Archbishop Carr appealed to Renan as belonging to the class of "unbiassed critics." In his lectures of 1895 he quoted Renan, and in the same mutilated form now so well understood. Then, in 1896, he again quoted Renan, and in the same peculiar shape. Now Renan is not any longer the sunshiny spot in the Archbishop's horizon.

DR. CARR'S LETTER I.

GROWTH OF THE SACERDOTAL ORDER AND POPEDOM.

To the Editor (of "Argus" and "Age.")

Sir,—I cannot help feeling flattered by the succession of representative writers who have undertaken in turn to reply to my lectures on the Primacy of the Roman Pontiff, for each of them has, by implication, confessed to the failure of his predecessor. The latest champion of a desperate cause must, by this time, have convinced his Anglican friends of the danger of relying on soldiers of fortune, who dearly love the din and smoke of battle, but who too often in the end turn their swords against those who have enlisted their services. If Anglican controversialists are content with Dr. Rentoul's refutation of the claims of the Roman Pontiff, and with his defence of his own and their position, I assure them that I do not envy them the help they have received from their new ally, and I can in all sincerity say that I am more than pleased with the character of that refutation and defence. The cause is desperate indeed that in the hands of so able an advocate as Dr. Rentoul could not find stronger or more consistent arguments in its favour. When a skilful dialectician abandons sober reasoning and seeks to obscure the real issue by the variety of his irrelevancies and the offensiveness of his epithets, we may be sure that the cause he advocates is a losing one.

I do not think that there is one real difficulty raised by Dr. Rentoul regarding the primacy of the Roman Pontiff which I have not answered by anticipation in my recent lectures. As, however, I hope to have these lectures published in book-form early next week, I will avail myself of the opportunity of developing these answers to meet the special phases of the difficulties which have been most recently presented. But I have no intention of allowing myself to be drawn by any controversialist from the subject on which I have been engaged until that subject is finally disposed of. In the meantime, however, when I am accused of changing "the peaceful attitude" of former days, I must take the earliest opportunity of repelling that accusation, and of reminding my accuser of the defiant public challenge, and the gross calumnies against the Catholic Church spoken in high places, which provoked the present and former controversies. Above all, he must have overlooked how applicable to one of his own combative disposition are the familiar words of the classic poet—*Mutato nomine de te fabula narratur.* I must also at once notice the grave personal charge of having represented Renan as a Protestant, and of having suppressed a part of his testimony for the purpose of making him witness to the Roman claims for the Papacy.

In reply, I must express as strongly as I can the deep sense of pain and wrong which such a deliberate and unfounded accusation causes me. First, so far from representing Renan as a Protestant, I explicitly referred to him as a typical representative of the rationalistic school; and secondly, I quoted him not at all as favourable to the Roman claims for the Papacy, but as a *hostile* witness who admits the *fact* of its existence before the end of the second century. With that admission alone was I concerned, and the omitted words in the quotation indicated by the usual signs, had no bearing on the point under consideration. Immediately before, I had quoted Neander as another hostile witness, and then followed these words—

"Little as we may admire the methods of rationalistic writers, we must at least regard their admissions in favour of the Roman primacy as the irresistible outcome of the facts of history. The Catholic Church, and she alone, has consistently condemned their wholesale and destructive criticism of revealed truth, while Protestantism seemed satisfied if Rome suffered equally with revelation. Renan may surely be taken as a typical representative of this school, and there is no room for mistake in these words. 'Rome,' says M. Ernest Renan, 'was the place in which the great idea of Catholicity was worked out. More and more every day it became the capital of Christianity, and it took the place of Jerusalem as the religious centre of humanity. Its Church claimed a precedence over all others, which was generally recognised. *All the doubtful questions which agitated the Christian conscience came to Rome to ask for arbitration, if not decision. Men argued—certainly not in a very logical way—that as Christ had made Cephas the cornerstone of His church, the privilege ought to be inherited by His successors.* . . . The Bishop of Rome became the Bishop of Bishops, he who admonished all others. Rome proclaims her right—a dangerous right—of excommunicating those who do not walk step by step with her. . . . At the end of the second century we can also recognise, by signs which it is impossible to mistake, the spirit which in 1870 will proclaim the infallibility of the Pope."

The italics are mine, and they serve to emphasise the unfairness of Dr. Rentoul in charging me with deliberate suppression, whilst he himself was in the very act of omitting from my quotation a sentence which clearly shows that Renan was represented as personally hostile to the claims which he admitted were advanced before the close of the second century.

Finally, when Dr. Rentoul charges the Catholic Church as falsifying history, and seeks to set up Presbyterianism in its stead as the primitive form of Christianity, I would remind him of the words of one who, perhaps more than any other man of this century, knew Protestantism in all its history, phases, and varieties:—"So much must the Protestant grant, that if such a system of doctrine as he would now introduce ever existed in early times, it has been clean swept away as if by a deluge, suddenly, silently, and without memorial, by a deluge coming in a night and utterly soaking, rotting, heaving up, and hurrying off every vestige of what it found in the church before cock-crowing, so that 'when they rose in the morning' her true seed 'were all dead corpses—nay, dead and buried'—without grave-stone. 'The waters went over them: there was not one of them left; they sunk in the mighty waters' . . . He must allow that the alleged deluge has done its work. Yes, and has in turn disappeared itself. It has been swallowed up by the earth mercilessly, as itself was merciless."—Newman's *Development of Christian Doctrine.*—Yours, &c.,

+ THOMAS J. CARR.

St. Patrick's Cathedral, May 18.

I.

DR. RENTOUL IN REPLY.

To the Editor (of "Argus" and "Age.")

Sir,—I will discharge at once the first portion of Archbishop Carr's letter. It consists of rhetorical sentences made up of phrases such as "latest champion of a desperate cause," "soldiers of fortune," "offensiveness of his epithets," "seeks to obscure the real issue," &c. These phrases will not advance the Archbishop's cause. Let me turn at once to the only substantial matter in Dr. Carr's letter.

1. He suggests that the Anglican controversialists have "enlisted" my "services," and that in argument they have "by implication confessed to failure," in conflict with the Archbishop. The delicate modesty of this assertion is memorable. The insinuation conveyed in it is at once unworthy of a responsible speaker, and is absolutely contrary to fact. It is enough to say that in all matters connected with this controversy I have not, either directly or indirectly, received any communication or expression of opinion from any Church of England clergyman.

2. Archbishop Carr says he hopes to have his "lectures published in book form," and he will there develop his "answers to meet the special phases of the difficulties which have been most recently presented." Very good. Right glad I am to hear this. I also will publish my lectures in full form. And I shall be happy to examine the "developed answers" of the Archbishop. I venture to suppose that they will require "development." For the difficulties which front the Archbishop and his Roman claim are solid and unanswerable historic facts

3. I come now to the one thing of genuine moment in the Archbishop's letter, viz., in reference to his statements regarding his "quotation" from Renan. Archbishop Carr makes two strange complaints. He asserts he did not imply Renan was a Protestant. Now turn to his lectures. The first lecture sums in succession a list of Protestant writers and historians, who are represented as bearing testimony in proof of Dr. Carr's positions:

(a) that Peter was in Rome; (b) that he finally fixed his see in Rome; (c) that his primacy was continued to successors. It closes with the historians and Renan, and then passes on at once to the "first uninspired document," viz., the letter of St. Clement to the Corinthians. Now turn to the beginning of the Archbishop's second lecture, and read there his own statement and representation of the men he had quoted from :—" In my last lecture I quoted exclusively Protestant testimony to prove :—1. That St. Peter was in Rome; 2. That he finally fixed his see in Rome : and 3. That his Primacy was not temporary, but was continued after the admission of the Gentiles into the Christian Church, and was transmitted to his successors in the Roman see. I next addressed myself to the testimony in favour of the Roman Pontiff, which is contained in the first uninspired document which has come down to us, viz., the letter of St. Clement to the Corinthians."

Just think of that! The Archbishop himself here affirms that the testimony, up to his dealing with Clement, was exclusively Protestant testimony; and yet he is not happy when I point out that Renan was not a Protestant. True, the Archbishop says he called him a "Rationalist." Does the Archbishop imply that to call a man a "Rationalist" is to say that he is not a Protestant? Unfortunately, the Archbishop's express words stand there to confute him.

4. I pass on to the much graver aspect of this matter, viz., the Archbishop's quotation from Renan. He says that Dr. Rentoul had "charged him (the Archbishop) with deliberate suppression, whilst he himself (Dr. Rentoul) was in the very act of omitting from my (the Archbishop's) quotation a sentence which clearly shows," &c. Now let us turn to the facts. I shall simply quote the passages, and ask the public to judge. (1) Here is exactly, and *verbatim*, the passage purporting to be from Renan as quoted in the Archbishop's lecture published Monday, 9th March :—"Rome was the place in which the great idea of Catholicity was worked out. More and more every day it became the capital of Christianity, and took the place of Jerusalem as the religious centre of humanity. Its church claimed a precedence over all others which was generally recognised. . . . The Bishop of Rome became the Bishop of Bishops, he who admonished all others. Rome proclaims her right—a dangerous right—of excommunicating those who do not walk step by step with her. . . . At the end of the second century we can also recognise, by signs which it is impossible to mistake, the spirit which in 1870 will proclaim the infallibility of the Pope."

(1) Now this is also word for word the quotation from Archbishop Carr's lecture as given in my first lecture (see *Argus* [and *Age*], Monday, 4th May). How Archbishop Carr can affirm that I " was in the very act of omitting from his quotation a sentence," &c., I cannot in the least explain. It is as amazing to me as a good many of the Archbishop's other assertions.

(2) Take, now, the quotation in the Archbishop's letter in the *Argus* [and *Age*] of to-day (19th May), in which it will be noted the

Archbishop inserts two sentences not in his quotation as originally given, and yet it is not a full quotation from Renan. I mark within square brackets the new sentences:—"Rome," says M. Ernest Renan, "was the p ace in which the great idea of Christianity was worked out. More and more every day it became the capital of Christianity, and it took the place of Jerusalem as the religious centre of humanity. Its church claimed precedence over all others, which was generally recognised. [All the doubtful questions which agitated the Christian conscience came to Rome to ask for arbitration, if not decision. Men argued, certainly not in a very logical way, that as Christ had made Cephas the corner-stone of his Church the privilege ought to be inherited by his successors.] . . . The Bishop of Rome became the Bishop of Bishops, he who admonished all others. Rome proclaims her right—a dangerous right—of excommunicating those who do not walk step by step with her. . . . At the end of the second century we can also recognise by signs, which it is impossible to mistake, the spirit, which in 1870 will proclaim the infallibility of the Pope."

(3) Then here is the true and actual shape of Renan's words and meaning, as quoted *verbatim* by me from Renan's book in my first lecture, and I pointed out the pages, and urged the laity of Melbourne to read it for themselves (*Hib. Lect.*, pp. 172, 173, 174, in the [*Argus* and] *Age*, 4th May):—"Rome was the place in which the great idea of Catholicity was worked out. More and more every day it became the capital of Christianity, and took the place of Jerusalem as the religious centre of humanity. Its church claimed a precedence over all others which was generally recognised. [All the doubtful questions which agitated the Christian conscience came to Rome to ask for arbitration, if not decision. Men argued, certainly not in a very logical way, that as Christ had made Cephas the corner-stone of His church, the privilege ought to be inherited by His successors. By an unequalled *tour de force* the Church of Rome had succeeded in giving itself the name of the Church of Paul also. A new and equally mythical duality replaced that of Romulus and Remus.] The Bishop of Rome became the Bishop of Bishops, he who admonished all others. Rome proclaims her right—a dangerous right—of excommunicating those who do not walk step by step with her. [The poor Artemonites—a kind of Arians before Arius—have great reason to complain of the injustice of fate which has branded them as heretics, although, up to the time of Victor, the whole Church of Rome was of one mind with them. From that time forth the Church of Rome put herself above history.] At the end of the second century we can easily recognise by signs which it is impossible to mistake the spirit which in 1870 will proclaim the infallibility of the Pope."

The square brackets mark the passages omitted by the Archbishop in his lecture. The above is the great and crushing passage of Renan in full. "Look on this picture and on that!" Look at the shape, garbled from its connection and drained of all its main meaning, in which Archbishop Carr gave it to the public, as if Renan were witnessing to the truth and strength of the claim of the Roman papacy! Just above this passage Renan has said in part I. of that lecture that in Rome "men had reached ideas which would have revolted Paul!"

I will not make any comments on these quotations. It is enough to put the exact facts before the public and let them honestly judge. With the sad criticisms at present filling the London press on Romanist modes of controversy, in view of Cardinal Manning's autobiography, I do not wish to speak further on the subject.

Archbishop Carr closes with a quotation on the Early Church's Presbyterianism, and the quotation, amusing to say, is from a Romanist cardinal! I have in my lectures said no word about, or on behalf of, my own Church. But may I now quote a sentence from a vastly greater man than the cardinal, viz., Pitt, the great Earl of Chatham, the greatest Englishman of his age, and a Church of England man :—"The ambition of Presbyterians is to keep more close to the College of Fishermen than to the College of Cardinals —to the Doctrines of Apostles than to the Decrees of Bishops. They contend for a Scriptural Creed and for a Spiritual worship."—I am, &c.

J. LAURENCE RENTOUL.

Ormond College, the University, 19th May.

II.

ARCHBISHOP CARR'S SECOND LETTER.

TO THE EDITOR (OF "ARGUS" AND "AGE.")

SIR,—If, as I am sure he meant to do, Dr. Rentoul had "put the exact facts before the public, and let them honestly judge" for themselves the value of his statements, he would have saved me the necessity of replying to his letter of this date. But, unfortunately, many of Dr. Rentoul's "exact facts" are the very reverse of being exact.

First, referring to my quotation from Renan, he says :—"I also quoted the Archbishop's exact words from beginning to end." This is not an "exact fact." It is not a fact at all. As I pointed out in my former letter, Dr. Rentoul omitted from my quotation from Renan the sentence which clearly shows that Renan was not quoted by me as being in favour of the Roman primacy. Such a statement or insinuation would have been preposterous on the face of it. He says he cannot in the least explain how I can affirm that he has omitted this sentence from my quotation. My direct statement ought to have had some weight with him. But if he had taken the ordinary precaution of making a little inquiry, as he was bound to do before making such a serious charge, the mystery would have been solved. He would have found that *The Argus* report of my lecture which he quotes was but an epitome, in which the quotations were necessarily abbreviated, and that the lecture was published *in extenso* in the *Advocate* of the 14th and 21st March. In the lecture, as anyone may see by looking at the *Advocate* (copies of which I will send to any inquirer), the sentences omitted by Dr. Rentoul are found.

Before making a similar charge against him I should certainly feel myself bound in both justice and honour to inquire whether a full report of his lecture could be procured. Dr. Rentoul is not more fortunate in his surmises than in his facts. He surmises that *The Argus* report of my lecture was from my own "careful abstract." But as I gave no abstract of the lecture, careful or otherwise, his surmise is as unreliable as his "exact facts."

Secondly, Dr. Rentoul repeats that I implied that Renan was a Protestant, and by way of proof he quotes from the beginning of my second lecture the following sentences :—

"In my last lecture I quoted exclusively Protestant testimony to prove (1) that St. Peter was in Rome, (2) that he finally fixed his see in Rome, and (3) that his primacy was not temporary, but was continued after the admission of the Gentiles into the Christian Church, and was transmitted to his successors in the Roman see. I next addressed myself to the testimony in favour of the Roman Pontiff, which is contained in the first uninspired document which has come down to us, viz., the letter of St. Clement to the Corinthians."

And then he comments thus on the quotation :—

"Just think of that! The Archbishop himself affirms that the testimony was exclusively 'Protestant testimony,' and yet he is not happy when I point out that Renan was not a Protestant."

Will Dr. Rentoul be good enough to read my words again, and he will find that I have not quoted Renan for any of the three propositions for which I have quoted exclusively Protestant testimony. I quoted him as I had quoted Neander immediately before, as testifying to the antiquity of the claims put forward by the Roman Pontiffs, and as thus admitting, Rationalist though he was, an important fact which tells in favour of the Roman primacy. So far was I from identifying him with the Protestant authorities I had quoted that I expressly contrasted him with them. Here are my words :—

"Little as we may admire the methods of Rationalistic writers, we must at least regard their admissions in favour of the Roman primacy as the irresistible outcome of the facts of history. The Catholic Church, and she alone, has consistently condemned their wholesale and destructive criticism of revealed truth, whilst Protestantism seemed satisfied if Rome suffered equally with Revelation. Renan may surely be taken as a typical representative of this school, and there is no room for mistake in his words."

I now ask any impartial reader to say whether I implied that Renan was a Protestant.

But Dr. Rentoul asks me, "Does the Archbishop imply that to call a man a Rationalist is to say that he is not a Protestant?" I answer, with all due deference to Dr. Rentoul's more extensive knowledge of Protestantism, that I have always believed that to call a man a Rationalist is equivalent to saying that he is not a Protestant. Protestants believe in, and argue from revelation, and the latest dictionaries give us as the meaning of the word Rationalist, "One who accepts Rationalism as a theory or system," and Rationalism is defined to be "the doctrine or system of those who deduce their religious opinions from reason or the understanding as distinct from, or opposed to, Revelation." But perhaps Dr. Rentoul knows better.

Finally, Dr. Rentoul might have shown more reverence for true greatness by not coupling John Henry Newman's name with an offensive epithet, and might have shown more judgment by not comparing things that have no common measure.—I am, &c.

+ THOMAS J. CARR,
May 20. Archbishop of Melbourne.

II.

DR. RENTOUL'S SECOND LETTER IN REPLY.

To the Editor (of "Argus" and "Age.")

Sir,—Archbishop Carr struggles stoutly to extricate himself from the meshes of difficulty in which he has placed himself by his "quotation" from Renan, and his statements regarding it. But my primary affirmation remains unaltered and unshaken, viz.:—

"I am surprised at the Archbishop's boldness in quoting from the brilliant critic Renan in support of the Roman claim for the Papacy. I am more surprised that the quotation was so maimed and mutilated that it gave almost the opposite sense of what Renan intended to say. I must protest against the implication in Archbishop Carr's lectures that Renan was a 'Protestant.' He never was. He was educated for the Romish priesthood," &c. (Lecture 1, *The Argus*, May 5.)

I have read very attentively and with genuine wonder the successive utterances of Archbishop Carr in reply to this. But the fact stands out still, and no amount of words on the Archbishop's part can alter or gloze it over, that, even taking the quotation as he now gives it, my charge made then, and made now, remains good and unanswerable. The professed quotation from Renan "is so maimed and mutilated that it gives almost the opposite sense of what Renan intended to say."

This is the grave and serious part of my charge. I have already unanswerably proven it by contrasting *verbatim et literatim* the Archbishop's quotation with the exact words of Renan. I now do so again.

In the *Argus* [and *Age*] of Wednesday last, 20th May, I printed at full length the shape of the Archbishop's quotation from Renan as given in the long abstract of the Archbishop's first lecture published in the *Argus* of 9th May. Then below that "quotation" I gave the shape of the quotation as presented in the Archbishop's letter in the *Argus* of 19th May, and as he declares it was given in his lecture. (He now for the first time tells us it was thus given in the lecture as "published *in extenso* in the *Advocate* of the 14th and 21st March.") That form of the quotation has two additional sentences. In my last letter I marked these two additional sentences in square brackets, and showed that, with these two sentences included, "it is not a full quotation from Renan," but still leaves Renan's tremendous passage in a "shape, garbled in its connection, and drained of all its main meaning." And I say this strongly and earnestly still. I further in the same letter printed the whole passage of Renan, drawing special attention to the all-important sentences which had been excised by Archbishop Carr, so altering the entire meaning and impression of the sense.

But the Archbishop says I should have read the account of his lecture as published *in extenso* in the *Advocate*. Now, I must frankly reply two things—(1) I thought I had really got "extension" enough of the Archbishop's characteristic "quotations" when I had waded through two columns of them done into small, compact, clear, and definite type in the *Argus* newspaper. 2. I do not read the *Advocate*. I find that it is far safer to trust oneself, in all that pertains to candour, truth, and sacred fair play, to the daily newspapers than to trust to the denominational organs. In the *Argus* the Archbishop's lecture stood, with its "quotations" unchallenged by him, from March 9 until May 4, when in my first lecture I began to analyse them. Furthermore, I have now gone to the *Advocate* and studiously read "*in extenso*" the Archbishop's lecture. But this does not in the least improve the Archbishop's position. The so-called "*in extenso*" quotation in the *Advocate* is exactly the same as the second shape in which I printed it in the *Argus* [and *Age*] of last Wednesday. The charge I brought against the quotation in my first lecture I bring against it still. There have been cut out from the heart of it the two passages which give meaning and colour to the whole as Renan wrote it and intended it to be understood. Here is the one passage, in which Renan declares that the Roman tradition on which the whole Catholic Roman claim is built is as legendary and mythical as the old pagan legend of Romulus and Remus:—

"By an unequalled *tour de force* the Church of Rome had succeeded in giving itself the name of the Church of Paul also. A new and equally mythical duality replaced that of Romulus and Remus."

That is the one passage which the Archbishop cut out. And the other is this:—

"The poor Artemonites - a kind of Arians before Arius—have great reason to complain of the injustice of fate which has branded them as heretics, although up to the time of Victor the whole Church of Rome was of one mind with them. From that time forth the Church of Rome put herself above history."

Those two great and crushing passages are the inmost fibre of the statement of Renan, of which Archbishop Carr professed to quote, to a great public audience, the testimony. Yet not a trace of them, or a hint of the interrelated meaning of them, is to be found in the quotation as given *in extenso* in the *Advocate*, or as given when the Archbishop spoke his lecture. When at last I unveiled, in my first lecture, the real contents of this part of Renan's book, as a sample of the Archbishop's quotations, it caused intense surprise. And it causes intense surprise still.

The surprise ought to deepen when one reflects that, in this same book of Renan, it is declared in a chapter entitled "The Legend of the Roman Church: Peter and Paul"—"If there is anything in the world which Jesus did not institute it is the Papacy." And it is further declared that "nothing can be less admissible" than "the unfortunate chronological scheme which according to Catholics brings Peter to Rome in the year 42." It is further declared that "Peter had not yet arrived in Rome when Paul was brought there—that is to say, in the year 61." It is further declared in the chapter from which Dr. Carr purported to quote, that the success of Catholicity at Rome rested upon the notion that "docility is salvation." It is further declared that the supremacy of this notion was due to means such as are described in the following two sentences (p. 175):—

"Every kind of authority, every kind of artifice served her (Rome) to that end. Policy never recoils from fraud, and policy had always found a home in the most secret councils of the Church of Rome. The vein o apocryphal literature was constantly worked," &c.

Truly, a quite amazing book from which to quote in support of the historicity of the Roman Papacy; and to sustain the thesis which the Archbishop, a few sentences above his quotation from Renan, affirmed, that, at the time spoken of, "according to the generally received Protestant teaching, the faith of the Church was pure, and the sanctity of the Roman pontiff conspicuous." This is said in special reference to Milman's "testimony." Neander is quoted immediately after. And then comes Renan. Then the Archbishop passed on at once to the other and second part of his lecture, viz., the "'testimony' of the Early Fathers." And he opens this part thus as an immediate sequent on the "quotation" from Renan:—

"And back beyond the close of the second century to the very dawn of uninspired Christian history we can trace the primacy of the Roman pontiff."

This is one of the three things the Archbishop took in hand to prove, and which he gave the long string of Protestant "quotations" to buttress.

When my pamphlet is published, it will be seen that I have analysed a few more of the Archbishop's quotations. And they will afford a few pages of curious and interesting reading.

The other matter, stoutly contended for in Archbishop Carr's letter, is of much less importance. He tries to maintain that in his lectures he did not "imply" that Renan was a Protestant. Now, I have done my best to look at Archbishop Carr's words, and their necessary implications, in the most favourable light; and I say, when read intelligently, they bear no other construction than the sense in which they first conveyed that meaning to me. This is necessitated by the whole balance of the first lecture, in its two parts, by the words which usher in Renan's quotation, and by the distinct statement in the opening of the second lecture. There the Archbishop himself distinctly states that he did two things in his first lecture; he "quoted exclusively Protestant testimony," and "next addressed himself" (please mark the words "next addressed") "to the testimony in favour of the primacy of the Roman pontiff, which is contained in the first uninspired document," &c. (viz., Clement of Rome). Why, the very name last on the list of quotations, before the Archbishop "next addressed himself" to Clement of Rome, is Renan himself.

But Archbishop Carr begins to define "Rationalism," as the last straw to clutch at. Very well! I only ask your readers to go to the *Encyclopædia Britannica* (last edition) and read there the article on "Rationalism," and see it treated as a great phase of Protestantism, and see Kant's definition of it. Renan, rightly speaking, was not a "Rationalist," and he was not a Protestant. He was a Pantheist. The whole make-up of Archbishop Carr's words, with his special fling at Protestantism being "satisfied if Rome suffered equally with Revelation" from the influence of Rationalism, left the distinct implication that Renan was both a Rationalist and a Protestant

Turning away from these things, Archbishop Carr says that I " coupled John Henry Newman's name with an offensive epithet." May I ask where and when.—I am, &c.,

J. LAURENCE RENTOUL.

Ormond College, 21st May.

III.

DR. CARR'S THIRD LETTER.

To the Editor (of "Argus" and "Age.")

Sir,—As I am unwilling to question Dr. Rentoul's candour, the conviction forces itself upon me that the heat of controversy has considerably warped his judgment. If he had considered the matter dispassionately he must have seen that all the "crushing passages" and "tremendous sentences" with their "interrelated meaning," which he quotes from Renan with amusing iteration and vehemence, so far from weakening my argument, only serve indirectly to strengthen and confirm it. Indeed, if such passages as Dr. Rentoul quotes were not to be found in abundance throughout Renan's lectures I should not have thought of quoting him at all. The special value of his testimony is based on the fact that he was a renegade from the Church, and belonged to a school whose "wholesale and destructive criticism of revealed truth the Catholic Church, and she alone, has consistently condemned." For this very reason, as I said, "we must regard their admissions in favour of the Roman Primacy as the irresistible outcome of the facts of history."

Renan, then, was cited to give testimony not to his own belief or disbelief in the Primacy, but to historical facts. What were these historical facts in support of which Renan's testimony was adduced? They were, as the context most clearly shows, the claims put forward by the Roman Pontiffs, and acknowledged by the Christians of the first three centuries. Here is the immediate context:—

"Neander testifies to the antiquity of the Papal claims to a Primacy of jurisdiction.

"'Very early indeed,' he says, 'do we observe in the Roman bishops traces of the assumption that to them, as successors of St. Peter, belonged a paramount authority in ecclesiastical disputes.'

"His evidence is not the less valuable, though, like other Protestant controversialists of far less note, he writes of what he calls 'the assumption' of the Roman bishops. We are not to forget that he is dealing with those very ages in which, according to the generally received Protestant teaching, the faith of the Church was pure and the sanctity of the Roman Pontiff conspicuous. And as we shall see in the course of our inquiry these 'assumptions' were filially recognised by those primitive saints and doctors to whose writings, when it suits their purposes, Protestants so confidently appeal."

Then, passing from Protestant testimony to a class of testimony even more telling, because the witnesses were still further removed from any sympathy with the Catholic Church, I immediately added :—

"Little as we may admire the methods of Rationalistic writers, we must at least regard their admissions in favour of the Roman Primacy as the irresistible outcome of the facts of history. The Catholic Church, and she alone, has consistently condemned their wholesale and destructive criticism of revealed truth, whilst Protestantism seemed satisfied if Rome suffered equally with Revelation. Renan may surely be taken as a typical representative of this school, and there is no room for mistake in his words."

The admissions in favour of the Roman Primacy to be found in Renan's "Hibbert Lectures" are not confined, as Dr. Rentoul seems to insinuate, to the passages quoted by me, but are numerous and emphatic.

Page 124.—Of St. Clement, Renan says :—"He is the first type of Pope which Church history presents to us;" and (page 125) of Clement's letter to the Corinthians, written towards the end of the first century, about thirty years after St. Peter's death, he writes :—

"Already the idea of a certain primacy belonging to his Church was beginning to make its way to the light. The right of warning other Churches and of composing their differences was conceded to it. Similar privileges—so at least it was believed (Luke xxii., 32)—had been accorded to Peter by the other disciples.

"A very ancient tradition ascribes the composition of it to Clement."

Page 127.—"Its letter to the Corinthians is the first manifesto of the principle of authority made within the Church," and in a note, "few writings are so authentic."

Page 128.—"Some years ago a great outcry was raised against a French Archbishop, then a senator, who said from the tribune, 'my clergy is my regiment.' Clement had said the same thing long before."

Page 150.—"The centre of a future Catholic orthodoxy was plainly here. Pius, who succeeded Hyginus, showed the same firmness in defending the purity of the faith. Cerdo, Marcian, Valentinus, Marcellinus, are removed from the Church by the sentence of Pius. In the reign of Antoninus the germ of the Papacy already exists in a very definite form."

Antoninus reigned from 138 A.D. to 161.

Page 175.—"This precedence of the Church of Rome only became more marked in the third century."

Page 176.—"The tradition of the Roman Church passes for the most ancient of all. Cornelius takes the first place in the affair of Novatianism. We see him, in especial, depriving Italian bishops, and nominating their successors. Rome was also the central authority of the African Church."

Page 180.—Speaking of Pope St. Victor's time, at the close of the second century, Renan says, "The Papacy was already born, and well born."

Page 198.—"That Roman Primacy, which is so brilliant a fact in the second and third century, ceases to exist as soon as the East has a separate existence and a separate capital."

Just immediately after the passage which Dr. Rentoul so unfairly complains of me for mutilating, Renan bears this striking testimony to the pre-eminence of the Roman Church. It will be observed how he translates the famous passage of Irenæus. *Primacy* is his rendering of Rome's *Principalitas*:—

Page 173.—"The writing, of which the fragment known as the Canon of Muratori formed a part and which was produced at Rome about the year 180 A.D., shows us Rome already defining the Canon of Scripture, alleging the martyrdom of Peter as the foundation of Catholicity, repudiating Montanism and Gnosticism alike. Irenæus refutes all heresies by reference to the belief of this Church, 'the greatest, the oldest, the most illustrious, which possesses in virtue of an unbroken succession the true tradition of the Apostles Peter and Paul, and to which, because of its primacy, all the rest of the Church ought to have recourse.'"—(Irenæus, iii., iii. 2, pp. 173-4.)

In the "Hibbert Lectures" there are several indirect testimonies to the existence of the Roman Primacy in the Early Church, as well as several references to that Church's purity of faith and morals. But these I have given will suffice to show that I was under no necessity, as I certainly had no wish, to mutilate or garble quotations from Renan or any other author.

Now, in face of this abundant testimony, is it not "pitiable" to find Dr. Rentoul straining out a gnat when he has to swallow a camel? With what in another would appear to be assumed earnestness, he asks why did I omit these tremendous sentences. I answer, because they had no possible bearing on the matter in hand; because they regarded not what I was dealing with, namely, the claims put forward by the early Roman Pontiffs to a primacy of jurisdiction, but the well-known opinions of Renan concerning the Papacy; because they regarded not the early existence, but Renan's views (of which I gave sufficient indication), in relation to the origin and character of the Primacy. The question at issue was not what Renan believed, but what he witnessed to, regarding the admitted claims of the Roman Pontiffs to the Primacy in the confessedly pure ages of the Church.

I have considered all that Dr. Rentoul has said, and I now deliberately state that I am satisfied that these "tremendous sentences" were properly omitted as being entirely irrelevant.

I thank Dr. Rentoul for the information he gives regarding the Rationalism of Protestantism. This patting on the back of Rationalism by a distinguished Presbyterian divine of our day is indeed new to me, but it serves to explain much that I could not previously reconcile in the faith and practice of some Protestants.

In return I beg to inform Dr. Rentoul that he applied an offensive epithet to John Henry Newman when and where he described him as a "Romanist" cardinal, and that he repeated the offence to Catholics as often as he referred to the "Romish" priesthood. I cannot help wondering that Dr. Rentoul was ignorant that these epithets are, and are intended to be offensive.—Yours, &c.

+ THOMAS J. CARR,
22nd May. Archbishop of Melbourne.

III.

DR. RENTOUL'S THIRD LETTER IN REPLY.

To the Editor (of "Argus" and "Age.")

Sir,—Through the huge haze of words with which Archbishop Carr has striven to envelop the reality, some solid facts now stand forth clear and indisputable:—

(1) The one vital matter at issue is the truth or falsity of the Roman claim. That claim is that the Roman Papacy rests on a twenty-five years' bishopric of Peter at Rome, and that from this bishopric a line of successive supreme bishops ruling at Rome, with "a primacy of jurisdiction," descended in unbroken succession in the first and second centuries.

(2) In support of this daring claim Archbishop Carr professed to cite a large number of accurate and trustworthy "quotations" as impressive "Protestant testimony." In connection with, and as the *finale* of, this cumulative "testimony," he tried to make it appear that even the "Rationalistic writers" had, by "their admissions" confirmed and made unanswerable this claim. He accordingly gave what purported to be a genuine and reliable quotation from Renan. To make it more impressive, Archbishop Carr introduced it by the declaration—"There is no room for mistake in his words."

(3) It is now proven that the professed "quotation" from Renan, instead of being reliable, or favourable, or a testimony to the Roman Papacy as "the irresistible outcome of the facts of history" was made to appear so only by a drastic mutilation of Renan's sentences —a mutilation so drastic that it cut the backbone and living heart out of Renan's meaning.

(4) It is now proven that Archbishop Carr's attempt to shield himself behind the *Advocate* report has not in the least improved his position. That report gives what Archbishop Carr has declared to be the accurate shape of his quotation; and it presents the passage of Renan still mutilated so as to convey just almost the opposite meaning of what Renan intended.

(5) The entire passage of Renan, had it been read without mutilation, would have declared that the Roman Papacy rests on a huge legend "equally mythical" with the pagan legend of Romulus and Remus. Had this been frankly quoted to the audience to which Archbishop Carr spoke, it would have fallen upon them with dismay.

(6) The whole context of Archbishop Carr's "quotation" makes the mutilation still more surprising. Just a few sentences above his "quotation" from Renan, Archbishop Carr had declared that in the times of which he was speaking "the faith of the Church was pure and the sanctity of the Roman Pontiff conspicuous." But in his quotation from Renan he cuts out a passage which declares, as a fact of history, that in those very times, and up to the time of Victor, the whole Church of Rome was of one mind with them," viz., with "the poor Artemonites, a kind of Arians before Arius."

Now this discussion might here determine, for the facts above stated are unanswerable. But in his last letter Archbishop Carr attempts two things, in explanation of his mutilation of the "quotation" from Renan First, he says he "omitted these tremendous sentences" only "because they had no possible bearing on the matter in hand; because they regarded not what he was dealing with, namely, the claims put forward by the early Roman Pontiffs to a primacy of jurisdiction, but the well-known opinions of Renan concerning the Papacy," &c. This ingenious distinction will not stand a moment's investigation. Higher up in his letter, Archbishop Carr had stated his object in quoting Renan, viz., that it was testimony "in favour of the Roman primacy as the irresistible outcome of the facts of history." Now, Renan showed that the Roman primacy, instead of being "the irresistible outcome of the facts of history," was the ecclesiastical and sacerdotal outcome of a huge legend as mythical as that of Romulus and Remus. But Archbishop Carr deftly cuts out of the "quotation" all reference to that fact. And so also with the other statement of Renan about the actual facts of the state of the faith of the Church of Rome in the second century. Archbishop Carr deftly cut that also out of the quotation. I am bound to say that you could make "quotations" prove anything whatever if you were allowed to make "quotations" by this method.

The other effort of Archbishop Carr is to make a number of new and irrelevant quotations from Renan with respect to Clement of Rome, &c. I wish I had space to set these, each in its true connection, before the public. But, as the Americans tersely say, "they don't belong here." I was the first in this controversy to give the name of Renan's book and the page and the facts and the connective meaning of it. I urged, and I urge still, the public to get it and to read it as a whole. It shows clearly how "the episcopate," and then the Papacy, arose out of the original simple "presbyterate," until at last the most potent "bishop" made himself a "bishop of bishops." It shows also that the Papacy is mainly due to "a vast

Ebionite legend" about Peter, which arose just shortly after Clement's death. "A vast Ebionite legend arose in Rome, and, under the name of 'The Preaching, or 'The Journeys of Peter,' took a fixed shape about the year 130 A.D.—that is to say, 66 years, more or less, after the death of the Apostles." And it testifies that in the letter of Clement of Rome prior to this movement—"We find no trace as yet of a *presbyterus* superior to, and about to dethrone, the rest." And Renan proves these things by documentary facts.

In Archbishop Carr's reference to "Rationalism" and Protestantism he is equally unfortunate. Instead of Protestantism "patting on the back" Rationalism, it was the Archbishop who first manufactured Renan into "Protestant testimony," and then into a "Rationalist," and then represented Renan as patting on the back Roman Catholicism. It will not do! I pointed Archbishop Carr to the *Encyclopædia Britannica* to let him know that the much-misused word "Rationalism" may, rightly used, imply no rejection of the facts of Revelation. Protestantism, as history proves, is not kin to what the Archbishop seeks to call "Rationalism." It is kin to "Reason" on the one hand; and, on the other hand, it is kin to "Faith" that rejects superstition and credulity. Protestants say, as Christ said, "Search the Scriptures." Archbishop Carr is on perilous ground in talking of Protestantism and disbelief. Has not he read the statement in a recent magazine, from one of our greatest living masters in the philosophy of religion and of history:—

"It is now as then (the eighteenth century). It is Catholic countries that show the most radical revolt of the intellect from religion, and a revolt, not at one point, but at all."

I need not enlarge on this tragic and palpable fact. Renan himself is too striking an instance of it.

Archbishop Carr completes the serio-comedy by confessing that the "offensive epithet" he accused me of applying to John Henry Newman was to call him a "Romanist Cardinal." And this from an Archbishop who has flung "epithets" all round him of a very sardonic kind against his Protestant antagonists! And he himself also has spoken of the "Roman See" and the "Roman Pope." Evidently, the Archbishop was hard up for something to complain of. I used the term "Romanist Cardinal" without thought of offence. But if the umbrage at it implies the assertion on the part of Romanists that they have any better right to the name "Catholic" than Anglicans or Presbyterians or any Protestants have, then I will use it again.—I am, &c.,

J. LAURENCE RENTOUL.

Ormond College, The University, 25th May.

IV.

ARCHBISHOP CARR'S FOURTH LETTER.

To the Editor (of "Age" and "Argus.")

Sir,—Allow me to reply very briefly to Dr. Rentoul's last letter. I will not add a single word to what I have already written regarding the main points of the controversy. I am perfectly willing to abide by the judgment of those who have attentively followed the whole discussion. But I may inform Dr. Rentoul that he takes undeserved credit to himself for being the first to give the name of Renan's book and the page, &c. If he will take the trouble of turning to my *Replies to the Anglican Bishop of Ballarat and the Rev. Canon Potter*, published last year in pamphlet form, he will find that I gave the full name of Renan's book (*Hibbert Lectures*), the date of delivery (1880), and the very page and passage in which the disputed quotation is found (*Lecture II.*, p. 37-8). Everyone knows that it is not usual to give many references in a newspaper report of a lecture, particularly when the matter is to be afterwards published in permanent form. But if Dr. Rentoul honours me by reading the first lecture of the late series, as it was already printed in sheets before his first lecture was delivered, and as it will soon appear published with the other five lectures of the series, he will find the name of Renan's book and the date and page given as exactly as he can desire.

Catholics, I may observe, have no objection to the title "Roman," indeed they glory in it as indicating the centre of their unity. But if Dr. Rentoul will persist in calling us "Romanists," and our doctrine and priesthood "Romish," we must try to bear the offensive epithets, as we have had to bear many other hard things he has said of us. In conclusion, I sincerely hope that however we may differ theologically, at least, in the amenities of life, the proverb may be fulfilled in our regard: *Amantium iræ amoris integratio est.*
—Yours, &c.,

+THOMAS J. CARR,
Archbishop of Melbourne.

St. Patrick's Cathedral, 26th May.

IV.

DR. RENTOUL'S FINAL LETTER.

To the Editor of the "Argus."

Sir,—I have no desire to prolong this controversy. With the only new matter in Archbishop Carr's letter of to-day I will deal briefly. He says that I "take undeserved credit to myself for being the first to give the name of Renan's book and the page, &c."

This, I must say, is another instance of his lack of accuracy. What I said was that I was "the first in this controversy to give the name of Renan's book, and the page, and the facts, and the connective meaning of it. I urge, and I still urge, the public to get it and read it as a whole. Even the title of the book, if given in full, would indicate its meaning."

I am exceedingly surprised at Archbishop Carr's courage in referring me to his "Replies to the Anglican Bishop of Ballarat and the Rev. Canon Potter," published last year, in reference to a quite different controversy, and quite different antagonists. I have consulted the Replies, and my surprise at Archbishop Carr's courage is deepened. The professed "quotation" from Renan on that printed page (p. 40) is mutilated just as in the recent lectures. I had not dreamt that the Archbishop had once before presented that strangely garbled passage to the public as the "testimony" of Renan.

Then, again, another astonishing thing is that, in the Replies (pp. 37-49), Archbishop Carr distinctly declares, just as in his recent lectures he "implied," that he was quoting only "Protestant testimony" when including Renan. He says (p. 37) that he will "anticipate Canon Potter's objection to Catholic authorities," and will "confine himself to Protestant historians." The five to whose "testimony" he then proceeds to confine himself are Dr. Nevin, Hallam, Milman, Neander, and Renan. Let the reader attentively compare this part of the Replies with Archbishop Carr's recent first lecture and his assertion at the opening of the second lecture that he had "quoted exclusively Protestant testimony."

The most surprising thing of all, however, is that, in his Replies, Archbishop Carr actually calls himself and his co-religionists by the name "Romanists." Says the Archbishop—"The Romanists are not the only denomination likely to interfere with the good bishop's hope of union." (Replies, p. 10.) Truly a prelate of much versatility is Archbishop Carr! In two series of lectures he pigeon-holed Renan along with the "Protestant testimony." In another mood he objected to me for pointing out that he had placed him there. In his Replies "published last year" he calls himself and his Church "Romanists." This year, when I courteously call a gentleman a "Romanist Cardinal," he terms it an "offensive epithet."

Archbishop Carr, oddly enough, complains of the "many hard things" I have spoken of the Roman Catholics. Surely he should be the last to speak thus. Any "hard things" I have spoken have been about the Roman Catholic claim, not about the men and the people. But read Archbishop Carr's writings! You find them made up mainly of two things—"quotations" and "hard things" about the great names and men all Protestants and liberals revere. Even Wycliffe was a "hypocrite;" Tyndale, the martyred translator of our English Bible, "was a most irreverent mind," and was "the very man to pervert the meaning of Holy Scripture;" Foxe "was a deliberate falsifier of history." This is the Archbishop's mildest. No wonder that in his eyes Dr. Littledale is "a discredited controversialist." These be "hard things!" What if we retaliated by telling some facts of history about the double line of Pontiffs and the lives of Popes? But we have not done so.

With this I am content to leave the matter to the public, asking them to remember that all this concerns the one point in my lectures which Archbishop Carr has ventured to controvert. Of one thing I am quite sure—Renan will not again be quoted in Melbourne as "testimony" to the historicity of the Roman claim. Rather will he be remembered as having likened the basis of that claim to the "equally mythical duality" of Romulus and Remus.—I am, &c.,

J. LAURENCE RENTOUL.

Ormond College, The University, 28th May.

www.ingramcontent.com/pod-product-compliance
Lightning Source LLC
Chambersburg PA
CBHW022016220426
43663CB00007B/1104